A KIWI
ON A
KENTISH FARM

Life on the Farm

and

Characters of the Hundred of Hoo

KATHY MACLEAN
Author of The Bay and Beyond

Copyright © Kathy Maclean 2024

The right of Kathy Maclean to be identified as author of this work has been asserted by her in accordance with the Copyright, Designs and Patents Act 1988.

All rights reserved.

No part of this publication may be reproduced or transmitted in any form or by any means, electronic or mechanical, including photocopy, recording, or any information storage and retrieval system, without permission in writing from the publisher.

Front cover photo by Ian Maclean

About The Author

Kathy Maclean was born in the sunny idyll of Hawke's Bay, New Zealand, the fifth child of busy orcharding parents. Day-dreaming was her forte, with inspiration all around, whether blossom or beach. Her imagination ran free and with it, her writing began.

The passion continues. Having had success with her first book of memoirs, *The Bay and Beyond*, (available worldwide on the Amazon marketplace) she has enjoyed editing more of her saved favourites to fill the pages of *A Kiwi on a Kentish Farm*. Five decades have passed in a flash; each one eventful, each dramatic and each worthy of a wealth of stories. The memories stacked up and Kathy was urged to share them.

Her first book, *The Bay and Beyond*, in two parts and with an Antipodean theme, comprised firstly of short stories relating to her carefree barefoot childhood in Havelock North. In Part Two there were accounts of courageous journeys of early explorers who crossed the world looking for the great southern continent and found instead the beautiful paradise of New Zealand. There were many other tales of brave British emigrants in the nineteenth century and more still of her own travel adventures in the mid-1960s. There was endless material for her to dwell on. Travelling solo and making her own decisions was character building and fulfilling. This particular period culminated in a shipboard romance on board the *Northern Star*. The ship then was on its way to New Zealand, and was full of 'Ten Pound Poms' with hope in their hearts. Kathy was returning home after nine months of what was known as an Overseas Expedition, thankful to be in time to enjoy a sea journey before the skies became full of Jumbo jets.

Two years later Kathy was back on the same ship, engaged to that certain young farmer from Kent. She arrived in England a young and nervous soon-to-be-bride. 'This was an adventure after all,' she told herself, surrounded by fields of wheat and fluffy lambs, with not an apple tree in sight.

It seemed a sensible thing to do, to write about some of it; the good and perhaps the bad, although thankfully there was very little of that. The idea of a second follow-on book emerged and *A Kiwi on a Kentish Farm* eventually took shape.

Kathy lives with Ian, her husband, now a retired farmer. He takes the word 'retired' lightly and he's never happier than when he is amongst cattle, or lending a hand to the family who have taken on the acres. With the farm surrounding it, Kathy's home is central in the village so she feels part of the picture and part of the action. Her garden is large and tending it is a time of reflection and pleasure. From her writing room she can see the colourful results of her labours.

Her two children and four grandchildren are local and give her much joy.

Acknowledgements

To Ian, Amanda and Spencer.
For their encouragement, patience and help.

I offer sincere thanks to my large global family for urging me to write a sequel to *The Bay and Beyond*. And to our many friends who have enjoyed learning more about my wonderful birth country, this is your chance to picture life on a farm, an English farm.

My thanks also to Liz Carter for her expertise in design and formatting.

Contents

Life on the Farm	11
Preface	13
Introduction	18
Happy Landings	21
Settling In	25
The Farm and I	29
The Village	33
A Marsh Summer (in 100 words)	40
West Point Beach	42
The Sunset	48
Anonymity	50
And Then We Were Four	52
Flock to Our Door	57
The Long Haul	61
The Honey Pot	65
My Equestrian Years	70
Time For Tea	77
Fun at Minnis Bay	81
The Last Visit	86
Thick Pile Lasagne	92
Sage	94
Moby	97
The Thirteenth Duckling	97
Monty	102
Educating Adults	106
No Comfort in Kent	111
It's an Ill Wind	115
Breakfast in our Farmhouse	118
Catastrophe	121
The Picnic	124
Baby Elephant	129
Fear is a Flat Door	132
The Therapist	134
Marsh Magic	141
A New Dawn	145
Victory Dance	149

Lakeside Dining	151
Short Listed for Take Off	156
Flutterings of a Farmer's Wife	160
What Price?	164
St. Mary's at Christmas, 2014	167
Headway	171
The Move	176
On Reflection	182

Characters of The Hundred of Hoo — 185

Introduction	187
The Legacy	192
A Tempting Trade	198
In Memory of Robert Gunning	203
who died in the garden of St. Mary's Hall, August 6th, 1828	203
Mary Prouse	205
Robert Gunning	212
Robert Gascoigne Burt	216
Henry Pye	219
Justice For George	226
Douglas Packman	234
The First Born	241
Game-keeper George	245
Stan The Man	252
Dear Dorothy	255
Edie Hassell	261
Doctor Mac	265
Doug Bradford, Snr.	273
Percy's Perks	277
Dave Fletcher	282
Arthur at No. 7	287
The House and Garden Machine	291
Little Man, Big Heart	296
Ross Farmhouse	299
The Hat and a Rat	303
Mr. Potter	306
Let Us Reflect	310

Part One

Life on the Farm

Collected stories from 1968 - 2021

1

Preface

I had a dream when I was little, of a big farmhouse with a pine dresser – of a Labrador sleeping by the kitchen range, and a rainbow of washing dancing on the clothesline. There would be hollyhocks and roses in a sweeping garden, with a wondrous view beyond it. I carried on dreaming - fuelled by my mother saying things like, 'you could do a lot worse my girl, than marry a rich farmer.' Thinking about what might be kept me going for years, until fate played a hand and with no help from my mother, I bagged myself a farmer's son. She was right of course; I could have done a lot worse. The trouble was, he was only rich for five minutes.

1966, Southampton

When I'd climbed the gangplank of the Shaw Savill ship, the *Northern Star* on a bleakly wet and foggy January afternoon, I had little intention of returning to the United Kingdom any time soon. My travels had been amazing, but my one thought then was a return to the Southern Hemisphere, to South Africa and then onwards to Sydney where heart and home lay. I left the chilly deck, where tearful passengers had grouped to wave their farewells and throw bunting, and descended the handsome spiral staircase to find the Writing Room. Scribbling postcards, I bade farewell to England and waited for the off. I sighed a not unhappy sigh to be leaving, for I was rearing to get on with my wonderful adventure – namely my year-long Overseas Expedition, with Durban my next stop. I'd seen even more than I'd imagined possible, travelled thousands of miles, worked at multiple desks to replenish fading funds, and generally had a marvellous, fulfilling nine months. Now it was time for the next chapter, the final part, which was to explore the southernmost country of the huge continent of Africa and spend time with my two elder sisters.

Little did I know that fate would disrupt my plans within hours. It came in the form of a cheerful young chap, who was braving the choppy English Channel for the journey's first meal. We met over soup, on Table 83. We'd both been late visiting the Purser for our seating arrangements, and had been allocated Table 83 for second sitting meals. It was apparently one of the least favoured tables, right by the galley. Our Scottish waiter was frequently drunk and was therefore imminently facing a nautical sacking. In spite of the carefree crashing and banging of plates and Jock's jokes and spillages, there followed sixteen days of delicious fare, and much conversation. The fourteen hundred passengers were treated to cinema nights, ballroom dancing, keep fit classes, quizzes and foreign language lessons. There were deck games and a large swimming pool and endless lazy hours to get acquainted with the young people on board. And yes, they seemed mostly to be young.

Once I reached Durban it was time to say goodbye to Ian. This was just a much-maligned shipboard romance I told myself, though I was not really convinced. What would become of my existing romantic connection in Sydney? I was confused. Ian continued on to Wellington to begin two years of working on a hill farm in Hawke's Bay. In an amazing coincidence, this property was a mere twenty miles from my home village of Havelock North. I meanwhile, planned a three-month whirlwind period of touring in South Africa. And so it proved to be – I packed endless excitement into every day, except for the ones where I was forced to find secretarial work to supplement my meanderings. My sightings of numerous magnificent beasts and birds in the famous safari parks were diligently noted in a diary, for me to recall such a privilege.

In exactly three months the *Northern Star* made port once more in Durban. I hitched a ride across the Indian Ocean, enjoying the ship's familiarity. This vessel, slightly smaller and younger than the *Southern Cross*, was alleged to be less reliable. It had been hastily built by Shaw Savill to cater for the huge demand in the scheme to transport emigrants to the Antipodes – the Ten Pound Poms, wooed by posters of a paradise awaiting. Although there were stories of the ship's frequent repairs and stoppages, my memories of the three sailings on the *Northern Star*, are of wall-to-wall joy.

After several reflective weeks in Sydney, the *Wanganella* spirited me across the Tasman Sea to Wellington. The four days on the Tasman Sea were bumpy, rather like my love life. Casting off boyfriends was not my forte, and certainly not this time. Whatever had I done?

However, it wasn't long before Ian's little green Fiesta was negotiating the winding road between the Te Aute farm and Te Mata Road, Havelock North on a regular basis. I introduced him to Friday night promenades in town, Sunday driving (a Kiwi habit), the glorious Hawke's Bay beaches, hokey-pokey ice creams, and Hastings' famous milk shake parlour. I couldn't persuade him to sample the Invercargill oysters which Dad and I loved, but he was definitely morphing into a local guy. Weekends would finish with tea around the Joneses' kitchen table and then we'd all watch the only television channel available at the time. Something pretty corny no doubt, but as we didn't know any better, it suited us just fine.

Like all romances we had our rocky times, but mostly the sun shone and the way forward seemed clear, especially with the appearance of a sapphire ring and the promise of a newly vacated farmhouse, (with a Labrador, a clothesline and a view beyond.)

1968

Having negotiated several tricky conversations with family about an imminent wedding in Kent, and not in our lovely Havelock North Presbyterian church, our departure date arrived. This parting seemed more final of course, possibly because it was. The beautiful strains of 'Now is the Hour' – a Maori farewell - added melancholy to the occasion. Ian was much more upbeat than me for he was going home, while I was beginning yet another journey, this time to cross the world to be married, leaving behind much that was dear.

Six weeks of lazy days on the familiar and cossetting *Northern Star* followed. Travelling by ship was still the fashion then, and the obvious option for young people with time on their hands, or families on a budget. Around that time Jumbo jets began to provide the other rapid and considerably more expensive option for world travel, until gradually the lazy, lengthy voyages across the seas were all but phased out. Under the UK Government's Scheme, emigrants from the late sixties were flown across the world, arriving a mere 28 hours later at Auckland's Whenuapai Airport. Meanwhile, our Shaw Savill fares were £245 each – Ian in a four-berth cabin and me in a six berth. They were basic, with tiered bunks, a few cupboards and a wash basin. A Cabin Steward brought tea to us every morning. Bathrooms were down the corridors, basic and few. Stopovers were an interesting bonus, starting with the tropical paradises of Fiji and Tahiti; and the fascination of the Panama Canal, followed by Acapulco, Jamaica and Curacao thrown in for good measure.

Oh, what a topsy-turvy world we live in. The girl from Havelock North village was to circumnavigate the globe to live on a farm on the gently sloping North Kent marshes. Ancestors who braved the seas all those years ago to start a new life in New Zealand, would be fascinated that a more recent family member jumped ship, deciding that England was the utopia after all. And how very different were our journeys!

A Kiwi on a Kentish Farm, set in a quaint little village in north Kent, will allow you to peep at our busy life over the decades. From arriving as a nervous newcomer in 1968, I take you on a journey through the years, as my story evolves.

Part Two acknowledges the importance of the local residents of the past, and the legacy they left for all to admire. The land was fertile, the road was rocky for some but the journey was theirs for the taking.

2

Introduction

Part One will allow me to share with you the pitfalls and challenges, along with the joyous peaks of farming and family life in a quaint little village with the even quainter name of St. Mary Hoo. Life for any farming family is fulfilling, healthy but hard. Dedication is a prerequisite, and danger is never far away. These tales have mostly been stored for years, and are just itching to be told. They describe my adjustment as a new wife, then a mother, gardener, cook, bottle-washer, counsellor and writer. They constantly refer to the two-thousand-acre tenanted farm when it was in our care. These glorious acres were purchased by the Church Commissioners of England in the mid-1850s. Their first tenant was an influential young farmer called Henry Pye. After his death in 1909 - and interim care for a decade, the farm was let to Lachlan Maclean of Thong, Gravesend. Until April 2021, it had been the way of things for three generations of Macleans, in a timespan of one hundred years. Now that we have reached retirement age and new tenants have taken over all but a few of the glorious acres, it is time to tell all.

I have always loved to write and on completion of a new story it would join a growing pile. Therefore, Ian and I and our children, Spencer and Amanda, plus the characters in the stories are now mostly all much older, or sadly in Part Two, deceased.

Our children say they had the best childhood ever. They climbed haystacks and roamed for hours, rode horses and bikes for miles. There were kittens and puppies to fuss over, little routine, and even fewer rules. Perhaps it was rather like my very own childhood at the Orchard House in Havelock North. Most of the stories are written as if we are still in the big old farmhouse, and farming the acres. I feel sure the new tenants will be forgiving of this minor aspect. And after all, we have only moved five hundred yards.

As I type this on my trusty computer, I can see the river Thames and the shoreline of Essex across the water. Huge container ships and smaller craft are moving on the tide. If I swivel in my chair, the river Medway is right there too, behind me and in view. This phenomenon is possible because we live on the Hoo Peninsula, a narrow isthmus between the two rivers.

The greater part of the Hoo Peninsula is sometimes referred to as The Hundred of Hoo. 'Hundred' was the name given to the divisions of the old Shires – plotting the country into so many hundreds in order to provide provisions to the King. Thus, the parishes of Hoo St. Werburgh, Cooling, High Halstow, St. Mary Hoo, Allhallows and Stoke make up the Hundred of Hoo. (Historically, the parish of Grain was in the Hundred of Gillingham.) This is an area of historical interest, due in the most part to its closeness to London, Rochester, Canterbury and the important Chatham Dockyard. The latter is now a tourist attraction after its closure, but in peak production in centuries past, it saw the building and launch of some of the most famous sailing ships of all time, most notably from a New Zealander's point of view, Captain Cook's *Endeavour*.

The mighty Thames, from its estuary at Grain, ebbs and flows with each tide all the way into the City of London. The marsh lowlands, adjacent on both sides of the river for many miles of its length, are protected by a seawall which thankfully has not been breached since 1953. When the weather is kind, these marshes produce good grass where sheep and cattle thrive, or provide acres of flat land for quality cuts of hay and silage. The more fertile upland fields multi-task, with livestock rotation, wheat, crops and the production of hay. The animals are terrific but transient, for every fluffy lamb grows into a less lovely adult, every adorable calf into mouth-watering maturity. We are governed by the vagaries of the weather, which is usually one of the main topics of conversation in the farmhouse, ours and everyone else's.

The air is fresh here and the view is great. Read on, into the heart of the harvests and haymaking, and the village life of St. Mary Hoo. It is one of the smallest villages in Kent, but so full of character, and characters too. St. Mary Hoo begs to be immortalised!

3

Happy Landings

Springtime, 1968

Once more in England, stepping off the much-loved *Northern Star*, we were surrounded by a welcoming family, a new family for me. This time there was no fog, and the sun shone as we set off for Kent. We were back in the real world after six weeks of make believe. The rest of our lives beckoned, stretching ahead in a grown up, and for me slightly overwhelming way. Southampton docks had been covered by a sea of boxes, cases, trunks, porters and mingling passengers. Two years before I'd been dismissive of that same busy port – now the chaos took on a new significance. My carefully selected worldly goods, in a huge tin trunk which I'd purchased in Hastings, New Zealand, along with Ian's hefty trunk of boarding school vintage, would be delivered to St. Mary Hoo later. I don't remember a limit to the amount of luggage we were allowed by Shaw Savill, but I had been as ruthless in my selections as in my discarding. It had hurt to throw away my treasures. I was a child no more.

Wedding arrangements were soon in full swing. I was absent for a great many of the lesser details and even some of the finer ones for I needed to find work, and quickly. I approached Stoy

Haywood, Accountants, in London and found to my delight I could start immediately, and at the same desk I'd occupied two years previously. It was a relief to be employed, but as temporary office work was available at all the agencies then, there would have been other options. The familiarity of Stoy's appealed. Secretaries it seemed, were ever welcome. Every Friday night I caught the train down to Strood in the Medway towns, to spend the weekend at the farm. Ian would regale me with progress; of how things were going at home and on the farm, for he was adjusting too - settling back into the old routine. He was full of the new ideas he had picked up from Jim Robertshawe in Te Aute, though he knew he must introduce them slowly, or possibly not at all, being a very new partner.

Our future farmhouse had been conveniently vacated by Ian's uncle prior to our arrival. It was enormous, with barely a lightbulb or a stick of furniture, save for two huge dressers painted oddly, in two shades of green. In an empty kind of way, the house seemed in need of love. We started painting over the bright colours, taming the wallpaper, argued about carpets and thought about curtains. My prize for sewing at high school would prove useful once my Husqvarna came out of the trunk. Choosing material for the curtains was easy enough, for I worked just five minutes from the Oxford Street Selfridges store. This and other stores were magnets for lunchtime strolls.

There was a welcome-home party for us, where I was introduced to a sea of unfamiliar faces. People so kind, and all of them wanting to peep at the new and novel addition to the family. I say novel because anyone from thirteen thousand miles away makes for very novel. I was feeling so homesick for the hills of home in spite of their collective kindness.

To counteract that feeling I immersed myself in learning to keep house, make pastry, arrange flowers and sew curtains and lampshades. The latter seemed at odds to my outdoorsy disposition, but those lightbulbs needed covering up and there was actually a waiting list to join the class. An Aga cooker was installed in St. Mary's Hall and I cooked my first duck (badly.) Ian showed me over the farm, driving through the stock, describing the breeds, sometimes lambing a ewe, and explained the geography of the land, with its unique position at the estuary of the Thames. Then there were the three small beaches to admire, below a seawall which bordered the river, and which kept the one thousand acres of marsh safe from rising tides. He explained the significance of the position of our acres, so close to the estuary and gave me a history of the small brick huts alongside the wall, used for storing ammunition in WWII. The Thames was the main path into London for the loaded German aircraft, which hit fierce resistance from guns and soldiers stationed at an Army barracks within St. Mary Hoo village, or from a watchful and enthusiastic Home Guard. Enemy planes jettisoned their bombs directly overhead, over the river or over the farm's marshes if they were hit, before attempting to fly home. Soldiers patrolled the seawall for the duration of the war and the skies above the farm were alive with action. The marsh was pot-marked with bomb craters and occasional wrecked planes. Not that Ian was privy to any of the action, having been born in 1946, but being a natural tour guide, he revelled in the telling of it. 'Dad was in the Home Guard,' he told me then.

If there was any spare time amongst working in the city and all of this learning, at weekends there were box hedges to clip around a series of garden squares, and a large area to maintain and prepare for the Big Event. A marquee was booked for the garden which would be ours. And there was endless painting indoors – the Hall being a very large house, with rooms of way-too-bright colours.

We were married in the autumn, in a thirteenth century church just over the garden wall. It was a country wedding in a farming community, with me floating around in the marquee on the lawn – a novelty newbie bride amongst a sea of smiling yet mostly unknown faces. I was, however, pleased to have amassed twenty guests of my own, some on their overseas expeditions, and a favourite cousin who was one of our bridesmaids. My parents were unable to travel the great distance from Havelock North as they had made the journey to South Africa and Europe for my sister Glenda's wedding three years previously. 'Money doesn't grow on trees,' my dad sadly told me, which was fairly apt, coming from an orchardist. That was upsetting of course, but special mention went to my sister Janet, who represented the Jones family by flying over to Kent from Johannesburg. The wedding day was a wonderful mix of sunshine, showers and even a thunderstorm which rumbled during the service. Ian's father gave me away. It was a gloriously happy, if slightly unreal occasion; then Lofty Fuller's taxi drove us three hundred yards to the marquee. (I have no idea why we didn't walk.) Ian's speech started with a thank you to his brother Robert for postponing the Dung Cart until Monday.

Covered in confetti, we caught the six o'clock train to London, leaving behind our guests who most likely departed at the same time. That was the custom then, with none of the late-night celebrations and riotous parties which accompany weddings nowadays. Corsica provided another taste of make believe. It was our honeymoon choice.

Farming and keeping house beckoned. Let married life begin.

21st September 1968

4

Settling In

Now we had the keys, Ian made a minor move of five hundred yards from The Moat, the home of his birth, while I had moved considerably further from mine. This was new territory for a couple of twenty somethings, but we were rearing to go. We knew we had a task to end all tasks ahead of us. It was daunting enough, with Ian working long hours and me with little practice in all things domestic.

The side door off the yard opened into a long entrance hall, with ancient black and white tiles on the floor. The hall had a high ceiling, and was empty, but for a lightbulb dangling sadly. That led to a central passage where the downstairs rooms meandered off in all directions. St. Mary's Hall was almost certainly one of the first houses in the village and was, way back then, in the possession of the family of Bardolf, then Sir Nicholas de Poing, followed by his descendant, William de Holden who died there in 1377. It had at least nine eminent owners after that before being bought by the Church. It boasted a moat way back then, though nothing of that was evident for us. Very little of the original house, save for a huge chimney stack and fireplace in the kitchen and very thick walls throughout remain to this day. A large extension was added in 1800 and various alternations had taken place in the years since.

Grandmother Maclean, on her arrival in 1921, announced it was far too dark for her and insisted on larger windows on two sides of the house. The original sash windows from the 19th century remained in place upstairs, though their efficiency was always doubtful.

Since 1850 it had been the family home of Henry Pye, his wife Elizabeth and their children. Clearly pencilled on the back of some of the pine doors of the Hall was the name 'Pye' and the two large pine dressers which remained were made to his design. Not surprisingly, sixty years after he left, it was still possible to feel his presence. His name was always mentioned in local history conversations, for he was an 'everywhere man' at the time. I have written about Henry Pye in length, in Part Two, The Characters.

The house was extensively added to soon after his arrival, offering four handsomely huge rooms to the front. This gave it a Georgian appearance. Subsequent families have made changes over the years to the much older back aspect. After Henry died in 1909, his adult children remained there until the Macleans arrived on the scene as tenants of the Church Commissioners. Ian and I eventually became the third Maclean couple to live in the Grade II listed house.

There were bare rooms everywhere and we badly needed furniture. We rattled around amongst echoes and emptiness, and space which needed filling. Trips to London or Rochester for a choice of merely the basic necessities seemed so alien for someone who had spent months in a small tent just a few years earlier. And for Ian it was also a quantum step after the basic wooden shearers' cottage on the Te Aute farm. Being suddenly so grown up didn't seem to fit at all.

As the first grandchild to be married, Ian was able to rummage in his Granny's barn for a pick of the furniture from her large vacated farm house. It had been stored for a decade and so was dusty and damp. I returned from my London job to inspect his choices. A large snooker table all but filled up the dining room. 'It has a top for dining,' Ian told me, waiting for approval, 'but nothing much else would fit on the trailer.'

A local carpet fitter was pleased to get the order to cover the old, uneven floorboards, while my sewing machine went into overdrive. Painting was endless and messy. I was also busy in the lampshade class. Would we ever finish the task? It seemed a challenge. And then there was the garden. First to face the chop were the box hedges, criss-crossing around four large squares of lawns. They needed careful clipping, which was fine when grandfather Maclean could afford a gardener or two, but not so great for us at the time. We installed sixty chickens in a new area once those hedges came out, and gleefully sold the eggs to a shop in Rochester. Ian's Labrador Sue ran riot in the cleared spaces. Old and loyal, she had waited patiently for him to return from his travels. I rescued a cat, who turned out to be pregnant; soon she became Momma-puss. We were constantly on surveillance to ensure the chickens were safe from marauding foxes. Gates were kept shut so our new seedlings were safe from the hens. These new-found responsibilities were endless! Heaven help us if we ever had children.

The early years were a time of huge adjustment, when of course I'd left behind everything and everyone I held dear. I missed the colours, the hills and beaches, the clear air and the fruits of the orchards. My writing began in earnest. In the days before the internet and mobile phones I didn't have the benefit of emailing messages or texting to make communication easy. I needed to keep in contact with family and friends, so writing was the obvious, and practically the only option. I discovered it wasn't a chore, and to my delight I enjoyed keeping in touch in this way, tapping away on my trusty Imperial electric typewriter for hours, ever thankful for a touch-typing training. Long Christmas newsletters from Kent were eagerly awaited and comments were favourable. I realised perhaps there was a smidgen of skill lurking and enrolled on an Adult Education writing course. In fact, one course followed another, and I was hooked.

New Zealand tabloids printed my articles on farming and family life; joys and dramas from across the sea. Three lengthy, factual episodes detailing the dreadful Foot and Mouth crisis made the front pages of several major newspapers. They were well received, not just by the farming fraternity, but by a nation whose resources rely on primary produce. I felt their concern, for our farm did not escape – being just two kilometres from an affected property. My short stories of happier times have also made their way to the Farmers Weekly magazine, and from their publishers I received my first pay cheque – for Thick Pile Lasagne, which is featured in Part One. Later, I joined several writers from Kent to produce a well-received Anthology.

I embarked on a university degree course in Creative Writing, which instilled necessary discipline. The modules forced me to attempt different genres, even if they felt alien. Poetry I found possible, writing for children pleasing, but I was soon to learn that my favourite direction was pointing towards memoir writing. And that is where my overflowing memory box has been called upon.

It seems one of the smallest villages in Kent is an endless source of material for writing.

With faithful dog, Sue

5

The Farm and I

The Early Years

As I write this in 2023 the farm **now** is so very different to what I was introduced to just after we were married, when I became witness to the hard work of a new husband, and different also from the gushing of an engaged person, on our tours of it, before I swanned back to London to my job. Oh yes! Now there were acres of mud everywhere, agricultural substances clinging to clothes, sock lambs in the kitchen and all manner of things to become accustomed to. Lambs, I learnt, chose to be born in puddles and calves timed their arrivals for the middle of the night. It wasn't at all like my old life on the orchard – once those apples were in their cases, we could retire inside for the duration, or at least for the night.

In 1968, with the Church Commissioners our landlords, our tenancy covered nearly two thousand acres. It was a time of change, however. The partnership of Ian's father and uncle came to an end while Ian was working in New Zealand. That freed up St. Mary's Hall for us. The new partnership between Ian, his brother Robert and their father commenced as soon as Ian returned to the UK. Two large farmhouses, barns, yards and eight farm workers' cottages were part of the tenancy. There were eight men on the payroll; two shepherds, each tending 750 ewes, two stockmen, two tractor drivers and two or three students. As he'd often caught those youngsters chatting, Ian's father had a saying, that *'one boy's a boy, two boys are half a boy, and three boys are no boys at all!'* In spite of that, during harvest, the farm employed several students. Usually, after interviews, three were chosen from Writtle Agricultural College, and almost always the boys were sons of Zimbabwean farmers.

One thousand head of cattle comprised of cows, calves, yearlings and ten Aberdeen Angus bulls. Rams completed the livestock picture, and a couple of horses were kept for exercise and pleasure.

Soon after our return, the Government introduced a scheme offering 86% assistance to tile drain the marsh acres currently in grass (they amounted to one thousand), create deep ditches and plough the entire area. The assisted process included cropping these acres in a rotation of wheat, rape and peas. The scheme proved profitable, especially when Great Britain joined the Common Market in 1973 and the price of grain doubled. The good times did not last alas, as the soil structure deteriorated. Even the application of gypsum – though helpful, proved too expensive as an option. Around that time there were also catastrophic floods on the marsh, so the decision was made to revert back to grass and graze livestock once again. On the uplands there were fertile fields of wheat. Acres of spring greens were grown for Covent Garden market in London, sometimes making good money and sometimes having to be disced in. Ewes grazed under the watchful eyes of the shepherds. Their lambs would be frolicking by springtime.

The farm's acres spread around the ancient village church, and the parish shared a vicar with High Halstow and Allhallows. Sometimes the congregation swelled to six. As the population of the village shrank, and the worshippers dwindled even further, the lovely old church was sold to Mr J.A. Lapthorn in 1977, before beginning its conversion to a private dwelling. The village school where the Pye children, the children of all the farm workers, and Ian's father and Uncle attended, closed in 1947 as it was felt the children would benefit from being enrolled in larger schools of learning. The School House was then converted into a family home. Not so very many years before Ian's birth, the pond at the junction was where the draft horses were led to be washed off after a day's ploughing, and to ease their loyal legs. I would have loved to have seen that – now their stables and hay racks remain empty. There were so many things to discover on my walks and so much history for me to absorb.

The farm tractors of the time were Massey Ferguson 1200s, the combine harvester was also a Massey Ferguson, while Ian drove an old American D4 caterpillar crawler for ploughing. These machines were given to farms of any size during WWII, with instructions to plough up all grass fields and crop them, to assist with the feeding of the nation. The D4s remained with the farmers as 'useful' white elephants. With these varied machines in use, and with an abundance of men for the allotted tasks, my offers of assistance were quietly ignored - though the old house, the profusion of mud, agricultural substances creeping indoors, and grafting with a duster and broom kept me occupied, but not exactly stimulated. I felt rather like a square peg in a round hole, or a sapling expected to grow well in foreign earth. It was a testing time in fact, but I was determined to meet the challenge. I suppose I had expected there might have been a cow to milk, or a sheep to shear, cattle to round up and myriad farming tasks to undertake, but I was gently told that there was now no cow, that Ian could do the shearing alongside the shepherd, and tractors were far too large for an un-coordinated newbie to contemplate driving. Sometimes I was called out to help Ian if a cow was having a difficult birth – inevitably in the middle of the night. Wherever possible I watched other activities from the side-lines, noting the action was relentless, seasonal and interesting.

Within three years there were two children to keep me busy and focused, but more about Spencer and Amanda and all manner of new focuses in the chapters to come. And I quickly learnt farming never stands still, just like the seasons or the ebb and flow of the Thames tide. It will be a joy to share these tales with you, as the Maclean family moved on through the decades, and the farm evolved as all farms were forced to do.

Cattle on the sea wall

6

The Village

St. Mary Hoo, quiet and quaint, is often likened to 'stepping back in time.' It remains one of the smallest villages in Kent. The oldest part of the village, near the Church, can be reached a short way up a narrow no-exit lane, named Hall Road. There is also a group of post war semi-detached houses midway along the main road to Allhallows. These were originally council houses, but most have now been privately purchased in a scheme introduced by Margaret Thatcher. There are more houses near the pub, at Fenn Street. The country lane soon meets a T junction, and turning right into The Street, one meanders past the Church, before coming shortly to an abrupt end at a farm gate. There is no shop nearby these days, though there is evidence of a small store which served the village a hundred or more years ago. Glass bottles and old china pieces have been found in a pile, and a hostelry shows up in ancient photographs. The legendary Edie Hassell had a store, cafe and post office along the main Ratcliffe Highway, and when she sold up in the seventies, 'Lofty' Fuller added a petrol pump to his business there. Amid the sands of time, pump and post office closed and a private residence emerged.

During the middle-ages, St. Mary Hoo and the surrounding district formed a reasonably peaceful farming community, though the area provided a health risk from the stagnant water of the saltings and creeks by the river Thames. It offered a stretch of fertile land near to London, and it could be reached easily from the river. Farmers then grew mainly fruit and hops. To this day the land has remained as farmland, rather than being gobbled up for residential use, though indications are pointing to the sobering fact that will change. Fields of oil seed rape stretch for many acres either side of the road. Everything is green and growing. Driving or walking uphill on Hall Road for half a mile, heading towards the church, a big house sits to the left. It is surrounded by farm buildings and is painted white. It seems rambling yet impressive. St. Mary's Hall is Grade II listed and had been the home of four generations of Macleans until the last couple (Ian and I) moved out several years ago. Now the Hall has new tenants and is getting a much-needed facelift.

There was definitely more bustle and activity a century or more ago. A village band was formed from aspiring musicians amongst the families in the mid 1800's. A barrel organ was purchased, a resident played the concertina, and a harmonium from the school was carried into the Church each Sunday. There were enough men in the workforce to make up a cricket team. There were gardening competitions, and there was a Home Guard formed of local farm workers during WWII. Ian's father Ronnie was an Officer in that regiment. In the 'good old days' Grandfather Lachlan Maclean provided a field for cricket, had a pavilion built, and games and fetes kept the children entertained. His wife, Margaret regularly made cakes and sandwiches for these events. Or probably kitchen maid Maud baked the cakes. Farming this land before the war apparently allowed for these luxuries in the big house. They included a cook, housekeeper, two gardeners, a chauffeur, a man to milk the cow and a boy to clean the shoes. Tasks Ian and I slotted into easily and with no help, apart from trusty Cyril who mowed the lawns – we inherited him from Uncle Charlie Maclean - while our daily milk was delivered courtesy of Bourne and Hillier Dairies.

In days gone by there was an avenue of towering elm trees each side of the Hall Road. Sadly, one by one they succumbed to Dutch Elm Disease. The large green space by the road is regularly mown and the dying tree roots of old have created slopes and dips. More trees have been planted and they are nicely established. Daffodils in spring, irises in summer are optional extras. A bench entices walkers to sit awhile and enjoy the peace. The quiet is everywhere until a rare passing car or tractor trundles by. Ours is the kind of village where we can abandon locks, alarms and bolts before setting off on our walks. That is a rarity in a crime ridden country and we treasure our good fortune. There have been no new houses built up here and it has remained special and small because of that. The rules of any Conservation Area apply, and they are strictly enforced. In High Halstow, the next village which overlooks the river Thames, there seems to be little restriction and building is gathering pace.

The Parish Church of St. Mary's has a nave and a Norman tower, both of which date back to the thirteenth century, as did the original chancel. The present chancel was rebuilt during or around 1881, the same time as the porch. The Church stands proudly, right in the midst of everything. I often linger at the graves of the three young servicemen, lost in WWII. These graves are maintained by the War Graves Commission. The other headstones are so ancient the inscriptions have all but faded. There is a small but grand section in a corner of the graveyard where members of the Pye family are buried, and an engraved slab to the memory of Robert Gunning, the poor young man who lived and died just over the wall. Then there are the sad little graves of children who succumbed to marsh ague. Traditionally, two yew trees have been planted by the Church gate, just to ensure their poisonous effect will keep any farmer from grazing his livestock in the graveyard. As if we would.

The village and the Church enjoyed a relatively peaceful period, with no connection to great events until the eighteenth century, when Robert Burt became the Rector of High Halstow and St.

Mary Hoo. The Prince of Wales (later to become George IV) fell hopelessly in love with a Catholic divorcee, one Maria Fitzherbert and demanded they be married. Unable to find a clergyman of the Church of England prepared to commit such a felony – the marriage of a Catholic to a Protestant - he paid the debt of Reverend Burt who was lodged in Fleet Prison for owing £500. The reward for conducting the service in December 1785 (in utmost secrecy) was a Domestic Chaplaincy in the Prince's household, before being presented to the living of Twickenham. However, after a year in dread of the part he played being disclosed, and with considerable means now at his disposal, he could buy the livings of two insignificant villages and settle down unobtrusively, with no questions asked. His secret was kept until his youthful death in 1791, when he confessed to his family. There is no doubt that the part their former rector played in the famous romance was known to some of the parishioners of St. Mary Hoo, although it wasn't until 1900 that it was conclusively proven. His fine Rectory, The Hall and Newlands Farmhouse are the three listed buildings in the village – the latter being the home of the Chancellor of the Exchequer, having been built for him in 1746.

With the 20th century modernisation of farming practices - machines replacing horses - combine harvesters and tractors becoming ever larger and faster, the need for a big workforce dwindled considerably. Worshippers for services each Sunday failed to fill a single pew and eventually it was deemed necessary to sell the Church and its large graveyard. The new residents transformed the building with love and care into a stunning home. Part of the purchase agreement stipulated that the public be allowed access to the gravestones at any time, so folk wander in and out through the ancient iron gate, taking photographs and generally making themselves at home. Luckily, the owners smile accommodatingly.

There seems gentle controversy as to whether St. Mary Hoo should be known as a village or a hamlet. It has credentials for both, being quaint, small and friendly, with few houses. It is also remote and surrounded by farmland. An existing place of worship or a community building would deem it a village, and in the absence of these, it would be classed a hamlet. What is perhaps confusing now is that the church is a private home, and there is no community hall or shop. Perhaps we, the contented inhabitants, can choose whichever one applies. I shall go with village.

We have a Victorian Post box - one of few such boxes in Kent still in use. Set into the wall of the oldest house, the residents accommodate its shape in their dining room, happy to have a piece of history close at hand. The box is cleared twice daily by patient postmen who wait for tractors, horses or combine harvesters to move through before they can negotiate the narrow road, namely our high street, which comprises of just eight houses.

A school, opened in 1868 by the wife of Reverend Burt Jnr. and with the Reverend and Henry Pye as Wardens, was needed when the collection of small farms which surrounded the village at the time employed manual workers, grooms, shepherds and gardeners. They and their families swelled the residents to well over two hundred. The building consisted of a large single classroom with mezzanine floor accommodation for the sole teacher. I've been told that pre-WWII, the terrifying Miss Henry spent a great deal of time leaning over her upstairs balcony, tapping her stick whilst sternly urging the seventy children below to concentrate. The toilets and play area for the children were across the road in the garden of The Red House, which three centuries ago served as a Poorhouse. The Schoolhouse doubled as a Sunday School until it was sold off in 1947. It was thought the local children needed the better facilities of another school, a bus ride away. It has been a private residence to several different families ever since, the large former classroom providing a perfect venue for village parties.

Opposite the Church is a pair of cottages of ancient vintage. They are charming. One is the home of our daughter Amanda and her family, and the other to country-loving Charlotte and James. In the next plot the semi-detached cottages are newer, having been built in 1938 for the workers on the farm, each with many children to fill the tiny bedrooms. They have been relinquished from the needs of the new farm tenant and are privately owned. On the bend of The Street, Ross Farmhouse looks imposing. It is our house, having been reconstructed cleverly from a pair of 1930s semis. Its name derives from the location of one of the tiny farms of old.

If we venture further along the lane, it gives way to a farm track, quite a robust one, and one well used by the farmers and their machines. At the first gate it would be impossible not to be impressed. For the view is glorious and unhindered. Most days when visibility allows, we look to the Essex coastline, and depending on the tide, the Thames river traffic moves in each direction. Tilbury is near, and to the right is the estuary. The magic is in the broad picture, the panorama of land and water.

This place is indeed a hidden treasure. Unbelievably, the marshes are a surprise to many people. They gasp in amazement whilst wondering how it is they had little idea of their existence. Although it is private land there are public footpaths where walkers have access. Plenty do, but many don't take advantage of this. Some show respect, and some do not. Gates are left untied or open and rubbish, bottles and picnic scraps are left lying around. Balloons float in on the breeze, tangle in fences, and their long ties are a danger to livestock. We sigh, but accept it all, for it is the price we must pay to have the farm in our care.

Houses seldom come up for sale in our village, for once a family buys into its charm, they are normally here to stay. I am sounding as if there are roses around every door, pristine lawns and swept, immaculate paths and gardens. That isn't the case at all. There are weeds, there's dust and leaves, overhanging branches and dying elm trees. In winter, inevitably there is mud. Some of the gardens need a little work on their overgrown aspects. So why, I wonder, is it so loved? It's all down to the ooze. It trickles out like a spider's web to sprinkle a little charm; an ooze which blasts through the overhanging branches to work its magic. It takes the arrival of the dustcart, a Tesco delivery van, or waste disposal lorry to ensure that it is a real and working place.

There's a pond at the T junction where a pair of mallard ducks hatch a brood annually, after sitting on their nest in the fork of a willow tree for three long weeks. Then the chicks plop into the water below, only to disappear with their enthusiastic but foolish parents when they are a mere day old and vulnerable. Much more successful are generations of moorhens who become tame, are fed and nurtured and who seem more adept at parenting than the ducks. Both species do not co-habit peacefully and early morning battles are frequent. Willows hang effortlessly over the water and reeds offer cover for the moorhen chicks, black and scuttling. When gossiping with a neighbour on the pond corner, the sight of ten little mallard chicks cascading out of their nest high above me will remain one of the most amazing sights I've witnessed in the village. And somewhere in the murky depths there are carp which we spot when rains fill the pond to an appreciable level. Frogs make their presence felt with their night-time croaking.

In an ever-changing world, we are proud country folk, thankful that our special, peaceful place refuses to join the urban upheaval.

St Mary's Church, from our garden

7

A Marsh Summer (in 100 words)

With renewed and unexplained enthusiasm, we breathe the air and see for miles, further now the rain has stopped. The air smells sweet with a fragrance of cow parsley and gorse, growing wild along the fence. Today there is time to stop, to pause and reflect on our surroundings in comfort, without the marsh winds. Warm sun kisses our arms and pale faces. Looking to the heavens as clouds fluff their chests proudly, only an aircraft signifies the amendment - for our forebears, celebrating the arrival of summer, would have witnessed just such a welcome seasonal change and vista, but for that plane.

Soft Autumn Focus

You gasp
for it's glorious;
this year, last and ever before.
The view towards our village
unchanged for centuries,
to the church on its gentle rise.

Gold bales, now caressed
by grainy sunlight,
stacked on bare brown earth.
Dappled autumn colours,
a mellow image
in soft focus.

Nothing moves or breathes
Until a swallow darts
high above
And a leaf falls
To join a carpet.
Then stillness returns.

8

West Point Beach

It isn't much of a beach, and neither would it win any prize as a bay. It has a nondescript name and a somewhat tatty appearance, striped as it is with seaweed and assorted debris. But it is there, a constant, a couple of miles upstream on the Kent side from the estuary of the Thames. Comprising of just one hundred yards of sand with a sniff of the sea, it is as quiet as a church even though it is only twenty-five miles from London town. West Point beach is accessible to a mere few lucky people, and that makes it a very special place. It lies at the bottom of the farm, so driving through grass fields, wheat crops or livestock to reach it is restricted and always on a trust basis to friends or family. Walkers can access it from the seawall, and as the coastline below the high-water mark is public property, we can't prevent those strolling through to admire and sit for a while. What we hate is the rubbish they leave behind, or the flotsam which floats onto the beach with each tide – a legacy of the river traffic. Why people use the river as a dumping ground is beyond us.

Important history

Where the tides of centuries have ebbed and flowed, twists and turns on the shoreline have formed tiny sandy reaches, mudflats and banks. Some are dissected by saltings and narrow creeks where watercress grows, and samphire and sea lavender flourish. The four little beaches at the bottom of the farm would have many a tale to tell. The Thames after all, was the motorway to London in those far off times and every vessel on its way to the London Docks sailed past Coombe Point, West Point, St. Mary's Bay, Egypt Bay, Cliffe Point and others on the Kent side, all just a few miles from the river's estuary. Merchants, men of high birth, highwaymen, whores and even royalty would have had need to sail the river. Some would have chosen to transfer to a small rowing boat, or lighter, a mere mile below our village and navigate one of the channels, thus saving a great deal of time and avoiding the hurly-burly of the city docks. In the middle-ages, and until a seawall was erected, the thousands of acres of ours and neighbouring marshes were tidal. Those early travellers, making use of a high tide, and wishing to make haste to Rochester or Cooling, each with a fine castle, needed merely to walk uphill for a mile before taking advantage of any hostelry or comfort there most certainly would have been in St. Mary Hoo. The village was considerably busier in bygone days.

Smuggling

It was through the well-rehearsed tidal channels of West Point or Egypt Bay that seventeenth, eighteenth and nineteenth century smugglers made their stealthy way inland with contraband goods. Unscrupulous merchants would anchor their ships near to the shore, having received a welcome signal from a lookout. Smugglers would then row little boats laden with liquor, tea, sugar, spices and other prized and highly taxed items into these creeks through the gloom and reeds. At a given point they'd be met by an accomplice and taken by cart to the taverns of Gravesend and the Medway town of Rochester. Though smuggling was a punishable offence – to the prison hulks off Grain, the gallows, a workhouse, or transportation to Australia for example, it seemed a risk worth taking to folk with very little. And it continued in spite of the threat of capture. Smuggling was such big business that bribes were often paid so that goods could change hands without apprehension. Wool from British sheep was coveted in Europe and was a major commodity frequently loaded illegally into waiting craft. No mercy was shown to those who were caught – a small packet of tea in the pouch would be enough to ensure a passage to a penal colony, or a rope around the neck.

London was renowned as the biggest and busiest trading centre of the world in the middle centuries. All shipping negotiated the Thames, bringing goods which were highly taxed to be sorted and traded at moorings, namely the East and West India Docks. It was a busy, disorganised and cruel area where smuggling was rife and crime constant.

Huge money was made by unscrupulous merchants who facilitated the transport of three million Africans to America and the Caribbean. Slave traders and their families became hugely wealthy and showed no mercy. The revenue from the taxed slave-harvested goods that returned to the docks – sugar, tobacco, liquor, tea, coffee and cotton for instance, ensured that the situation continued for decades. The dreadful trade continued until 1807.

The original docks were eventually not able to cope as world trade increased. Victoria Docks were dug out of marshland, followed soon after in 1880, by the Albert Dock. These latter Royal Docks, constructed during the nineteenth century, catered for decades until the port of Tilbury was opened to ease congestion in London and the east end. It was also proving difficult for containers and larger ships to navigate as far as the Royal Docks. Tilbury was a perfect site and being downstream, it conveniently shortened their nautical journeys. It is now the third largest container port in the UK.

With innovative architecture the London Docks have been transformed into stunning and desirable residential areas.

It is impossible not to feel at least some of the mighty river's history, even though modern usage has changed the outline of the shore. Inevitably, progress has insisted on developing some of what was once so precious. Nowadays with the high seawall, erected about one hundred and fifty years ago keeping out even the highest spring tides, those marsh acres (once tidal) are able to provide good grazing, and excellent grass for hay production.

The seawall is effective prevention, apart from one very serious high tide in the spring of 1953. That night, with no adequate warning, there was a tragic loss of life on the Essex coast and livestock in large numbers perished on ours and other marshes. The wall was then strengthened and rebuilt with clay from the diggings of an adjacent vast ditch, or delph. This feature stretches from Coombe Saltings to Egypt Bay and receives water from the farm's drainage systems. A sluice gate operates to allow an overflow into the Thames. The delph, with its gentle contours and prolific reeds providing cover, is a perfect habitat for moorhen, swan and geese.

On one boundary of the farm, at Swigshole, there is a path with a fascinating name. Bessie's Lane, now sadly overgrown, is where Queen Elizabeth I was carried uphill from the marshy creek after her royal coaster had gently deposited its passenger. As I said, it's impossible not to dwell sometimes on the historic past of these north Kent marshes. Thinking about the souls of centuries ago - furtive or famous - alighting from the ships which came up river or down is spine tingling.

And later

Once on the beach – it is best to visit at high tide – the magic lap of the water is as tranquil as any other beach. Birds delight as they take flight or swoop for food. There is a thick strip of assorted seaweed to welcome us, although caught amongst it is glass, driftwood and the curse of plastic bottles.

Watching huge ships coming up the Thames, while we barbecued close enough to see activity on the decks was always hugely exciting. Especially so in the evenings, when their illuminations were reflected in the water. We miss them, though the occasional exceptions are welcomed and news of their imminent passage is broadcast. Now the river traffic is mostly confined to an endless procession of enormous containers from abroad, ferries or smaller cruise ships destined for Tilbury on the Essex coast. A huge Container Port has been erected nearly opposite West Point with four cranes constantly in use. This ambitious undertaking involved dredging and massive infilling. Consequently, the coastline on the Essex side at the point of construction was drastically altered. It has also altered the fishing in the river, and its flow. Local to our little beach no eel has been seen and few fish have been caught in the last few years. Ian's recent eeling expeditions have proved fruitless.

On the beach at low tide there is always work to be done, pre-barbecue. Walkers have invariably left their picnic debris. Each high tide has deposited shoes, false teeth, buckets, driftwood, old lifejackets, toys and endless plastic pieces; once even a body, and occasionally drugs. Ronnie Maclean once found a tortoise on the beach, obviously jettisoned mid-river. Alive, and as energetic as a tortoise ever is, it was given a forever home with a friend. Jet skis would have zoomed over on the tide from Southend, with a picnic on board and a bottle or two of beer or wine. These would have broken into many pieces, for invariably they were left behind before the skiers started their return journey.

We take a few minutes to clear a space so that we can enjoy and absorb what should be sacred. We watch oyster catchers, curlews and redshanks scamper over the mud, pecking and scavenging. And we take in the peace, feeling instantly calmer. This is our therapy, free of charge.

From birthdays, anniversaries, mid-summer parties and village get-togethers, to a solitary contemplative visit, West Point has always been a favourite spot. For the celebrations it 'merely' involves trestle tables, chairs, a rug or two, food, drink, charcoal, grid, a spade and a box of matches. We need a favourable forecast and muscles to carry that lot down the seawall and onto the sand. And, of course, we have to visit earlier with refuse bags to clear the beach of all debris, except driftwood from which we build our fire for the barbecue. Children prefer a low tide when they can wallow in the mud, emerging unrecognisably, to the horror of their parents. At high tide the river is safe for swimming, although some would dispute that. Perhaps the best advice is to swim with mouths firmly closed, and not to venture out too far as the rip tide is a threat.

Then, when the eating and swimming or mud-larking is done, everyone gathers around the fire. Darkness settles and the villagers flop into their folding chairs to watch the dying flames or the moon on the water. At times like these, West Point becomes a place to dream, in spite of the other folk and their flotsam.

West Point Beach, with Sage and Rosie

9

The Sunset

I stand with the others on the seawall. Thirty villagers and a jolly mix of dogs; black, brown and indifferent. While the dogs pant and shake in excitement, we are in awe. Overwhelmed by the burning redness of the spectacle before us, we are consumed by its passion. I feel insignificant against the strength of it, dazzled by the dynamics being played out way over there. How far, I wonder? If I stretch just a little, could I touch it? For somehow, this display seems accessible. It's surely exclusively for us, a finale to the annual village barbecue. How thoughtful of the producers to stage their show as our own personal backdrop.

There is nothing between us and this wonder. Nothing that is, except a horseshoe bay, wading birds and swallows, saltings, ditch banks and a patchwork of farmer's fields. Perhaps a few bundles of hay. Nothing to dilute the fire. No chimneys, buildings, traffic; no noise save for our endless compliments, until we are depleted of adjectives. Then we stand in dumbstruck silence. No one wants to leave the wall - it acts as a primitive grandstand in an amphitheatre. We know that at any moment the show will be over. It is too fragile to last; too perfect to be repeated in its present form. Perhaps in another, for the kaleidoscope changes constantly as we observe it. And then slowly, it weakens and dulls.

The dogs are bored now. One of them nudges the ball down the slope and waits for attention. Mere mortals cannot ignore these antics or their enthusiasm, now that the sunset has faded. The colour tumbles away down that mystical slope we call the horizon. 'Wow, that was something else,' say some newcomers to the village. 'We never got sunsets like that in town.' They thank us as if we've arranged the colourful extravaganza just for them. 'We moved out here for all this space, and seeing that huge sky was incredible.'

'Well, you must have had big sunsets too,' I suggest, amused, 'but they're certainly easier to admire down here on the marsh.' And that's the difference. A sunset is flawless enough in all its glory, to be just as nature intended, with no frills, no fetters, no nothing at all.

The dogs shake sand everywhere, and the car boots close on the barbecue debris. The small convoy snakes along the top of the seawall, finding the farm tracks through the twilight, and onto the upland fields leading to the village.

'It was beautiful down on the beach tonight,' I murmur. 'What a sunset!'

'A red sky at night's a shepherd's delight,' answers the farmer predictably, from his store of folklore. 'The weather's set fair, there'll be another display tomorrow, you'll see.'

10

Anonymity

Written in 1971

Not for me, the anonymity
Of ambling carefree in a crowd.
You're not from round here then, they say
As I start to speak, out loud.

On the phone, or in a shop
In welly boots, or in a frock
Just as soon as I open my trap
Out it comes, the jolly map.

It's usually Oz, or maybe Africa
South I mean, or p'raps it's Canada?
Give us a clue, it's somewhere out there.
They fret and puzzle, getting nowhere
Until I declare, with utmost glee
That I'm a bona fide Kiwi.

And I just bet, after years and years
They will pause and quiz me still.
I can't escape. It seems my fate
For fifty-three pence change I wait.
Before you go, just tell us so
Where are you from? We'd love to know.

Do you know my aunt, she's called Meg Smith?
She lives in Sydney – a bit north of it.
I've been there, but I'm not from Oz
I groan in answer; I'm cross because
To me the accent's chalk from cheese
Do not confuse, I beg you please.

Don't get me wrong, I love it all
The Antipodes, wall to wall
But why in a country with myriad voices
Does mine provide such a question of choices?
I'm bewildered, I do profess,
To be the cause of so much guess.

Novel or nasal, lilting or soft
When I try to talk local it doesn't come off
I am who I am
And my voice is my own.
But sometimes, just sometimes
Anonymity's my goal.

11

And Then We Were Four

'These things happen,' said Mac, our lovely family doctor. 'Easily for some people, apparently. You're pregnant!'

I was stunned and delighted, and naively surprised. 'What?!!'

'You'll be a busy girl, that's for sure.' Mac knew everybody in the district, their health issues and lots more besides. He'd known just what to say when I was homesick on arrival in the country. He was a Maclean family friend, which added extra comfort. 'Two babies under thirteen months – is this going to be an annual event?'

I assured him it wouldn't be, and drove home in a daze.

Amanda narrowly escaped being born in the car, so speedy was her arrival. 8am was not an ideal time for a flustered expectant couple to arrive at a maternity home, with the night shift finishing and the day shift about to start. By 8.05 we had a daughter.

It will be similar to having twins we were told, and that's how we coped. Sleep deprivation would double and so would the towelling nappies. Everything would be in duplicate, including a timetable of bed, bath and play. It worked beautifully most of the time. Spencer and his baby sister were wonderful companions throughout their childhood. He called her Bubba. Together they hatched many mischievous adventures in the glorious freedom of a large garden and a warren of rooms in the farmhouse. The first two years of parenthood were negotiated with maximum noise and minimum fuss. Our kids ate well, slept well and grew lots. There were few jars of baby food in the cupboards – Ian merely carved a couple of slices off the joint each night and into a jug they went with vegetables and gravy. Then a wondrous little machine called a Bamix whizzed it up ready for the babies' Peter Rabbit plates. There just wasn't the time for the complications of fussy eaters at the dining table.

The nearest I ever had to the luxury of a nanny was in the reliable form of our shepherd's sixteen-year-old daughter, Glynis. She would come home on the school bus, alight at the bottom of Hall Road, walk to our place and spend a couple of hours with our 'twins.' She helped to feed, bath, settle them down and read them a story. The children adored her. She knew by then that she wanted to be a children's nurse, and I knew for certain she would be perfect in that role. And having a helping hand at bath time, with two soapy babies slithering around is surely one of life's essentials.

The children each had a pet lamb, and always there were cats to cuddle. Momma-puss had given birth to two kittens and the children, after much thought, had called them Fatty and Slimmy. We had sheepdogs to fuss over and sixty chickens, although that number fluctuated as Mr Fox was always on the prowl. Amanda wanted a pony but we resisted her request and persuaded a friend to share lessons. A neighbour also allowed the children to ride adorable little Nobby, who was invited to Amanda's eighth birthday party, coming briefly through the back door to join in the fun. At around that time I acquired my beautiful mare, Lady and was thrilled to have Amanda's help with the grooming and stable duties. At sixteen hands there was some growing needed before Amanda could ride her.

Both Spencer and Amanda say they had the best childhood. They had room to spread, room to grow and room to roam on their bikes. They did a lot of that in all weathers, and were able to disappear down the farm as far as the seawall and feel completely safe. And it was almost a traffic-free zone. They knew early the rules which come with gates and livestock, and about tides and trespass. We trusted them to be sensible.

For Spencer's sixth birthday we joined forces with the parents of five other birthday children in his class at school. Fifty children in big open trailers were transported down the farm to the beach for a barbecue. The girls were in one trailer, with a monitor, trundling from Sally's house along the main road. (Her dad organised insurance for that journey.) And the boys were in another trailer from our home. Though they were so excited, they were all well behaved for these rides. We thought it best that the tide should be out for the occasion. We arranged sack and potato races, running and wheelbarrow races before the feast, but mostly the children just wanted to scavenge among the rocks looking for crabs and shells. One birthday father, a butcher, optimistically supplied 50 lamb chops. Sadly, half of them ended up in the sand. To this day, our beach party for the birthday children is remembered fondly. There were so many facets to the occasion; what with trailer rides, races, rocks, crabs and Thames mud. All so irresistible to six-year-olds.

Although the farm was always a drawcard for school friends from the Gravesend Convent, where the children attended from four until eight and ten years old, and there were many playdates and sleepovers, options and choices for further education split up these young friendships. They sadly watched as their buddies went in different directions. We enrolled both children at boarding schools about an hour from home. This was something totally alien to me but Ian and his siblings had all gone away to school and that was what we would do, thank you very much. Spencer had his father's trunk and tuckbox and after a lengthy session with nametapes, off went our little eight-year-old in a smart grey uniform. He took to the life lots better than his sister, who missed Nobby the pony, our cats, no doubt us, and generally had a miserable time.

During their holidays, our rural community seemed bereft of children their age and life on the farm became isolated. That was to change when they passed their driving tests and of course when they attended Loughborough University. Spencer studied Sports Science – he had decided against becoming a farmer – and Amanda chose Media Communications. At every opportunity they drove down to Kent, usually with a car full of university friends anxious to breathe some country air and let off some steam. And as we always had three agricultural students helping out at harvest time, they would join up in the evening for tennis and barbecues. There was nothing isolated about their university life.

Ian and I adjusted to a large and rather empty house and yet we remained as busy as ever on the farm. I'd long ago discovered that I loved gardening and spent hours shaping and tending the huge space we'd inherited. But it wasn't enough. I enrolled on a Creative Writing course and allowed my imagination to run free. I became hooked on playing around with words, attempting different genres, and learnt to take the tutors' criticism on board. But still it wasn't enough. I decided to become a Counsellor, and so began three years of study, reading and placements. The two courses worked nicely in tandem, each aiding the other.

With farming, gardening, horses, writing and counselling and not forgetting housework, from which there was no escape in the big old house with its dodgy roof and haphazard insulation – my days were full to bursting.

Our two babies

12

Flock to Our Door

We often said that there must have been a sign at Heathrow Airport in the early days of our marriage, with an arrow and instructions pointing to our little village in Kent. It seemed to us, the first stop after Baggage Reclaim for many passengers off the early morning flight from New Zealand, was our farmhouse in St. Mary Hoo. Of course, there were the Kiwi brothers, sisters, and cousins, then the neighbours of all the above, and school friends past. All of that was extended by neighbours of neighbours, forty-second cousins and anyone with the vaguest connection to any of these categories.

As I had worked for a couple of years in Sydney, and Ian had worked for two years in Hawke's Bay, we had our own friends from both countries who flew in with astonishing regularity. They too had seen the sign and were most welcome – and as it seemed to them, were their own forty-second cousins and neighbours. Word of our Kentish welcome mat had spread.

With six lazy, sun-baked weeks on the *Northern Star* on our return to England having provided an excellent opportunity for generating friendships, they had also ensured yet more eager knocks on our door. Travelling was so easy in our and their twenties before the arrival of offspring. As soon as children arrived, it put paid to long haul flights, or at best turned them into a nightmare of planning. Actually, we didn't mind hosting Hotel St. Mary's for we had plenty of room and space to spread. We were kept up to speed with news from home and it helped maintain my accent for a little longer. My stoic washing machine was forever needed to cope with anything from the sands of tropical stopovers to the ingrained grime of a backpacker's rugged wardrobe. For every guest on their first morning with us ventured downstairs after a luxurious sleep with a huge pile of laundry and a sheepish grin.

They arrived at our door singly, in pairs and in family groups. We even had a mini bus surprise us one afternoon; so big that it blocked out the sunlight. Its eight young occupants assured us they were self-catering and we mustn't worry about them, not one little bit. However, when I discovered that contents of their food store amounted to a loaf of bread and half a packet of cornflakes, it was clear this would need topping up. They were part of a football team, with corresponding appetites and thirsts, sent by a brother who thought it would be a grand idea for the lads and their coach to see an English farm.

The next mini bus to arrive, more of a camper actually, comprised a large farming family sent on the same brother's recommendation. Our little daughter was crimson deep in a bout of measles, but they weren't put off by that and mucked in happily, even helping out on the farm. For that was how it had to be - farm work doesn't stop for guests. Watching livestock being fed, the combine at work harvesting the wheat or rape, or hay being baled was a major attraction to most of them. Every once in a while, there was a sniffy remark about the fragrance of farmyard manure if the wind was in the wrong direction. We chose to ignore such comments. It went with the job and there were a hundred bonuses to compensate. For all of our guests, a few days on a peaceful farm on the banks of the river Thames, were just the wind-down needed after a long flight or several weeks backpacking around Europe. And for rest and relaxation after a few days of frantic sightseeing in London - our little village could happily provide that in abundance.

We would receive advance warning of a visit by letter (there were no emails then) brimming with excitement, telling us of a gap in their itinerary, when London and the farm would/could be fitted in. Sometimes the letters gave flight details and we would drive to Heathrow to fetch the travellers. After the numbers grew to include neighbours of distant cousins and random penfriends, all possibly with the same fetch and carry expectations, we decided to restrict the red carpet airport welcome to close family. To meet a flight from New Zealand required a dawn start, careful planning and child care, so a trip to the local train station made life considerably easier.

So many people came in the summer season, and all keen for a tour of the farm; Ian could have taken up guiding professionally. He was a natural; same route, same talk, same stock. They all loved it. Being by the Thames added a new dimension, especially when a high tide lapped the seawall and cruise liners and coastal shipping could be observed at close quarters.

Then the visitors tailed off for a while, busy at home with nappies and night feeds. But one by one, or possibly two by two, their offspring, friends and partners became teenagers and decided to come to Europe on their own Overseas Expeditions. The trickle started all over again, only with a different generation this time around.

Overseas guests often arrived bearing gifts, ensuring we had a goodly supply of New Zealand tea towels, calendars, recipe books, Marmite, bubble wrapped sauvignon blanc and paua shell souvenirs. All of them were presented with an Antipodean flourish which preceded a bag full of travel weary clothes, ready for our in-house care. The most bizarre gift came from an Australian farmer – a cousin of a friend - and a reputable polo player. We were bemused until we read the label. It was a purse made from a kangaroo's scrotum. It made an excellent gift for a puzzled recipient at our next Secret Santa opportunity.

Then years ago, when fetching my very young children from nursery school, my front seat passenger was a Kiwi farmer with film star looks. I'd fetched him from the station and (that brother again) had assured him, a breeder of stud bulls, that Ian would give him a take on cattle rearing, Kentish style. The other mothers took more notice than usual as I parked up and collected my small charges.

Now we've moved – a mere five hundred yards – just across the field from The Hall. We have less bedrooms in our new house but still welcome visitors from far away, though possibly not a flock of them. Thankfully it is years since we've seen a backpacker's rucksack or a mini bus full of hopeful tourists on the drive.

A Welcome Mat

13

The Long Haul

Now and again, in between the influx of visitors coming our way, we made the trip ourselves, though ours was in reverse of course. In the dead of winter, when the livestock could be tended more easily by a shepherd or cowman – for they were tucked up in barns – that's the stock, not the shepherds and/or cowman Dave – and when it was summer in New Zealand, we made the long flight home. I say 'home' for I was confused as to where to pin the label for many years.

There was no quick and easy way to make the journey. It was tedious with no stopover and even a little wearisome with one short break, however exotic. Jet lag and body clocks were not a marriage made in heaven. Time aboard seemed to stop, while engine noise continued. Pristine fellow passengers became dishevelled as they too tossed around searching for slumber. But recovery was quick, thankfully. After a few gulps of clear Auckland air, we would soon be speeding away into the sunshine, followed shortly after by a sound sleep. Nothing more was required before Kiwi time took over.

Although I have no proof, I'm sure the longest ever 'supposedly direct' flight in the history of Singapore Airlines was in December, 1973. It was one I was booked on with our son Spencer, then aged three. Full of anticipation, I checked our luggage in at Heathrow, only to be told after a short wait there would be an overnight delay. The nearby hotel, courtesy of the airline was comfortable. Apart from not having any nightwear, it was an adventure of sorts. Next day and gleefully airborne, but for a mere two hours, there was an unscheduled stop at Rome airport, due they said, to engine trouble. We were told to be patient and obviously how very sorry the flight crew were to have inconvenienced us. Four hours later, having been treated to a free sandwich, we were airborne once more. Our relief lasted for a mere two hours. A small audible explosion was followed by an announcement. One engine had 'gone' (I think they said 'lost') and we would be returning immediately to - guess where? - Rome. Disembarked and shepherded into buses, we were booked into a reasonably adequate hotel for three days, but it was so tricky with a small child and still no clean, cooler clothes. He was hardly interested in the catacombs, the free tours laid on for us, or the pasta served up three times daily. The city was losing its appeal. A replacement engine was flown into Rome from Singapore, to be strongly strapped to the defunct one. Suitably trussed, the same poorly plane flew to Singapore as the next stop. By then we were a plane load of bemused, bedraggled passengers, less than pleased with proceedings. Some had decided to book another flight, thinking ours was jinxed. At peak pre-Christmas-time, this rescheduling was proving difficult, but at least the freed-up spaces gave us room to spread. And there was a camaraderie developing amongst those left behind. Spencer was being stoic and was less frazzled than his mother.

    Singapore welcomed us and at last we were reunited with our luggage. We gladly abandoned our winter garb and were able to change into summer clothes. The hotel was spacious, fragrant with flowers, there was a pool in which to cool frayed nerves and we were shown genuine hospitality, but that wasn't the point. For my 'direct' flight, this annoying delay was not part of the plan. The plane was still out of sorts and it was another two days before we took off for Sydney. Airport officials there informed me of two things: a) that my flight had been 'lost' for a time - that staff in Rome had said it had left, while Singapore had advised that it hadn't yet arrived - and b) that my connecting flight to Auckland had long since gone.

'Where on earth have you been? We can't get you to New Zealand until after Christmas.' It wasn't the news I wanted to hear. The tears of a weary young mother worked their magic. A suggestion was made that I fly to Melbourne from where just one seat was luckily available on a flight to Auckland the next day. So that is how I arrived. Careworn - with a brave little boy, and a very bad headache. Nine days to cross the world on a direct flight was surely an unfortunate record. Nothing could give me back the week I lost.

Air travel is all very well; it's (mostly) quick, fairly comfortable and convenient, but as such is neither epic nor intrepid. Speaking of courage, none of the problems on my ill-fated flight could possibly compare with any of those of the nineteenth century travellers to New Zealand. I was fed, watered, warm and in all probability safe – (it was just a *small* explosion) and these were conditions those brave folk were never assured of in their precarious sailing ships.

Since all of our guests who stayed at St. Mary's Hall in the early days of our marriage flew into Heathrow, none had the pleasure or enjoyed the magic of a long sea journey to reach British shores. We were so fortunate to have scraped into that era for our overseas expeditions before the skies filled with Jumbo jets, and everybody was in such a hurry. To date we have enjoyed the company of so many Jones relations from four generations who have stayed with us over the years - some more than once. And there will be more. That they all inherited Richard William Jones's adventurous genes there is no doubt. Their journeys here were certainly less arduous than his, en route to Bluff on the *Zealandia* in 1872.

From Mangaweka to Melbourne, from Durban to Dunedin, Auckland to Akitio, Brisbane to Bulgaria we continue to welcome little flocks of visitors, and we love it. Perhaps the sign at Heathrow is still there.

Trips to New Zealand tailed off for a few years for Ian and me, which was a shame. Myriad reasons contributed to this and there often seemed to be yet another spanner in our travel plans and dreams. The farm provided us with some lean years and it was such a monumental task to organise the care of the livestock in our absence. We also needed a multi-tasking house sitter. One who liked cats (three) and dogs (two) and who wasn't averse to mucking out a stable with equine duties attached. Such a person was like gold dust to find. The responsibility was so great. For the dreadful winter of 2001 the farming community was ravaged by Foot and Mouth Disease and we were victims too through no fault of our own. We didn't move very far that year, either.

In 1990 I commenced training to be a counsellor, and simultaneously enrolled on an Open University Degree course for Creative Writing. With these commitments encroaching on my time; clients, case studies, modules and portfolios requiring intense study and writing, I welcomed the arrival of our internet to communicate by long emails to family and friends abroad. Newsletters at Christmas were and are still an example of this. In this way I was able to practise my developing writing skills.

When we did venture to the glorious South Pacific, we relished the opportunity and made the most of every minute. Every corner we turned, every coastline we followed, each valley and hillside we viewed, we exclaimed, not in surprise, but in delight for we'd always known how lovely our journeys would be. However, there is no road which to me conjures up more delight and excitement than that of Napier Road, driving from Napier city towards Havelock North. For miles, way ahead, there it stands - Te Mata Peak, as serene and welcoming as ever.

'We're nearly there,' I always say. 'Look! There is the Orchard House.'

14

The Honey Pot

After my own lengthy flight disaster, Ian was in no hurry to arrive early at Heathrow with our two-year-old, Amanda. We'd decided that we would fly to New Zealand separately, swap children for the return journey and I would spend more time in my birth country with Amanda. I even planned to spend a week in Sydney on the way home, to visit friends from my time working in the city. I had been so homesick for Down Under and this indulgent arrangement seemed just perfect.

At the Singapore Airlines check in desk, Ian was offered accommodation in First Class as a consolation, for he'd wasted no time in reminding them about their shortcomings; namely his wife's recent trauma and her precious days lost. This upgrade was a welcome bonus for a young father who could only otherwise dream of real knives and forks on an aircraft, gourmet meals, a bed, and an abundance of beautiful air hostesses to assist him with his little daughter. And, for him, there were no airport delays at LHR. His luggage contained jerseys for all of us, as I'd rung to tell him that the weather in New Zealand was unseasonably cold. Naturally, he actually arrived in a heatwave. And so we were soon all snugly together once again.

It was the first time my mother had seen these two English grandchildren, numbers thirteen and fourteen in the pecking order. I think the novelty had worn off somewhat, although we attempted to keep the noise to a minimum. Optimistically, I was determined to catch up with every relative I possessed, wherever they lived. The rental car notched up many miles. Thinking back, I cringe when I recall landing on aged aunts with our two tinies, but they were easy-going children and as house trained as any puppy. We drove as far south as Dunedin to see two aunts, several cousins and flatmate Faye, from my time in the city. She had married a farmer too. Sadly, we discovered that one aunt was suffering from dementia and had no recollection that her sister Marjorie was my mother, or that I was her daughter. The other Otago aunt was ever welcoming and arranged an evening so we could meet as many of her seven children as she could pack into her busy schedule. The driving had been exhausting for Ian and a long early morning flight from Dunedin to Napier was very nearly missed. We'd overslept and had minutes to gather two sleepy children, their teddies, ourselves, pay at reception, hand in the car and flop into our seats. That night there was a reunion of girls from my class at Hastings Girls' High School. It was wonderful, even if I was bleary eyed.

Camping at Clifton beach was a trip down memory lane. We ate fish daily, swam lots and both children became tanned and outdoorsy. Sleeping in a caravan was a remembered novelty, especially with the water lapping tantalisingly close. Days were reliably sunny. One morning, I left Ian in charge of the children and joined a trek on horseback to Cape Kidnappers to see the gannets. It was enormous fun, so the next day it was Ian's turn to travel there, this time on a trailer pulled by an old Massey Ferguson tractor. It would be a toss-up as to which was the preferred means of transport. There were others – walking, for instance, or driving overland. Any which way, it was a special outing. It was humbling to be dwarfed by the magnificent cliffs in the meandering journey by the water's edge. And the end prize of the gannets in their rare habitat was well worth the trek. We ate crayfish and paua fritters at Akitio with my brother, Spencer, having dived for them just hours before. This lovely, wide stretch of beach was where he'd been Headmaster of the tiny school, built just yards from the water. He knew the best fishing spots and all the local farmers. Ian was interested to meet them and tour their coastal properties. We sat the children on Pania's knee (a famous statue) on Napier's Marine Parade, showed them the view from Te Mata Peak and feasted on the best ice-creams in the world at Rush Monro's in Hastings. Most of all, and significantly we introduced them to their Kiwi cousins.

One special uncle in Havelock North had a family business – Ashcrofts' Honey House – and a visit there was high on our agenda. We watched the extracting process, trying to keep Spencer and Amanda away from any wayward bees. And in a repeat of their mother's treat of many years before, they were allowed to dip their fingers into the glorious mix. We purchased a half kilo tin of creamy Manuka honey for Ian to bring home. It was time after all, for him to start thinking about his luggage, and to begin packing for the return journey. He would have charge of Spencer this time, and not a little girl in his care.

I bundled up all the obsolete jerseys, plus a couple of pairs of my high heeled shoes, (I have no idea why I thought I'd need them,) sundry items of underwear and several dresses. I was pleased to offload all this excess into his case. Dispensing of those clothes lightened my load for my week in Australia. His packing, with my help, went well. The tin of honey had been carefully sealed and labelled, and was a legal export at the time. As was Marmite. We wrapped them in a towel and tucked them amongst my redundant girly stuff. All was well. Oh, I nearly forgot to mention the kumara tubers. I'd missed kumara almost as much as I'd missed the view from Te Mata Peak, so I'd tucked a few of them into the shoes. Possibly not in the legal vegetable category, and yes, I was certainly pushing my luck with that addition. (Kumara are the New Zealand version of a sweet potato.) Four extra shiny paua shells completed the random extras.

Prior to his flight, Ian decided to take Spencer to the village barber – to spruce him up, he said. Maybe his haphazard English instruction set the man with the clippers on a path towards giving our dear little chap a short back and sides. The lovely locks were gone forever. I was not amused, though the deed was done. 'Move on,' said my man from Kent. 'You have to admit he looks more grown up.'

'He's only three,' I wailed.

Their flight was scheduled for an overnight stopover in Singapore. They spent their time in the pool and topping up their tans. Waiting at reception next morning, with the other half dozen Heathrow bound passengers, the group soon realised they had been overlooked. Time was running out and panic had set it. Emergency taxis were arranged. By now flustered and anxious they would all miss their connecting flights, their drivers turned up, to everyone's relief. Ian is not a naturally calm traveller at the best of times, and once at the airport he looked a perfect example of someone in a fix. Sure enough, the Singapore customs picked up on his sweaty demeanour and pulled him over for closer inspection. He'd tied his case up with twine – the type farmers use for their hay bales – and the whole caboodle looked decidedly dodgy. Anyone could see that. With Spencer howling loudly, and parenting skills at an all-time low, the contents of Ian's case were pulled out for all to see. By now a bright hue and wet with sweat, Ian watched helplessly as the dresses, the high heeled shoes, the floaty nightgown and on deeper inspection a well wrapped cylindrical object were discovered by the men in blue. At that point, the officers' fingers hovered over their pistols. A word which Ian roughly interpreted as being local jargon for bomb was dropped loudly into the equation. Protests about an imminent flight were ignored and the pair of them were marched off into a side room with the humble honey pot held aloft. It took an interpreter, an X-ray and a great deal of explanation before the situation calmed down. The kumara tubers were ignored, the Marmite and the shells bypassed, as it was obvious this young man with the shorn child was a cross dresser who merited pity. No-one assisted Ian in the repacking of his case. He was half way home before his blood pressure returned to something resembling normal.

His mother met the flight at Heathrow. 'You've lost weight,' she said to Ian. Spencer rushed up to her, looking relieved to have landed. 'Good grief, what have they done to your hair, little chap?'

The honey made it to Kent, and was all the tastier for the drama. The kumara did not thrive in our upside-down climate, and it was a contest at dinner parties thereafter as to whose flight was the more dramatic.

Children, this is Pania of the Reef

15

My Equestrian Years

When it became apparent that Lampshade classes and Flower Arranging lessons were not keeping me from pining for New Zealand, and the mop, bucket and broom were not the desired stimulation I'd dreamt of, Ian suggested that I learn to ride. There had been horses on the farm for ever. Eight heavy and handsome draft horses, loyal and loved, were employed to heave and plough until about 1950 and various ponies for the Maclean children had arrived over the decades. Before we arrived back in England, Ian's father had a couple of racehorses in training. They were not hugely successful and they were now living out their days in a field near our house. I fed them carrots, patted their soft flanks but that was pretty much it. As close as I'd been to a horse.

I guessed I looked the part in new boots, jodhpurs and riding hat, but it felt alien as I drove the three miles further along the Ratcliffe Highway towards Allhallows. The riding stables and clubhouse had opened several years previously at Slough Fort, an abandoned historical feature, built in 1867 to guard a stretch of the river during a period of tension with France. The fort, at the estuary of the Thames, was needed again during WWI and WWII. It was dark and cavernous, with brick walls and compartments giving out an eerie feel, but the horses seemed accepting of it. Most importantly, they were well-loved and cared for.

A neighbouring field had been utilised by the club for riding lessons and exercises. These sessions were taken seriously and were challenging, and definitely more interesting than housework. We were allocated different horses each week, some placid, others playful. Occasionally there was a gymkhana to test our developing skills. I never thought I was a natural, rather more middle of the road. When I won a silver cup in a novice jumping class, it was just the nudge I needed. The obvious happened shortly after. It was time to buy my own horse. After all, I lived on a farm, where there was space and acres of grass. Keeping it was going to be easy, or so I naively thought.

My first purchase was an ex-racehorse. It was not a successful choice, and Alfie was soon sold on to a girl who had enough experience to cope with the uncontrolled gallops which were his one speed.

And then I got lucky. A friend was shortly to be married. Already Jill was the proud owner of two horses, a mare of fifteen and the mare's offspring, a young gelding of four. It was more a case of her fiancé suggesting that 'I'll happily take you and one horse, but I'm not sure about the three of you!' Her beautiful Russian thoroughbred was therefore up for grabs, meaning the bride-to-be and her young boy, Fred could be incorporated into married life on another farm nearby. That left me in a bidding war of one.

Lady was beautiful, a chestnut with a kindly temperament and a white blaze down her lovely face. She was absolutely perfect for me. We bonded immediately. She had travelled by ship from Russia as a two-year-old, in a journey which had been so traumatic it had taken three days before she could be coaxed off the ship. Soothing words in her own language needed to be quickly learned. But not by me. By the time she arrived in St. Mary Hoo years later, she was calm and clever, had raced in point-to-point, evented and been pampered by two adoring lady owners. Now it was my turn.

When she was twenty, she gave birth to a colt we named Gigolo. He arrived in a horrendous lightning storm, in a field where he was to live happily for thirty-one years. His forever home. Drama was never far away however, although he survived each of them. His sire was Anglo Arab, carefully chosen. The combination of genes ensured that he was a fabulous looking fellow and bay in colour. He didn't have the placid temperament of his mother, and riding him was literally a roller coaster as he was often unpredictable. His field companions were ten stock bulls and they cohabited happily enough. Except for the one bull, who once tossed the annoying little chap over a fence, leaving him with seven lives still intact and needing a visit from the vet. Gigolo had a favourite bull, a Charolais, and would snuggle against him, both of them sleeping in the sunshine.

The huge expanse of marsh and seawall allowed him far too many gallops and he had his way too often. One of our fields offers an uphill gallop of nearly a mile, and is reckoned to be one of the best gallops in Kent. I admit we never walked it. Usually, I had a Labrador tagging along behind, quite some way behind, I confess.

For most of Gigolo's best riding years I had a succession of friends sharing the stables. He therefore had a variety of horse companions. Of course, for a start, there was his mother, Lady. Whenever possible I would venture out with Amanda, who could ride either of the horses well. There were wonderful outings with Dee, an accomplished horsewoman who shared the delights and the view of the farm from her beautiful listed house in the village. Over the years the picturesque acres drew many horse friends for our handsome Anglo Arab. His favourite was Maverick, owned by the lovely Sarah. Together the four of us enjoyed fun times for years and brilliant riding experiences.

It was a joy to be on horseback on the farm, and in forty years I would have covered every inch of it. Seeing the farm in all four seasons, and the marsh in every mood was such a privilege. It provided perfect riding in any season. The fields were large and if gates were shut there was usually an option to jump a fence. Once on the seawall there was an opportunity to admire river traffic; cruise ships large or small, coasters, tugs and fishing boats, constant birdlife and the occasional seal. A pleasant, easy circle of an hour could cover ten miles of farm and seawall. Sometimes we would take the horses down the wall and let them paddle in the water.

We often had dainty swifts follow us – not as escorts but to devour the tiny insects the flying hooves of the horses might provide, or nuisance flies they might attract. In the Delph (a wide, deep ditch which was dug for its earth from which the seawall was built, and which runs the entire width of the farm) swans glided gracefully, often with a brood of cygnets in tow. Some years there were sixty swans in family groups. They shared the Delph with moorhens and coots. Canada and greylag geese frequented the marshes, and never far away the occasional marauding fox would be after a tasty snack of hare or rabbit. We never took for granted the perpetual display of wildlife happening right under our noses.

We were spoilt then. It is very different now – the menace of rabbits has left many lethal holes at the fields' edges, while on the roads traffic has quadrupled, as housing estates have appeared in neighbouring villages. Some farmers have locked gates to discourage visitors, including four legged ones, meaning alas, horses.

Below us, the outstanding view from every field (but especially from one called Paradise) offered the wide stretch of the Thames, twinkling on a full summer tide, gloriously blue and bordered by an Essex coast which seemed within waving distance. But in winter with the tide out, the river took on a sombre brownish tone, uninviting but for the scavenging wading birds. Sometimes a low fog would drift in with a frightening speed, but with familiarity, and advice to stay close to fences for guidance we knew how to return home, even with almost zero visibility, whilst attempting to keep our horses calm.

Over the main road we had further options for our riding, firstly trotting through neighbouring orchards, with frost crackling underfoot, or admiring the blossom, and occasionally (I admit) plucking a juicy plum or apple from a branch. They were far too tempting to leave there, shining in the summer sunshine. We called it quality control, because sometimes we needed another one or two, just to make sure. Once through the orchard we could see the river Medway and a succession of different additional routes opened up to us. It was so easy to take in several miles on these rides, with just a little road work and minimal traffic to worry about.

Looking towards the river and to the left, we had the oil-fired Grain Power station, huge and imposing with its tall tower, supplying a million homes with power. The tower (the second tallest in the UK) was demolished in 2016 as the power station was no longer viable. It had already been replaced with a new dual coal and gas fired installation. On the skyline there were cranes in operation at Thamesport, and ahead of us was the huge Kingsnorth Power Station, occasionally letting off steam in a horrendous noisy burst. This station was demolished in 2012. The view over this side was industrial towards the river Medway and the towns along its banks; Strood, Rochester, Chatham and Gillingham, heavily populated and historical in nature. They were known collectively as the Medway Towns. We often rode along country lanes, narrow but safe enough, taking in Stoke, Allhallows and High Halstow and wherever possible, galloping along farm tracks, before returning to the quiet of St. Mary Hoo. Along the way we were frequently avoiding the bird scarers – gas guns with timing devices to deter flocks of pigeons. It was a brave horse who didn't flinch when one went off next to it. We soon learnt how long we had between explosions – usually in the region of fifteen minutes.

Amanda proved to be a competent rider when she was very young so she was able to discipline Gigolo while there was still hope! Lady lived a wonderful, well-loved life until she was nearly twenty-six (we had the joy of her company for ten years) and her beautiful boy grazed happily in his latter years in the field where he was born and lived for all his thirty-one years. I often think that must be a record. Mother and son were irreplaceable and played a huge part in my life.

Lady and I

Proud Lady with Gigolo

Gigolo with his friends

Amanda and Nobby arrive at the party

16

Time For Tea

For the first few Christmas-time visits back to New Zealand our luggage was always stuffed with presents for the family. Every crevice was packed with goodies of some random sort or another. Shoes were ideal depositories for little specialities from London stores. Harrods was a favourite - their fancy soaps, toiletries, biscuits and tea towels seemed perfect. Or I'd choose very mini models of the famous red double-decker buses, or Gentleman's Relish, which was packaged in lovely ceramic pots. The choice was wide and tempting. Generally, we packed 'things in things' with not a jot of space to spare. Shopping for various members, from babies to a granny, was a monumental task. We met it with enthusiasm, and the process needed to begin in November.

It had seemed a good idea at the time. The task on the particular year in question involved a jaunt by me to the historic market town of Canterbury, which lies deep in the Kentish countryside. It's about an hour from the farm. Here I knew I would spot most of the gifts on my lengthy list. Choosing presents for the babies and children was straightforward enough. I concentrated on trendy clothing which I optimistically assumed would fit. I was sure that they would be welcomed, especially if emblazoned with a motif of Britain.

But what about gifts for the adults? They always provided a minor conundrum. However, after merely a single circuit of Canterbury's High Street, and for me that's not long at all, I spotted an answer. A deliverance. With mounting excitement and lessening logic, I examined each and every model. Teapots! Not just your average plain and ordinary breakfast-table types, but brightly coloured china ones in the shape of bicycles, animals, fire stations and post offices, windmills, sewing machines and goodness knows what other designs. I became so smitten with glee that I completely disregarded the possible weight and size of the treasures. I purchased three immediately. They came boxed of course, and because I was so overly enthusiastic, (more so obviously than the average customer) the shop assistant wrapped each one carefully in copious amounts of bubble wrap and tissue. Seeing my delight and gratitude she tactfully agreed that I'd made a brilliant choice. Once home, the fervour didn't evaporate, although the size of the stack was a little daunting.

It was a relief to have finished the shopping, especially knowing that I had made such an innovative choice for my three sisters in law. I just knew they would absolutely love their sewing machine, country post office and beehive designs in multi coloured authenticity. My only regret was that I hadn't purchased another, this time for my mother, or even perhaps a fifth, for myself. But no, I'd stuck with the three. A patchwork quilt draped enticingly over the antique sewing machine, and since one sister-in-law was an expert quilter, it had seemed an obvious choice. The post office door was enchantingly festooned in a climbing rose on a trellis, daisies nestled by the step, and the windows were lead lined. (That one for Barbara who was garden mad.) What was not to like? And the beehive was, well it was a hive of activity – there were lots of bees humming happily. I was too - slightly euphoric at my cleverness.

The stewardess on the British Airways flight was accommodating, considering she probably had several such random requests on each or every flight. (Greek urns on the return journey from Corfu spring to mind.)

'Yes, I'll keep an eye on your teapots. They'll be fine here in my locker,' she assured me, smiling warmly, lipstick immaculate. That's the thing about cabin crew, they're so obliging. One year I had my grandfather's mantle clock, carefully wrapped for the return flight. That went into a steward's locker for safety. That it has never chimed two o'clock since then is no fault of his, I'm sure. A homemade Christmas pudding was similarly welcomed. I doubt such favours would happen as the 21st century progressed, trust being a wonderful thing, especially with a dome shaped, bomb-like pudding bundle.

During our two-night stopover in Singapore my smugness took a dive. A deep one. On a jaunt in the shopping mall near the hotel I noticed a display of teapots frighteningly identical to my treasures. So large was the display they practically obscured the window. There were even more varieties than in Canterbury, and worse still, they were half the price. There must have been twenty myriad designs. I had to admit it did take the shine off the Canterbury purchase.

'Oh dear,' said Ian, not sure how to placate me. There was no going back to Canterbury to buy other authentic British presents, though I took a little comfort in the hope that my lovely girls would not have visited Singapore in recent weeks.

Sadly, the situation deteriorated (though the girls were gracious on receipt.) In every town we visited during our month in New Zealand there was a display of the dreaded pots. There must have been a container load of them arrive from China to the docks in Auckland, and from there, distributed to every gift shop the length and breadth of the country. As for the specialist shop in Canterbury High Street, they had surely welcomed their own container load and doubled the price.

After that disaster, and because by then the family had expanded rather more than our 20 kilograms of luggage allowed, we gave up on presents for everyone.

We were soon to discover that New Zealand shops were stuffed full of a wonderful assortment of gifts – home grown or home produced – and some imported from England. The novelty of a tiny red London bus or a Union Jack tea-towel was in itself so mini, we settled instead for a fine bottle of local Chardonnay from a Havelock North winery and everyone was well satisfied.

17

Fun at Minnis Bay

For a hundred years, three generations of Macleans, with children in tow, had joined other farming friends on the Thanet coast in a quest for a large dollop of sea air. Nothing much had changed over the years. The beach was a huge hit with young and old and it seemed natural that Ian would want to take his little brood there for some sunshine and sand castles.

Thanet was therefore so familiar to north Kent farmers that several chose a Birchington prep school for their sons. Ian and his brother Robert were included in this plan, and from the age of eight they were packed off with their trunks, not to be reunited with mum and dad until half term, and then only for a day. Harsh rules continued with an enforced daily dip and a brisk march to the beach in swimming costume. With the M2 motorway a distant dream, and the road to the coast passing through each of the Medway towns, the journey to see the boys took hours. Parents preferred to stay overnight pre-visit, having a fine old time, while their attachment to the area developed accordingly.

Between the wars, Ian's mother and her six siblings had enjoyed holidays with their parents when they were children. The French* family rented a large house for the school holidays and the beach was inevitably full of farming families in a tradition which was followed year on year. Thanet was also predominantly an agricultural area and, in those days, farming was a friendly network of familiar fathers and sons. Ian, Robert and Janet were also able to enjoy similar idyllic bucket and spade holidays as children. Beach cricket, races, and crabbing were a serious business every day. And the ice-cream shop did a brisk trade late in the afternoon.

(*Incidentally, on the first night of meeting Ian, just after embarking on the *Northern Star*, he told me that his mother was French and his father Scottish. As a Kiwi I found that quite impressive, certainly intriguing, but of course French was his mum's maiden name. And Ian was given to exaggeration, I would discover.)

Minnis Bay, near to Reculver Castle is an hour from home. It's a pleasant drive, becoming less populated, before reaching the coast after passing through Birchington. It's sheltered at one end by high cliffs. The promenade is wide and inviting, allowing picnickers, sun loungers, strollers, bikers and pram pushers to jolly along. Once on the beach, the sand stretches for miles. There are beach huts to be rented, and some lucky few to buy. They are tiny, but are a precious commodity, keeping possessions safe and dry and giving the children a base to indulge endless appetites. There's a pub nearby and a fairly adequate toilet block. The children think it's heaven there, as the tide goes out for hundreds of yards, leaving a huge welcoming stretch of sand. There are crabs to be caught and pools to be examined, cockles to dig up, day after exciting day. The crabs get a reprieve but the cockles are steamed and enjoyed. The sea is seldom rough and swimming is mostly safe. Small people become tanned and outdoorsy in no time. Some dads show off with dinghies and boards if there is a breeze to snatch. So that is now…

Back then, in the seventies, it seemed sensible for us to purchase a tiny flat in a block of twelve. The flats, square and functional, inevitably arrived one after the other when the popularity of the heavenly spot spread to the masses. The little bay offered a small block of shops and a large playing area for mini golf, tennis and just frolicking around. Our flat was on the first floor of the oldest block, though its fine view was soon taken out by yet another block which was right in our line of vision. Progress has its disadvantages of course. Every morning the mums (dads were often back at home on their combine harvesters) would load little baby buggies with drinks, towels, lunch, jerseys, hats, sun cream and crab nets and set off on the short trek to the beach huts where one mum, more organised than the rest of us, would have rented one for all to share. That we resembled the raggle-taggle brigade as we walked the short distance was not lost on us, especially if a baby was squashed and complaining somewhere under the load. Naturally it was chaotic but all the more fun for that. The huts were as basic as any hut, with no electricity and a single water tap along the beach. There was always a scrum of wet sandy little people, trying to snatch a morsel, or babies having a nappy change. Often a nappy was all they wore all day.

Whilst we owned this small piece of Thanet real estate, we were able to welcome my brother Spencer and his wife, Jenny who were in England at the time. They were able to enjoy one of the beach side barbecues when about fifty people gathered for a riotous night. That it differed dramatically for them from eating crayfish at their nearby Akitio, Wairarapa beach idyll, added to their pleasure. Another huge Minnis Bay party, well remembered, was in honour of Charles and Diana's wedding. Any excuse, and the beach was soon a scene of celebration. My mother was taken there too on her first visit to Kent. She was able to relax when on sand castle duty and proved a reliable baby sitter. In a change from the beach, we ventured to nearby Margate with her, where Spencer and Amanda begged to visit Dreamland. With its arcades and funfairs, it couldn't have been more different than Granny's conservative home village of Havelock North.

In the ten years we owned the flat, Ian's visits were few alas. With a large herd of breeding cattle, it was difficult for him to take time away from the farm. I drove down whenever I could with the children or with their friends. On one occasion their friends were very local to home. Nigel and Tracey, much the same age as our two children, lived on the farm with their father. The five of us settled into the flat at Minnis Bay, with a promise of a visit to Quex Park in Birchington next day. It was advertising a Carnival Day which seemed irresistible to the four youngsters. The two boys, aged twelve, decided to head off on their own – with instructions to meet up in an hour and obviously with the usual warnings about taking care. Off they set with a pound each to spend (this was in the days when children were more secure and a pound went further.) We three girls stayed together. After an hour we waited at the given rendezvous and Spencer turned up, explaining that Nigel had dawdled so much, he'd left him behind. Oh joy!

Half an hour passed and there was no sighting of the gangly blond lad. I approached the Secretary who obligingly put out an announcement to the effect that Nigel was needed to meet his friends, and where. Another half an hour sped by, with me becoming very agitated indeed, wondering what I would say to his father that evening. What if he'd been abducted? Had he run away? Was he hurt? Another announcement, followed by yet another fifteen minutes later. Still no Nigel. A welcome committee of officials and our own little party sat in a stew of concern. There seemed little we could do, except panic. And we were most certainly doing that.

'There! That's Nigel, Mum. Look at him, he's wearing big funny ears.' Sure enough, Nigel had spent his pound on humungous Doctor Spock plastic ears, green and ghastly, and hadn't heard any of the panicked announcements. Neither, it appeared, could he tell the time. Worse, he was totally unfazed by the drama he'd caused.

Amanda was away at pony club camp, when as a special treat for Spencer, I booked a trip to Calais on the Hydrofoil. I parked up in Dover and we felt the unnatural motion of the craft, or flight, as we sped over to France. The sea was rough and became rougher. We purchased a few of the normal French go-to goodies, like cheese, mustard and chocolates and set about exploring the town. Back at the terminal we found the hydrofoil return journey had been cancelled and it was doubtful whether any space would be available on a ferry, or even whether it would also be too rough for the return crossing by that means. Along with all the other hopeful passengers, now displaced, we walked wearily to the ferry terminal and waited for hours. At least we had some cheese to eat! Finally, the sea calmed down sufficiently; we crammed on board, and many hours later we arrived back at Minnis Bay. More torment than treat for the child, but he was surprisingly accepting.

Once both children were installed at boarding schools and with school holidays differing slightly, we decided to sell the flat. It had been useful and enjoyable for ten years, but possibly under-used, especially for our farmer. Amanda's principal interest seemed to be equine, and Spencer was cricket mad. Mostly, they wanted to be at home on the farm in their holidays.

Minnis Bay continues to attract multitudes – generations of beach lovers with the same welcoming expanse of sand and wide inviting seascape. It's where memories are made, sun-kissed days are idled away, just as always. There are more blocks of flats and more people vying for the beach huts, it's difficult to find a parking space, but somehow there is room for everyone down on the sand.

18

The Last Visit

It was to be her last visit to England, the land of her birth. We picked her up from Heathrow at dawn, a confused old lady, attempting to look on top of the chaotic situation which greets every traveller on arrival. After Dad died my brothers had thought it would be a grand idea to bundle Mum up and send her overseas to spend a month with each of her daughters. It sounded simple enough, recuperative at best but the considerations of time change, baggage reclaim, hand luggage, medication, and paperwork had apparently slipped their minds. Some of these were missing, left randomly in airport lounges along the gruelling route. We got her home eventually and into bed and then wondered how best to accommodate a grieving, disorientated granny.

Her English grandchildren, Spencer and Amanda, were stars. Although they were numbers thirteen and fourteen in the tally, she showed gallant interest and joined in their games when possible. However, they were unfamiliar little people to Mum, along with the environment, and she was clearly homesick for Havelock North. I fervently wished she had been a better correspondent over the years for so much was new and different. Thankfully she was reasonably mobile and able to walk short distances, occasionally venturing off down the farm, though not always with the children. That was not to be encouraged, we decided.

'I do love this view,' she sighed, on one of their strolls, rheumy eyes straining into the distance. 'My father, that's your great-grandfather, left me his brass telescope and I wish I had it now. Those fields are such wonderful colours, and the river further down at the bottom of the farm – it's so bright. And the trees, there are so many of them. But I can't see the detail very well.'

'Dad's got some binoculars, but they're not brass. He'll let you use them.' Our small daughter was nothing if not generous. They leaned on the five-bar gate for a while, talking about nothing and everything, and looking down towards the Thames. It was a bonding time. 'Granny, are you as old as that oak tree?'

'Probably, dear.'

'There were lots more trees before half of them got sick,' Spencer told her. 'See all the wood that's fallen. About two thousand elm trees died.' Information overload from a seven-year-old. He was merely quoting his father, though Mum was impressed, apparently.

'What a dreadful shame. Thank goodness for oaks, willows, hawthorns and ash trees then.' Their old and once wise grandmother smiled.

'Gosh Granny, you definitely know about trees, don't you?'

'Well yes, I suppose I do. When my children were little – that's your mum and the others - we bought a whole set of Encyclopaedias and read up about a lot of things. Their favourites were the volumes about trees and nature, and we read them so often I got to know a lot about the trees of the world. Funnily enough, that volume's the only one left in the bookcase. All the others have disappeared, to goodness knows where.'

'We have computers now, and Mum helps us ask Google for the stuff we need to know. We haven't got a Paedia or whatever you called it, but I think you know more about trees than we do.'

'Mmm. Maybe.'

'Granny, why did great-grandfather have a telescope?'

'It was because he wanted to follow the route of the ship which brought him and my mother, and me and all the Ashcrofts to New Zealand in 1910. There were nine of us altogether, because my aunty Lizzie wanted to be part of the adventure. Everyone was excited, but still we all cried as the *Ruapehu* left Plymouth. It was Christmas Day when we sailed. The journey from England took nearly three months, so taking an interest in the countries we sailed past, and the other ships we came across helped fill the hours and days. It was a very long time to be cooped up on board a small passenger ship, but actually I was too young to remember any of it. I only remember my sisters talking about all the handsome young men on board, about to start a new life. It was called emigrating, if you want to look that up on your Google thingy.'

'Was it fun starting a new life, Granny? Were you scared? And now you've come back to England in a plane, and it only took a couple of days. That was much quicker. Does it feel like coming home?'

'So many questions! It was fun for me because I was too young to know of any struggles, but it must have been very hard for the grown-ups as New Zealand was quite primitive then, so long ago. And no dear, this doesn't feel like coming home. New Zealand is my home now. I only lived in England for a few years and can't remember a thing about it. We left because the weather was too cold for Grandma Ashcroft and she was always getting bronchitis. Do you know what 'primitive' means? Well, no computers, telephones, washing machines or anything like that. No aeroplanes either, and not many cars.'

'Was there a school?'

'Oh yes, we all went to school. It was a very good school and we all did well there. Our school in Otago was one of the first in New Zealand, and the Otago hospital was also one of the first. That was in Dunedin, where we lived for years and years. It was a wealthy town then as a lot of miners came there to look for gold and the money they brought to the town built great big buildings.'

The days whizzed by with the generations becoming re-acquainted, filling gaps enforced by the cruel reality of distance and travel restrictions, and each of us enjoying the hectic routine of summertime on a farm. Granny was bundled into the car for the school runs, on trips to the beach and to the zoo, and she tried valiantly to keep up. Sometimes her faraway look spoke of the pain of separation, from her home, the bulk of her large brood, and of course her beloved partner of many years. We ensured her days were full and happy. In no time it was the turn of another sister to welcome her on the second stage of the grand plan. This time the destination was South Africa.

The second and also the third sojourns with her remaining daughters guaranteed more adventures and took her into the hinterland of that great country. From safari parks to wild seascapes, from Table Mountain to a tin mine, Mum saw the lot. Then they said she was ready to go home.

She'd promised to write more often, and I'd suggested she resurrect the old typewriter from under my bed at home (that's my New Zealand home.) No way would she have been able to manage a computer. 'After all Mum, you were once a top secretary, and you taught me to type as a child. It'll be quicker than writing by hand. It'll need a new ribbon though.'

For a few years she managed to keep in touch with her three daughters. Having her irregular updates on the state of everyone's health was a comfort, though sometimes the arrival of an airmail letter heralded sadness. One by one the beloved pets of the family home died off and then it was my turn to lean on a five-bar gate and sadly reflect.

When her letters tailed off my brothers explained that she was getting a bit forgetful and that I should be more patient. 'She's just getting older, everything takes her longer now,' they said. It was all right for them, they could see her whenever they wanted and they did, but patience was never my crowning virtue. Months went by and nothing seemed to change - no answers were forthcoming. Eventually Ian said I must fly over and check. Doesn't that sound easy? To evaluate the situation and possibly instigate some changes into Mum's routine.

The Kiwi family met me at the airport, a semi-circle of support around a frail little lady whose sapphire blue eyes looked at me and beyond, trying to register and yet not totally succeeding. We drove in convoy back to the home I'd left years before. Over tea and cake – the teapot was chipped – I was soon to find most of the pretty dinner set I'd bought my parents was damaged or missing - I was brought up to speed with the extent of our mother's deterioration. Unhappy carers had left or been dismissed by the sweet person we once knew, who had now morphed into a cantankerous grumpy soul in a personality turnaround which is so typical of dementia.

'Here are the house keys; watch them like a hawk,' my brother said as he left for his home nearby. 'And don't let her near the stove. Good luck.'

One by one the family departed, and soon it was just Mum and me, but it wasn't a bit like old times. This was a near stranger, and neither of us felt comfortable. It was impossible to relax for a moment, and I felt very alone that first night in charge, and definitely not on top of the situation. It was a despairingly sad homecoming for me.

We needed a diagnosis and I obtained it from the family doctor next morning. After that the wheels were rapidly put in motion and a family conference was called to agree on the next move. Meals on Wheels were cancelled. I'd found custard pies in the bathroom cupboard and casseroles in the wardrobes. No wonder she had lost so much weight. My sisters-in-law came with me to look at several old folks' homes and unanimously we chose the one we felt was most comfortable. Her room was large, she could take some of her furniture, move in straight away and the view was wonderful. We began sewing nametapes. My brothers, now that I was there to steer them, could not have been more supportive.

At first Mum thought it was a great adventure, but after a week she thought it was time to return to her home. It became terribly hard to leave her there after each visit. I bought her tapestry, scissors and embroidery thread, Scrabble and books, but later learnt that she had cut up some sheets with the scissors which of course were then confiscated. And it was painful to challenge her at Scrabble when once she had trounced everyone in the family.

One of her favourite pastimes was to play with buttons and her few remaining pieces of costume jewellery. She loved the bright, happy colours swirling in the button jar and the shiny glint of her favourite blue earring as the morning sun cascaded through her big picture window. There were singalong sessions and piano recitals but more often the residents would sit in a huge square glaring at each other. Our mother was not the only one with a personality change.

I stayed a month; it was the very least I could do. I wish I could say it became easier, for her or for me, but she was safe and for that we were all grateful. There was much to do and we were all busy closing up the house and distributing little treasures here, there and everywhere.

There were no more escapades with scissors, but there was an incident involving an escape plan. Apparently, she rang for a taxi and left the home with another elderly patient. The driver thankfully sussed out her plan, drove them around the block and returned them soon after. I wonder if he'd done something similar before?

Reports from home appeared more settled and soon a year had passed since my hurried visit. At 3 a.m. one winter morning the bedside phone rang. It had to be New Zealand. And it was. Bad news always comes in the middle of the night.

It had been the same when a brother rang to tell me that Dad had died. Waving him goodbye from the deck of the *Northern Star* was to be the last time I saw him. How was I to know that? Unlike Mum, he was never to visit St. Mary Hoo or meet our children.

19

Thick Pile Lasagne

No-one can put a mother in her place quicker than a thirteen-year-old daughter. One of my classic put-downs was when Amanda returned from a short holiday in Edinburgh to stay with her pony club pen pal, Fran.

To my normal mumsy-ish greeting of 'Hello darling, had a good time? Lots to do and see? Lovely ponies? Lots of nice food?'

Her reply to all of that was to brush over the good times – Just assume that, Mum and say dramatically, 'I've never been so embarrassed in my life.'

On enquiring why, it appeared that on the first night she had been asked if she liked lasagne, and she'd had to reply that a) she didn't know. What was it, exactly? And b) that she had never been given the chance to try it. Thereafter, Scottish dinners proved to be a gourmet's delight for the deprived child.

Now, our particular man of the house – father of the deprived child – is a meat and two veg merchant. He's the original Bisto Kid. Anything that doesn't resemble a slice off the leg, shoulder or nether regions of a beastie in an unadulterated form, he just doesn't want to know. So, we all went along with that which meant that the kids didn't get their lasagnes, their curries or their carbonaras. I always intended to get around to it, but admit I hadn't by the time the Edinburgh holiday loomed. It seemed easier to go with the flow, his flow.

And it transpired that Fran returned the visit the next summer. Much polishing of ponies and tack went on outside, while inside I browsed through the recipe books planning my piece de resistance. For what seemed like hours I fiddled with sheets of lasagne. Forever the martyr, I'd made my own and discovered on rolling it out that the kitchen table was barely big enough. The pasta guru had advised the quantity was ideal and family-sized. Who was I to argue, but whose family was he thinking of? Eventually, The Thing was finished. Into the assembled gathering of thirteen-year-old friends, watched in awe by number one daughter and especially by Scottish Fran, it was carried aloft.

I'm not sure which was more spectacular; the flight of The Thing as it sped through the air, or the neat splat it made as it lodged in the thick pile of the dining room carpet, cheese down. St. Mary's Hall was full of little steps and stairs in the doorways and I misjudged them that evening.

'Wow!' said Fran, 'you sure do things different down here.' And that was it, she thought it was a marvellous trick and she even helped me pick the hairs from the sauce, before the crumpled creation was devoured and pronounced Not Bad.

Amanda was not as embarrassed as I thought she'd be, and could even raise a laugh about it, before adding, 'Well Mum, you've done MUCH worse than that.'

20

Sage

Sage was just one of the many dogs, cats and horses in residence over the years at St. Mary's Hall. They were all so loved, and were a big part of our lives. The next three stories, written at the time, are an indication of that. Then there were the hundreds of sheep, cute lambs, cows, calves, bullocks and Big Daddy Bulls. Yes, it was animal magic around the place.

She lies, most of the day, with her back pressed against the Aga, never seeming to feel its intense heat. Instead, as always, Sage appears serene yet territorial. Any ideas involving the family actually cooking something on the big old stove must accommodate her bulk, since the kitchen is hers really and she merely allows us to share it. Sometimes she twitches as a rabbit scuttles across her subconscious, but generally she just lies there, simmering and snoring in prone position. It's true her lungs have seen better days and her deep breathing can now be heard a room away, but she sees and hears mostly everything – if she wants to. We wonder sometimes if her more violent movements whilst dreaming, involve her first and last sensual encounter. She was not impressed with Toga's advances, but the resultant eight puppies gave her something to focus on for nine busy weeks. She nurtured and disciplined, and we all agreed she was exceedingly maternal.

They were beautiful, just like their mother, and we told her often. But never again, she reminded us.

This dog, in her prime, could put her mind to anything. Bringing up a family was merely another example of how she took life in her stride. We chose to keep the little pickle who kept escaping from the puppy pen and was always first in line for food and attention. At a matronly nine, Rosie is her Mum's best friend, though considerably more active. (Sage and Rosemary, get it?) As the years pass, Sage's sleep time increases, though she happily leaves her warm mat for an afternoon walk and for her supper. Most of the time, and especially when the floor needs sweeping or mopping, she tells us she positively can't get up at all, it's just too much effort. But tap a spoon on a dish and she's by our feet waiting for a crumb or a morsel. She tells everyone, 'I never get fed, I'm starving! Just look at my ribs.' No Sage, we haven't spotted your ribs in years. When we talk about her, she opens a rheumy eye to survey the speaker. She processes the discussion and unless it involves food, she'll return to the heady task of slumber.

It's all an illusion. I'm not the dog they think I am. True, my tum's expanded, but what am I to do when offered such regular bribes? They, foolish family of mine, talk to me in loud tones as if I'm decrepit, referring constantly to the resident cabaret – me! It's enough to give a dog a complex. If they don't move the furniture, I can find my way around with these rheumy eyes. What a pain they are, eyes and bowed legs; they'll do the splits one of these days when I scurry towards the dishwasher. But I can still hurry in a pre-breakfast run, in spite of their claims.

Basically, I'm the dog of my dreams; diving into a wide fleet to pick up a duck, swimming through the reeds to emerge triumphant, always. No-one can retrieve like me, though Rosie tries. It's in her genes. She's going to be trouble that Rosie – she's far too complicated, I say. They need to be patient with her and she needs to chill out more. Which reminds me, I'll snatch a nap now, by my cooker.

A brisk brush with a Dandy, borrowed from the stable, results in her smiling in sheer enjoyment. She loves this therapeutic attention and knows her coat will gleam, like faded black silk. In her younger days she'd hang out in the stable, walking confidently under and around the horses. Her party trick was to take the rope and lead her friend Gigolo out to his field. It never ceased to impress but she failed to comprehend the left and right commands, so the last part, that of getting the horse through the gate was a combined effort.

The old girl is motivated only by food. She has, as far as I know, only two dislikes – dish-wash powder and raw garlic. Otherwise, everything is hoovered up and enjoyed. She can be persuaded to do almost anything with a biscuit, but to leave her warm Aga, it frequently requires two.

Sage

21

Moby
The Thirteenth Duckling

I walked through the brick archway under the fig tree, carrying a basket to dig potatoes for supper. 'Maybe some beans too,' I mused, and started to search in the lower leaves. It was then I spotted the downy nest with its broken shells. In the middle of the pile was an egg, still whole, with a single crack from one side to the other. It was moving back and forth. 'Oh no!' I wailed, 'she's left one behind.' I searched for the mother, and listened for the newborn chicks. But it was too late, the duck was probably already at the pond with her little family.

In the walled garden, hidden behind the runner beans, and shaped with leaves and twigs, the nest was safe. The mother duck had lined it with fluffy down from her breast, then she'd sat tight for twenty-eight days. Not a single soul had seen her, even when she moved to feed nearby or to turn her eggs. Now something magical had happened. They'd hatched! All that remained were cracked shells where, one by one twelve ducklings had wriggled free.

I called Ian from the barn, and while we both looked at the abandoned nest, the egg rocked around. The chick inside struggled as the egg rocked back and forth. Ian took off his cap and settled the egg carefully into the lining. 'Let's go inside and put it somewhere warm. It's about to hatch.' I found a woolly scarf hanging in the hall and lined a small box with it. While we watched, the crack got bigger and the movement inside became stronger. There were urgent tapping sounds until a tiny beak broke through. After two more twists, a small head appeared, and three turns later, a damp chick wriggled out. It lay quietly for a moment to rest, before it tried to stand. It fell over, then did the same thing, all over again. When it finally stood on spindly black legs, it blinked with beady eyes, and seemed to be looking at us.

The chick was so small I could hold it in the palm of my hand. 'Back you go, into your box. For a start you need to be warm, that way you'll dry, just as you would under your mother's feathers.'

Ian scratched his head and looked thoughtful. 'The mum will reject it because it will smell of us, but she did leave it behind, after all. We'll have to keep it inside for a few weeks. It will be a lot of work. Are you sure you want to do this?'

I looked at Ian for help, but he just rolled his eyes.

'Feed it! Good luck!' He went outside to check on the harvest.

I asked for advice on rearing baby birds at the Garden Centre and came home with some chick feed and grit, enough to last a week or two. The girl behind the counter was interested in the tale of our tiny orphan.

I drove home to tempt the new baby with the special feed. Then I chose a spot near the Aga and lined a larger box with newspaper and a blanket. I left food and grit in one corner and a shallow bowl of water in another. 'There you go, little duck, you'll be safe and warm in there.'

The Aga kept the kitchen cosy all the time. Sometimes, newborn lambs had been snuggled up to it, if they'd been chilled on a frosty morning or in a snow storm. Wrapped in a blanket with their backs to its warmth, they usually recovered quickly. When Ian came in for his supper he watched as the chick searched and scratched, pecking at the feed. 'It's going well so far,' he said.

'He's adorable, and already so fluffy! I'm calling him Moby!'

Ian grinned. 'That's a strange name, and anyway, it might be female. We won't know for two months. Not until his bright colours show.'

'Hmm, we'll see. But Moby it is, either way.'

Next day the little duckling was sturdier. He cheeped happily as visitors picked him up. Everyone agreed he was gorgeous. He grew bigger each day, cosy in his cardboard box. 'Number 13 was lucky for you, Moby, but I'm not getting much work done!'

His favourite time was breakfast when he sat on the table with a bowl of cornflakes. Actually, he sat *in* the bowl of cornflakes, splashing and gobbling until there was nothing left. He also liked sandwiches, picking out the favourite parts, and scattering crumbs everywhere. Moby eagerly tap-tapped his tiny beak and flapped his wings in delight. On the table he left small puddles of milk. Sometimes Moby sat down right in the middle of it all, looking very pleased.

After our work was finished for the day, I settled him down in the big box until the first farmyard noises of the morning woke the household. Moby preferred me to anyone else, flapping his wings and cheeping a greeting when I came into the kitchen. He sat on my shoulder while I watched television or read the paper. By now he was two weeks old. He didn't enjoy being on his own during the daytime. Mostly when he gave a worried squawk, someone carried him around. The cats were bemused but thankfully did not stalk our little orphan.

'Today little duck, you're going to have a swimming lesson!' I half-filled the kitchen sink, and Moby launched himself into the water, cleverly using the instincts he was born with. 'That was excellent,' I told him and started to dry off his feathers with a towel - until I remembered that ducks always shake themselves dry.

'We'll try him outdoors tomorrow.' Ian broke off a corner of his toast and marmalade and offered it to Moby. 'He can't live in the kitchen forever. Soon he'll have to be taught how to be a duckling! What about that then, little chap? Are you ready for school?'

We watched anxiously, as next day Moby waddled and quacked on the lawn. When he flapped his wings, the other mallard ducks came to have a look, but Moby rushed back to us.

'We'll have to take him back inside for a while yet. It hasn't worked.'

We tried again half a dozen times, and gradually our little orphan became used to the wide spaces of grass and garden, and the noises on the pond. His first feathers grew in streaks of brown. Ian tried to explain. 'When his feathers change again in a month – if he is really a Moby, he'll have reddish-brown breast feathers and a curly tail too. Females stay brown and their tails are straight.'

'Come on, little duck,' I urged, out in the garden next day. 'Let's put you in the pond with all the rest. You're not a baby any longer, but you act like one.' Moby flapped in the shallows and the others swam over, eager to meet him. The pond mallards quacked and squawked and flapped their wings, sending water in huge spirals. It was too much for Moby. He scrambled out of the water, wet and frightened and hopped onto my lap.

'They're only trying to be friendly, Moby.' But he wasn't so sure. Back inside at tea time, as Moby recovered from his ordeal, we vowed to step up his education. He was now growing rapidly and we knew he needed to be with his own kind. 'And you're making too much mess,' I told him.

Every day after that, I tried Moby in the pond and each time there was an improvement. He was getting noisier with his quacking, messier with his splashing, and braver with his swimming and diving. 'He swims just as well as any of the others,' I announced proudly, 'and he's getting more confident.'

Then one day, a week later, Moby swam across the pond, all the way to the other side. He remained there for half an hour before paddling back towards me. For no more than a minute he stayed near me in the shallows, waggled his curly tail feathers, then turned and swam away again. We'd done it! Our little duckling had grown up.'

Most summer afternoons I visited the pond ducks and fed them bread. Moby always stayed the longest, flapping and splashing, before swimming away to join the others.

One morning, in the autumn of the next year, there was a special surprise at our farmhouse door. Moby, now a handsome drake with a beautiful green head and fine bright plumage, was waiting on the step. There at his side, a very pretty duck in shiny shades of brown, sat contentedly. They scurried after some toast and marmalade and stayed just long enough to be admired.

Moby

22

Monty

Green eyes stared from a tormented face. Why, they asked, why do I have to live with you? I want to go home to Mr Quigley. But Mr Quigley didn't want him, that was the whole point.

Monty began life in Brompton Army Barracks. He was loved, and he enjoyed a happy couple of years, up until the posting. Packing cases predominated, bustle beckoned, and Monty felt the vibes of change. It was a disciplined house, stiff upper lip and all that, though a few tears were shed when it was announced that Monty and his brother Rommel were not included in the move to Germany. The children pleaded and begged, wept and wailed, but to no avail.

So to the Animal Sanctuary went the sad pair, woefully waiting for a new family. The visitors tickled them under their chins, murmured approval, but said they'd rather have a kitten. These two tabby army boys were through adolescence and right out the other side.

In downtown Strood, Tom Quigley and his long-time neighbour, Dot Long, elderly and recently widowed were having coffee. It was bleak, miserable and raining outdoors.

'This weather makes me feel so lonely, Tom. I've been thinking of getting a cat for company. I'd like to rescue one, but I'm not sure how to go about it.'

Tom knew when he was beaten. 'Come on then, Dot. I'll take you to that sanctuary in Leybourne.'

There were so many kittens. Tiny, fluffy and all utterly adorable. But Dot didn't want a kitten. She wanted to bypass the messy stage. Then she saw Rommel. It was love at first sight. 'That's the one for me,' she said happily.

'Just a small donation will cover it,' said the lady in charge. You should get on just fine with him. His brother will miss him, though. They haven't been apart for two years.'

Tom gazed at the tabby now on his own in the cage. 'Dot, why not have them both?'

'I'd like to, but no … I can't. But why don't you have him, Tom?'

Rommel and Monty went home to Strood. Tom installed a fancy cat-flap. There'd be no strays for him. Rommel slept on Dot's bed every night, and Monty prowled as all insomniacs do. They preened every day in adjoining gardens, meowing and meeting up just like old times.

Then disaster struck. Rommel was mown down in the road. Dot was tearful, Monty was puzzled, yet Rommel wasn't replaced. Life went on nearly as before; Monty was out all hours, with no routine to speak of. He was a character, and Tom became a new convert to cat appreciation.

When he'd been missing for three days a worried Tom took the fancy device off the flap before he went to work. That evening, once home he hurried to the kitchen. There in the corner was a sorrowful bundle, one hind leg stretched out at an awkward angle. Tom knelt down to comfort poor Monty. He borrowed Dot's cat basket and with a heavy heart drove to the vet.

Obviously, the leg had to come off, as the X-ray showed 11 breaks, but since Monty seemed undamaged internally, the vet explained to Tom that cats and dogs live nearly normal lives on three legs. Tom wasn't so sure. 'We'll see,' he said, but without conviction.

'He's eating well and he's come through the operation nicely.' The nurse was encouraging. Tom looked down at his friend, wrote out the cheque to seal his fate, and walked out. He couldn't face life with an amputee.

'Now what?' Nurse Angela was a cat lover. Monty had come this far and she thought he should have a chance at least. The vet agreed to a fourteen day stay of execution.

No-one seemed to want him. And when Angela dropped in the bit about the missing leg, the shutters went down. On day eleven of his 'stay' I got to hear of the sorry saga, and long-story-short, when I asked what he was called (as if it mattered) I was signed up for the long haul. I've got a brother called Monty. It was time to save the day.

He came home to us one very wet Bank Holiday, with thunder and lightning thrown in for good measure. He was frightened and no doubt wished he was back at the vets. It wasn't long before we agreed with him. He wouldn't eat or drink and when we turned our backs for just one minute, he was off. We spent most of that Bank Holiday looking for him. He was fussed over constantly but flatly refused to enjoy life. On the plus side, his scar healed beautifully, gradually disappearing under a new downy coat. He was confident on his three legs.

'Please Monty, I begged, after rescuing him from under a wood pile. 'You're such a lucky cat, you've got a big garden, a farm to explore and very little traffic.' He wasn't convinced. For two months he ate only enough to sustain himself before rushing off to the wood pile to contemplate his dismal existence. The pile of wood was in the churchyard next door. I was well aware that at any time, men in white coats would be summoned to the strange lady in a dressing gown, who in the dead of night would leap from grave to grave, tapping a tin with a knife, while calling 'Monty, Monty, come to Mummy.' He was a challenge, and I was his last-ditch hope. If the knife on a tin trick didn't work, I'd shine a torch around the garden, until those large green eyes glowed. It wasn't much of a life for him.

And then he **really** went missing. Perhaps he's walking home? My daughter rang the police. 'I'd like to report a missing cat,' but the constable seemed barely interested. 'He's got three legs,' she added.

'Any other distinguishing features?' he asked her, while stifling a chuckle.

There was no three-legged cat to be seen on the home front, or marching back along the Highway to find Mr Quigley. Upset, we searched high and low and under wood piles too. The days went by and we started to lose hope. Then, from a ditch came a muffled meow. His collar glowed from the muddy depths. We were sure he could have climbed out, but that was the whole point. This was our test. We rescued him, scratching ourselves on brambles. He was hungry, but quite laid back about his ordeal. If we wanted him that badly, then possibly he'd make the effort and grow accustomed to us. We'd passed his test.

He's never looked back after that, no wood piles or boltholes, just comfy beds and sunny spots. His affection is open and constant, his is not a cupboard love. He cuddles tightly, his front paws around our necks. He careers around the house, up and down the stairs, in and out, taking life at the gallop. He ventures deep into the garden, hopping along at great speed. He's discovered cows, sheep and horses, is astounded by them but accepting. Try as he might, he just cannot master tree climbing, but he bears no grudge for his disability. He's a cheerful chappie. We're his family now.

Monty

23

Educating Adults

I have always endeavoured to attend a class or course in an attempt to keep body and brain in some semblance of working order. The list seems endless, thinking back, for it does span quite a few decades. And it's random – in a 'you name it, I've tried it' kind of way.

My first experience of Night School (or Adult Education as it is known here) was in New Zealand when I was in my mid to late teens. I enrolled on a cookery course – mum said it was a good time to learn, and parents in those days were always wanting to prepare their girls for an early marriage to some unsuspecting chap. I rebelled quickly and after a succession of lumpy sauces and pancake flat cakes, I switched to a shorthand/typing course. I could already write shorthand and I could also type, thanks to a Commercial Course at High School, but I wanted to be quicker, to pass an exam and enjoy the subsequent pay rise. That seemed more 'me', and I happily hung up my apron and handed the wooden spoon on to some other prospective bride material.

The Boys' High School, host to the mature students, came alive at night when the boys' books and endeavours were ingloriously pushed aside. It seemed bizarre for a choir to be full throttle in the science lab, or yoga meditation under way amongst the rugby or cricket paraphernalia in the gymnasium. In the typing room, rows of matronly women and young ladies sat and scribbled down their Pitman symbols from Hansard Parliamentary Debates, and tapped away at their transcription with varying degrees of speed and success. We all had the same degree of boredom, as Hansard was exceedingly dull.

I passed the exam, and the pay rise helped me save to cross the Tasman Sea to Sydney. One of my job requisites there was to hold a First Aid Certificate, so I found myself in another school attending evening classes, learning about pressure points and how to recreate two dozen shapes with a triangular bandage. This time I took the venue in my stride, stepping over football kit while coming to terms with bones, breaks and cuts. It was the solitary dark train journey to and from the school, through wooded Northshore suburbs which unnerved me. Perhaps a class in self-defence for me, next time? After ten first aid sessions, when I could tell the difference between a tibia and a tourniquet I left, clutching my Certificate.

The saving continued through the pay rise, and having been born into a family of intrepid travellers, I soon found myself in South Africa on a round-the-houses bus route home. One sister, Durban based, was currently attending Flower Arranging classes, so I went along to night school with her. 'You can choose,' Glenda said, 'flowers or Italian.' I'm not sure why, but I thought Italian would be handy. Florence had captured my heart after all. I toyed with the language, but there was something incongruous about a Kiwi sitting in a Durban school trying to get to grips with Italian vocabulary. I did not excel.

Back home – mum again - suggested a dressmaking course as the next step. (But Mum, I can already sew, thank you very much.) It wasn't long before I'd run up a suit, which actually fitted and included several pesky buttonholes, to my credit. It was time to leave on a good note and join a musical comedy group. Unsure whether I could sing or act, I gave it my best and had the greatest time trying.

Once back in England and married, with more thanks to Shaw Savill than my mother, the learning continued and classes beckoned again. We had stared at bare light bulbs long enough, and I was packed off to make lampshades. This time the sessions were in the morning in the living room of a dear elderly lady, with just the one sewing machine and one large table. Her red setter was a permanent fixture under the table and he suffered badly with flatulence. We were forced to endure, even ignore, as Basil was the lady's pampered significant other. Covering the bases was quite an art, and with fingers like pincushions signalling it was time to leave, I bade farewell to Basil and the other eager ladies. I'd completed a dozen shades, some frilly, some not. I moved further then, into Rochester to the town's Adult Education Centre, situated opposite the Charles Dickens building. The traffic-free cobbled area just screamed 'history.' Room 11 in that three-storey building beckoned. French, the notice on the door indicated. With no prior knowledge of French – Commercial girls were not taught languages – I lagged behind the others, and really, you'd think that my Durban experience would have suggested I'd knock on another door from the outset. Ian didn't help by telling me that there can't be anything worse than French spoken with a New Zealand accent. How mean of him.

And so on to yoga. Held weekly, these classes were always popular, and at last I was in my element. Yoga is not, as is often the misconception, hours spent tying oneself in knots, while chanting in meditation. The emphasis is on strength, flexibility and stamina, and we all benefited hugely from the postures (or asanas.) It is also calming, since it is claimed to be a fusion of mind and body. The poor old cinema in the Centre was structurally unsound, so with the outside corners of the room subsiding, our yoga postures involving balancing were compromised. Eventually, after continued moaning from pupils and tutor, it was transformed structurally into a tranquil place of pastel pink, with a pine floor and cupboards full of equipment. I'm still a yoga fanatic forty years later, after the pastel pink introduction per kind favour of Iyengar. Now, at a local gym, I practice Hatha yoga. Its benefits to me have been ongoing, as have the other classes and the social aspect of the place. These days I can be on a treadmill gazing over the river Medway. To the right is the huge motorway bridge. The river is wide and very tidal and there is continual traffic and activity in both directions. Swan and wading birds peck in the shallows. It is a prime position for any building. Ian and I are forever grateful that we made the decision to join this facility. We find it as friendly as it is useful in keeping away aches and pains, otherwise inevitable with birthdays which keep knocking on our door.

The Education Centre in Rochester was where I started my writing career. It was in a tiny room, home to a dozen hopefuls, who literally purred when the exceedingly nice tutor told us all that our work was 'wonderful.' Did I learn anything there? Well, yes, maybe so. I learned that talking marks go outside the full stops, and whatever we did, we must try to steer clear of clichés.

The kitchens there extended over the entire ground floor. The Cooking with Yeast course proved very useful for a farmer's wife. I took that knowledge home with happy results for many years. My favourite loaves were made in small terracotta flower pots, with their tiny bubble at the bottom. The big old Aga was so perfect for baking.

At the Hundred of Hoo School, I sat nervously in front of a word processor, being asked to 'name that file'. For ten weeks we 'older' girls strove to come to terms with our Nimbus machines, while the advanced work of the young daytime experts mocked from display boards. We pushed buttons and cursed cursers and eventually most of us passed the elementary examination, feeling anything but skilled. But it was basic training enough for me to put away my IBM typewriter for good.

When another creative writing course beckoned it was to be held at the Thomas Aveling School, some miles from home. We were given regular homework to be read out the following week. This was met with varying degrees of enthusiasm. Just when we thought we'd struck gold with a piece, half the class were asleep, signalling that the pot of gold was still a long way off. Still searching for the rainbow, I enrolled in an Open University Creative Writing Degree Course. This was grown-up territory and the learning was intense, useful and quite literally, wonderful.

Not content with studying just Creative Writing, I enrolled on a three-year Counselling course at the same time. It was an enlightening journey into self-awareness, involving many miles, different venues, much reading, challenging clients and hundreds of pages of word processing. The huge amount of writing required was inspired by the courses running concurrently.

Graduating for both was hugely rewarding. Perhaps the time had come to hang up my schoolbag and concentrate on becoming a self-aware writer. And I can't think of anything I'd rather be doing. This writing journey definitely beats my forays into dressmaking, cooking and learning a language.

Yoga in my garden

24

No Comfort in Kent

1987 was our Annus Horribilis, and for a lot of other locals too. There were two major disasters. This story, and the one which follows it, were printed in somewhat longer versions in the Hawke's Bay Herald Tribune, soon after each happening.

January, 1987

I have often wondered what living at the South Pole would be like … now I've just experienced it, shivering in the Big Freeze which was the South of England this January. For once the Met. Office was right, for they DID warn us to batten down the hatches, that something big was on the way. But we were far too complacent.

No-one prepared, and the snowflakes started. The wind in the east drove up the estuary of the Thames, straight over the marshes and the uplands of the farm, and right into the big house with its ancient, inadequate sash windows. The cold could not be tamed and it was soon apparent that the very worst weather was in the south. In particular on the Hoo Peninsula with its many villages; Allhallows, Grain, Stoke, Hoo, Cliffe, Cooling, High Halstow and St. Mary Hoo. Most of these became cut off entirely for three or four days.

Our farm was a winter wonderland, a photographer's dream, but a farmer's nightmare. Ian, with a JCB tractor and plough clearing a path, searched for his stock in the snow. This machine did a wonderful job of keeping our narrow village road open, and clearing our own and neighbours' drives. But when the blizzards sent the snow drifting, and our Hall Road into the village was buried fifteen feet under, it was time to give up and sit tight. Next morning, we woke to a wondrous scene, white, crisp and very deep. Sheep were under snowdrifts, the chicken wouldn't come out of their house, and the horses were bored and impatient in their stables. We were isolated by a wondrous ice channel of blues and greens. It could have come from a film set and was all that remained of our access lane.

Radio Kent set up a Snowline, which united listeners in a community spirit. The Hoo Peninsula remained at the epicentre of the snow and the Radio Station kept us up to date as best they could. The BBC News pictured a resident of St. Mary Hoo being picked up by an army helicopter and flown to an available dialysis machine. The local bobby gallantly attempted to drive by tractor to get supplies from town. From Allhallows, it proved impossible. Workers at Grain Power Station and at Kingsnorth Power Station, further up the Medway were cut off from their families, as all smaller roads were impassable, but they continued working to provide necessary power to the Peninsula.

Expert volunteers skied in with supplies, reporting that they'd not seen conditions as bad in Norway. The Army was called in to make several drops by helicopter. Supermarkets had donated basic groceries, pet food, baby food, milk, bread and coal. The trips were not wasted, for on their return journeys to less rural climes, two pregnant women were flown out, just in case.

Our turn for a helicopter drop came next day. A large craft circled our house and the Church before dropping deftly into the meadow behind. The five resident bulls were startled, as were the army officers, when they discovered who their field companions were. They'd brought 28 loaves and more milk. Someone was heard to gasp, 'gosh if we get sent any more, we'll be living on bread pudding for weeks.' One of our tractor drivers in his big Massey Ferguson battled overland and on into town, parking at Tesco's Supermarket. To the fascination of shoppers, he filled his tractor cab up with random groceries. At Swigshole, a tiny out-of-the-way hamlet down by the Thames, all looked bleak. Two babies were running out of milk powder and nappies. They were completely isolated and panicking. Rescuing them with provisions had to be undertaken on foot, negotiating the brambles in Bessie's Lane.

Ian was towed out of the village to the main road. Anxious to try out his new Shogun, he set off to rescue Amanda from her boarding school near Tunbridge Wells, an hour away. She had stopped thinking it was a great adventure when she watched news from home make television headlines. She wondered whether she would see us or her precious horses before spring. He said their return journey through the Kent countryside was as pretty as the loveliest Christmas card. Deep impassable drifts were the problem only on our narrow Peninsula lanes, so he went overland for merely that part of the way. The main roads were kept open with Council snowplough machines.

It was a fun time for children and dogs, not so good for horses, and the fracture clinics were full to bursting. Tiny birds never stood a chance. Pigeons became weaker as food disappeared under a white blanket, and any vegetable peeping through was soon decimated. We couldn't buy a leek or cabbage for love or money, and potatoes and carrots were supermarket gold.

The snow thawed slowly. Huge piles of blackened stuff heaped up by the machines remained intact as a reminder and a warning. It had been 25 years since Kent had suffered in anything like the same fashion. In 1963 the entire country was engulfed in many feet of snow, in a three-month period known as The Big Freeze. The sea off Herne Bay in Kent froze a mile out to sea, as did parts of the river Thames. It was the coldest winter on record and snow remained until early March. 20 years before that, in 1947, the river

Medway froze over and the entire United Kingdom was plunged into despair in below freezing conditions.

As we adults smiled through gritted teeth at the inconvenience, we resolved to be more organised next time. Perhaps we needed to give thanks that at least 1987 wasn't quite along the same lines as '63 or '47.

St. Mary's Hall, garden and chicken coop under snow

25

It's an Ill Wind

October, 1987

1987 will age me five years, Ian said, as we surveyed our garden at dawn on Friday, October 16th. His estimate was later altered to ten years, after we wandered sadly around the farm buildings, unable to take in the devastation.

The south east had done it again. We were in the news once more. The first signs of the hurricane came at 3.15 a.m. when tiny sycamore seeds from the many trees which surround our house began crashing into our bedroom window. Like rifle shots, thousands of them were whirling around. It was a dark night and difficult to see what was happening outside, though the sound effects made up for our lack of vision. Anything loose soon joined the seeds in their merry dance. Heavier objects could be heard connecting with walls and windows. My first thought was for the horses. Thank goodness I'd shut the top door of their stables, but would they be alright? There would be nothing gained by venturing outside to check, since the wind was by then gusting at over 110 m.p.h. I didn't fancy getting hit on the head by a brick or a stout branch. We could hear the trees trying to stay upright, their battles were painful and often unsuccessful. We heard many branches breaking. After a while, when my eyes became more accustomed to the dark, shapes could be seen lying spread-eagled over the grass tennis court. Twelve trees of varying size and vintage had come down and were scattered cruelly. Another twelve were at rakish angles, while two large ash trees were teetering. They were all old friends, and we were heartbroken.

Travellers in France and Belgium had been warned to stay off the roads and not to venture across the channel. That was so wise. Here in the South, we were merely told to expect a windy night. There was no mention of any impending gale, or warnings to take necessary precautions. I went to bed as normal. In our case, so much damage could have been prevented by shutting all the huge and heavy barn doors. Thankfully they were empty at that stage of the farming calendar. Battening down the hatches generally would have saved us a fortune. While searching for a scapegoat, the Met. Office seemed as good as anyone else to blame. In the understatement of the weekend, a spokesman said 'I wouldn't say we got the forecast wrong, but we could have done better.'

The County of Kent was plunged into darkness at 4am and neither was the City of London spared this indignity. This was its first blackout since the blitz. Looters were soon at work in Oxford Street and the law was hard-pushed to do anything by torchlight. The ensuing power cut lasted for days and our fridges and freezers gave up their contents. Telephones stuttered – 40,000 British Telecom customers lost their service. Engineers were in action at dawn; experts were drafted in from other areas to reconnect major towns. We couldn't say they weren't trying.

Work was soon under way clearing major roads of fallen trees and felling others in danger of toppling onto vehicles. Random houses suddenly had wondrous views after entire woods and copses lay uprooted. Sadly, there were several deaths when motorists were crushed, and countless stories of vehicles flattened in driveways. The timing of the storm was fortunate, however, for had it been raging during the daytime, the death toll and suffering would have been much worse.

Once again, Radio Kent kept us up to date with major damage and likely dangers – for instance, live cables severed and lying on the ground. All schools were closed for the day and several Headmasters reported classrooms full of trees. Sevenoaks town lost six of its famous oak trees. And that's the tragedy – knowing that while buildings could be mended, the replacing of trees would take a very long time. Tales of matchstick houses were familiar, especially among the many mobile homes at the resort of Allhallows. Over Radio Kent came a plea from a dairy farmer in Rainham, one of the Medway towns. His cows hadn't been milked since Thursday and they were getting very uncomfortable. Could any listener milk a cow, or would they like to learn as soon as possible – he'd be waiting. Our own livestock sheltered in the fields as best they could. They seemed none the worse for wear, and the horses were cosy enough in their stables.

No house in the village escaped damage, most losing slates and aerials. We lost a chimney pot which crashed onto its side directly above our bed. Luckily, Henry Pye's 1850 addition to St. Mary's Hall was sturdy enough and it didn't end up in the bedroom. I swear the house shifted slightly on its ancient axis – the windows didn't fit as they used to – yet that was never very well. The church had temporary plastic covering a gaping hole. Everybody was in the same damaged boat. It took a while to pick up the pieces, sort out the mess and breathe easy.

No, 1987 was definitely not a vintage year.

26

Breakfast in our Farmhouse

The Seventies

The farmhouse kitchen will be the hub of all things wondrous, I'd thought. So that was the dream, in theory. In practice of course it's different. Take mealtimes, and especially breakfast. For my livestock farmer, expectation of a regular slot around the table was fraught with hazards; some are minor distractions and some jump up and hit him at precisely the time the porridge is ready. After a night-time of semi neglect, the beasties save drowning, disaster and near-death experiences for the early morning round, and so over the years the man of the house has staggered in excessively hungry and usually late. So late, that the stables would have been mucked out, the school run would have been underway, and that bowl of porridge would've been a solitary, stodgy affair. 'Sheep, the darned things,' he'd moan. 'If there's one blackberry bush in the field, they'll queue up to get tangled in it.' And the same applied to the lambing meadow's deepest puddle. 'It's their favourite place to drop newborn lambs. A water birth – just perfect.'

Breakfast was always chaotic. That wasn't how I dreamt it. Neither incidentally, did I imagine I'd be uprooted 13,000 miles to find my kitchen dresser, and that the wondrous view would be the river Thames near its estuary, rather than a country vista in New Zealand.

Every drama or query in this village finds its way to our door (or window) at breakfast-time. Questions come in the form of a lorry driver lost, an engineer fixing the power supply or village water leak (apparently, we hold the key to both) or someone who needs directions to find a fault, any fault; the local bobby on the hunt for a drug runner, illegal immigrants on our beach, stock on the road, past employees' grandchildren – now living in Timbuktu and here on a visit. Would we like to see their photos/hear about their lives? On and on it goes, as Ian is the Mr. Fix-it around here, and there is 'that sign' on the door.

2015

Now that the children are doing their own school runs, and mucking out the stables of my lovely horses is sadly not on the agenda - breakfast is less rushed but more self-help than organised. These days we do rendezvous over yoghurt or whatever, if helpful walkers on the footpaths which criss-cross our land haven't let the stock out. Then we might scan the paper, discuss the price of cattle, our evening meal or the grandchildren, in random order. That's if the phone doesn't ring or a tapping on the window announces another drama.

And then there's indestructible flexitime Cyril, 85 years young. We inherited him with the farmhouse - Jack of all trades, master of plenty. He often pulls up a stool at breakfast times. Part of the furniture, is our Cyril. He would have to be the slowest person in the world to down a cup of tea, but that ploy gives him time to regale tales of the Falkland Islands where he worked for years, way back when Stanley was a two-bit town. What we don't know about Goose Green would fit into an eggcup. It's different now it's touristy, he says, and as he won't go back to check, we're stuck with the old hard-working, hard-living version.

Once breakfast is over our days start in earnest endeavour. It's the Good Life, our version!

Spencer and Amanda, off to university

Ian, off to a party

27

Catastrophe

February 2001

They didn't have names, nor were they individually tucked up in bed each night, but each had a value and each amounted to the life blood of a farmer. To have our livestock threatened in the most menacing way possible, through no fault of our own, was the worst kind of nightmare. The challenge we faced was the deadly foot-and-mouth disease which swept through rural England, bringing the farming industry to its buckling knees, and leaving devastation and heartbreak in its wake. As the outbreaks escalated, conversation in our house took on an even more serious note when news broke about infected animals at an abattoir in Brentwood, Essex, and on the adjoining holding farm.

Looking back

Standing on our sea wall at the bottom of the farm, we looked directly across the Thames to Canvey Island, while just along the Essex coast and still opposite, was Southend. Behind the two was Brentwood. It was concerning, knowing that viruses could be airborne. A bird could easily have carried the disease across the five miles of Thames to our grazing marsh cattle, in the strong winds which blew in the most untimely way. Temperatures plummeted that winter; frost was soon followed by snow. Cold was something foot-and-mouth thrived on – it stayed alive in freezing ground. Our large commercial herd numbered 600 then and we also had 1,800 sheep ready for market. Getting the sheep ready had been impossibly hard. Rains started in October and huge tracts of the country were flooded, including our usually low-rainfall area of north Kent. Soon the freak rainfall flooded the lowland and even our upland fields became one huge waterfall. And we still had five months of winter ahead of us. Into the slurry the first calves were born. The mud was crotch deep and like the best glue. We were fast running out of straw and our barns were full of heifers giving birth. It was the worst winter Ian could remember. And that was before foot and mouth hovered ever closer.

The national news became grimmer every day. The first animals to be infected (so the theorists maintained) were on a farm at Heddon on the Wall, in Northumberland. Pigs there were fed swill which contained scraps of cheap infected imported meat from a country which was in the aftermath of their own outbreak the previous year. Undetected, the sick animals then made the long journeys to the abattoir at Brentwood, Essex. Then, using the same lorries, livestock travelled to all the holding farms and abattoirs in Wales, the West Country and Ireland. Those long enforced journeys were the most blatant cause of the spreading clusters, but still Kent was spared - though at the two week stage the clusters numbered 124 and fresh outbreaks were getting closer.

As our farm surrounded the tiny village of St Mary Hoo, which obviously we shared with several families, each with vehicles and with jobs in the adjacent towns, or in London, we realised that people, vehicles and footfall could spread the virus just as easily. The farm was criss-crossed with public footpaths. Keep Out signs were hastily erected at all the gates and disinfectant mats were quickly placed on the approach road into the village. No horses were allowed near, and my own horse and his livery friend were confined to their field. It was a case of waiting and hoping, but hope was running dry as the numbers of affected farms increased at an alarming rate. News coverage was harrowing and difficult to watch, much worse for those suffering. Farming was on its knees. No-one was allowed near the poor farmers who had spent their working lives building up their herds, toiling long and hard, and latterly for very little. These same farmers were forced to watch dreams going up in smoke - imagine a huge tragic funeral pyre - only to return to empty, echoing barns and fields, which must by law remain stock free for six months. It could have happened here, we knew that. These farmers were like agricultural lepers, untouchable yet traumatised.

And then, just two kilometres away, from a neighbour's farm came the worst news. Several of their housed cattle were showing signs. It was devastating to be so close to what we feared might be impending doom and death to our own herd. And yet it was also a puzzle. The farmer was further away from Essex than we were, by two kilometres, so had the virus jumped our marsh to land in his barn? Could they have had a visitor with muddy Essex boots or jacket. They said not, but we would never know. A total ban on any stock movement was imposed. We had no straw left, no grass thanks to double our expected rainfall, a sea of mud everywhere, full to capacity barns and 1,800 sheep ready for market. There was no answer, no happy outcome.

Dear reader, this story does not get any better, alas. Tested to the very limit, we survived 2001, our cattle were spared at least, but it became our annus horribilis.

28

The Picnic

August the 13th. What a date to choose for a picnic. But it wasn't a Friday; the tides, according to The Telegraph, would be just right, so I went ahead and rang around. I randomly selected friends, about eighteen in total, all hardy outdoor types, and invited them to a beach barbeque at the bottom of the farm. The venue could be reached by four-wheel-drive vehicles only, or on foot, but with all the paraphernalia needed to cook the feast, plus tables for the plates, drinks and glasses, rugs and chairs, we would all need to have transport.

'Yes,' they all said, 'we'd love to come.' Naturally the weather played a big part in the pre-planning stage. What will we do if it's raining hard? That possibility was very real, quite likely in fact, and we muttered something about Sod's Law.

'We can't do much until the day.' Statements like that made up Ian's vocabulary, and drove me to nervous distraction. Not exactly negative, but not definite either. Picnics and planning were my department, and so was the nail-biting in the lead-up.

There we were, twenty people poised with sausages, steaks, freshly prepared salads and chilled chardonnay waiting for a window in the cloud. It came, big envelope sized in the late afternoon, and we seized it eagerly. An assortment of vehicles, ready and waiting for the off, meandered snake-like down the hill and tracks towards the beach. The terrain was rough and the path zig-zagged amongst crops and livestock.

Friends in the first vehicle unlocked the gates and someone in the last one, carefully secured them once again. Farmers can never be sure who they will get wandering around – trespassers, poachers and so on, up to mischief - all wanting a slice of space. Chains and locks are the new norm. The view as always was breath-taking. Assorted birds took flight, to be named and admired; egrets, lapwings, heron, tiny darting swallows and a soaring buzzard. Meandering slowly was the best way to enjoy the broad picture and our friends always appreciated the journey down to West Point. We never tired of it, either.

With a mere hint of chill, there was no heat haze; the colours were clear, the images sharp. The tide was coming in over the mud of the estuary, inching along the channels and gullies in its own ever changing individual pattern. Seagulls hovered overhead, intent on their search for a quick snack. Mid-way out in the estuary, slightly more than a couple of miles from the Kent and Essex shores, a container ship made its slow progress up the Thames towards Tilbury. Travelling down river, another container ship made the necessary manoeuvre to pass by on the portside. Today the Essex coastline seemed just a grasp away. Though we couldn't see the people who frequent those beaches, we could see their houses and other buildings. And the distance? Five miles. Three yachts and an assortment of dinghies bobbed along near Allhallows, catching a light breeze, seeming in no particular hurry. A fishing boat was following the tide in, ready to snap up any unsuspecting eel, sleepy from a day in the muddy pools of low water. With eels such a delicacy, I hoped he'd put the undersized ones back. To complete the scene, three jet skis, making too much noise for everybody's peaceful expectations, were looking for a base to rest up between circuits. We planned to beat them to our little beach and persuade them to settle elsewhere. Though they'd travelled from Leigh-On-Sea, through a busy shipping channel, their risky exertions made no difference to us. They could go somewhere else. To the locals there was nothing extraordinary about these everyday sights, but the eighteen guests on their way to the beach were fascinated by the activity on the Thames and the unique habitat of the marsh. From the top two meadows, one aptly named Paradise, the stretch of Thames, in glorious technicolour had a remarkable range. Our guests could see from Tilbury Docks to Allhallows at the Estuary, and faint random activity on the Essex coastline. It was not unusual to stop to take this view in, before continuing on – most visitors did pause awhile. There were exclamations of delight at sightings of birds on offer. It was as if the entertainment had started the moment they'd got into their vehicles.

Once on the beach the delegation of barbecue jobs began. Wood debris and pieces of driftwood were collected and a fire built. Some men, possibly remembering their Boy Scout training, quickly took charge. This freed up a large chunk of time for the wives. Most of us played at being helpless, settling into a wine-tasting session with enthusiasm, while the food was cooked Scout style over an open fire. Salads appeared from picnic baskets and trestle tables overflowed with produce from our vegetable gardens. Wine glasses were refilled. We relaxed deeply into our chairs, gazing over the peaceful twilight scene. A sprinkling of stars dazzled and the tide lapped near our toes. Nautical reflections from the opposite shore twinkled in shafts of colour. The brave amongst us swam in water which, though not as clear as the Algarve, was warmer than Antarctica. The jet skis had returned to Essex while there was enough light to make the journey and the fisherman had also taken the hint and shifted further along the shore. It seemed exclusive – just the twenty of us enjoying a picnic, feeling well fed and utterly content.

And then it came. The phone call. 'Your stack's alight.' We didn't need any more details, it happened every year, to some unfortunate random farmer, almost on cue around this time. The man with a box of matches had done it again.

'Oh hell! Sorry everybody. I'll have to go back up. I don't want to break up the party, but you know how it is. Can't stop to help pack things up. I'll leave the gates unlocked for you.' And he was off. Nothing indefinite about the farmer's speed now.

Somehow the chardonnay had lost its edge, and the lapping tide its magic. Despairingly, we gathered up the dirty plates, and remains of the barbecue, damped down the fire and folded the tables. One less vehicle now, but we loaded everything up and headed homeward, through the gates and away from the activity on the river.

Uphill was more urgent now, with a signal of smoke to guide us, and as we reached the top field we saw the flames, shooting thirty feet into the night sky, sparks crackling at the asbestos roofing and sending shards in all directions. Our barbecue guests made their reluctant exit. Our friends found Ian, now covered in smuts and smelling of smoke. 'What bad luck,' they said, knowing there was little more they could do or utter.

The fire crews were as organised as they could be. After all, they'd had so many arson attacks on straw and hay stacks to deal with. They could put out the fires eventually but none of the bales they saved could be used for feed or litter. Smoke and water damage made them unpalatable and brittle. Ironically, it was almost better to let the stack burn itself out once it had been lit. It was all a senseless waste, tiring and expensive for everyone, but awesome entertainment for the public who drove in to watch. They followed the fire engines and the beacon of flames. The arsonist too perhaps. It was very common for whoever lit the fire to return to gloat over their handiwork, to stand incognito in the background.

 Ian was a mixture of despair and resilience. 'That was the best hay we've ever made. What a bugger, eh? We have to take the bad with the good in this game, that's for sure.'

 It was a depressing, dramatic sight; the fierce heat barely decreasing for hours, even with the full force of water being sprayed at its core. This was a battle which couldn't be won, and was all the more soul destroying, for the obvious outcome could only be a monumental mess, and a huge claim on our insurance. There was asbestos in the roof panels. Clearing up would have to be done by a specialist team. As I hovered, shocked and not very constructive in my assistance, Ian walked over. I was angry and close to tears. It was such a terrible waste of cattle feed.

'Why don't you go home and make the men some sandwiches? They'll be here for hours yet.'

'How many men are there, then?' I sniffed.

'There's fifteen now, with another engine on its way.'

It took my mind off the drama for a while. The fire took sixteen hours to extinguish, and by then the hay was reduced to ash. Chunks of dangerous asbestos were spread over a wide area, in amongst the chaos. Just the stark framework of the huge barn remained, minus its roof. Twenty-one firemen were finally able to make their weary way home. No-one was hurt and no livestock was lost or injured, so it could have been very much worse. Though we were short of hay the next winter.

29

Baby Elephant

Joining the gym was the best of decisions. There was such a variety of classes on offer. Like a kid in a candy shop, I was keen to try as many as possible. And I proved that point by succeeding to hula hoop, and in the first session too. Euphoric! 'Really, Mum?' But I admit, I was younger then.

Co-ordination was always a concern though, and by five past eleven, I knew for sure. That Monday morning, early in my membership, I realised that I moved like a baby elephant. After all, my mother had told me often enough, though her tone was loving. I took the comparison on board through my early years and after that it would surface occasionally in my most embarrassing physical moments. Possibly alas, more than occasionally.

For reasons which I can't explain, a friend and I booked into a just-formed line dancing class in Studio One. Carol wanted moral support - in case she made a fool of herself, but by eleven fifteen it was a toss-up as to who was the bigger fool, her or me. She wasn't a natural mover, either.

I think I had a bag over my head when co-ordination was given out – I blame it on being left-handed, because I do love there to be a reason, a scapegoat. Messages for simultaneous movements of hands and feet always get so scrambled, so much so that anyone within a two-metre radius is in dire danger of being felled. With line dancing, I foolishly thought I was in with a chance, since most emphasis is surely on the feet, for that was my interpretation. I took note of the queue for the class and how enthusiastic they all looked. There is surely nothing more confidence-boosting than a happy queue. It was an all-shapes-and-sizes queue, and ages too, so I slotted myself into the line-up with only a moderate degree of self-consciousness. We gathered and chatted in anticipation. Carol and I pretended our knowledge of grapevines would suffice. She said she'd tried a few a couple of years back. I'd tried a few too, but more of the bottled variety.

'Could be fun; we'll give it a try, eh? Probably get the hang of it after a bit.'

'Mmm,' she said, but without conviction. 'It's the taking part which matters, so they say. Come on. We can do this!'

'Really?' I glanced at my neighbour in the queue, whose hips were already wriggling in a 'let's get in there, I can hardly wait' kind of way.

Scrambled would barely describe what was happening to the messages given and received that morning. The tutor did her best to encourage, even commenting to the pair of us, things like, 'Well done, you're doing SO well,' or 'You've nearly got it,' which only served to panic me more, out there on the end of my line. I interpreted her comments as patronising – though that could have had something to do with my sense of humour bypass at the time.

With forty-five minutes of torture remaining, I indicated the door with a surreptitious nod and a wink. 'Shall we do a runner, Carol?' I mouthed. Alas, my gesture was surely too obvious. The tutor had spotted my message plea, and she cheerfully piled more encouragement towards the struggling pair of newbies; obviously thinking it was worth a try, and smiling over-warmly to make us feel more at ease.

'You're really great for a first time. Just be patient, you've love it.' Then she spoilt that train of thought by saying to the rest of the class – the experts – 'Sorry these exercises are basic; it'll get more challenging next time, I promise.'

Mid-way through a confidence crisis is hardly the time for self-analysis, at least not when your feet are fecklessly flying, but I tried to bring myself to heel and even vowed not to be such a spoiled sport. It worked briefly, for half a dance, until I lost momentum once more. For fail, read flail. Forward now, shuffle back, grapevine left, right, together, kick. What on earth could be easier? I was beating myself up now, when all around me – with the exception of Carol, were synchronising beautifully. The large lass in front never put a foot wrong in the entire hour. I tried to follow her, but started to giggle nervously only to find the humorous approach not the way forward either. She, my front row role model, put her heart and soul into the steps, with a posture all of her own, and she radiated happiness throughout. With sturdy abandon, absorbed and perspiring, she had obviously found her niche.

We gritted our teeth, Carol and I, but it was hard. The smiles didn't come. Neither did the steps. The time dragged and we didn't perspire. You don't when your feet are all wrong. Maybe if my mother had called me a little nymph I'd have been working to a different agenda.

30

Fear is a Flat Door

I fear long periods of inactivity; dread enforced immobility, or restricted movement. I want daily to be able to stand on my head, run, jump or garden with spontaneity, making use of every inch of the free space I've gathered. Staying still would not be my favoured option. This excessive anti-geriatric attitude needs careful maintenance, so I push, twist, and sit-up in multiple yoga classes, creaking into unfathomable positions from which the only way out is up. Oh, the fun of it all, and it is definitely fun at the gym I joined twenty years ago, when I was already knocking on the door of middle age. I attend other classes there, but it's usually the yoga sessions I gravitate to.

I've had scares with broken bones, and can think of just one word which accurately describes their effect on my exuberant existence. Sobering. Yes, it was sobering to lie for weeks, waiting for lumbar three to nestle back where it belonged. No yoga or walking; no anything much at all. Just me lying there, on a door which we removed from its hinges - needing its flatness - waiting for the hours and days to pass until I could bend once again. Bending forward to haul out the bath plug, downwards to pull on shoes, sideways to get in a car, upwards to get back on the frisky horse. It's not great to lack bending qualities, and I could achieve none of the above for weeks.

Gigolo had jumped high over a ditch in a spectacular fashion. Mid-flight he bucked me skywards – up, up and away until I came crashing down onto the rocky bank. Riding slowly home was not the wisest decision I have ever made. Later I was told I'd suffered a compression fracture and was given the rules and advice attributed to such an injury. The hospital fed me soup through a straw, laid me flat for five days then sent me home with a back brace. That was the extent of their care, alas. What they should have done was have me lie on a shaped support, so the spine could start to recover with a natural curve. As they omitted to do that, my back healed ram-rod straight, rather like a broomstick, with the same degree of bend – that is, none.

The middle of harvest was not the best time for a farmer's wife to be flat out on a door, when her other half was flat out on the combine. For light relief I was allowed to stand upright to eat and walk robotically, just for short distances. There was to be no sitting for weeks. Prone or vertical were my preferred positions. Painful! A cup of tea felt like a lead weight. Pushing a small supermarket trolley was a challenge too far. The bath plug haul was still a long way off. As for shoes, socks or slippers, assistance was needed there!

During my long association with the frisky lad and his mother, Lady, I'd amassed more breaks – one to rearrange my nose – galloping into a low branch – that was down to bad timing – and several fingers are now wonky, owing to a fall and more subsequent failings in the fracture clinic.

 I'm a patient person, but an impatient patient. I was back on my horse within three months, and returned to my yoga mat as soon as I was able. It took many months before I was achieving postures competently but I persevered, knowing that if anything could get me bending, yoga could. And it did! I owe it everything for my nearly complete recovery. And it even put some curve back in my spine. As I slide into old age, I'm toting a hula hoop, a yoga mat and a bulging gym bag. I might be as batty as can be, but thankfully I'm bendy with it.

31

The Therapist

The client's name has been changed and the location of the particular prison omitted from this story.

You always remember the first. The first day at school, the first boyfriend, his kiss, the fluffy mother cat from way back, first job; that sort of thing. It was the same when I was in my final year of training to be a counsellor. The setting: Her Majesty's Prison. I was jumping in at the deep end, bursting with enthusiasm, and wanting to sort the world.

This was my Placement, a year-long necessary part of my training. I knew it wasn't going to be an easy ride. I was accompanied everywhere by a prison officer, apart from visits to the toilet, and the actual hour-long sessions with the inmates. There was much dangling of keys and clanging of doors as we negotiated barren corridors in all the wings.

I'll never forget my first client. The door to A Wing clanged shut behind me. An officer, displaying an undisguised suspicion of counselling, took me to an interview room. 'Sit where I can see you through the glass,' he instructed. 'Ring your personal alarm if anything untoward happens. Johnson is in his cell, so I'll fetch him. Remember, kindness will be seen as a weakness. These chaps are smart arses. Don't give them an inch or they'll see right through you.'

How very reassuring, I thought. Mental note to self. *Do not stray too far from your training. But if kindly fits, use it in moderation.*

'Thanks, I'm sure I'll be OK.' But my knees were actually knocking from wondering what he'd be like, this lifer – or any of them, most doing time for murder. My first 'kind' act would be to address Johnson by his Christian name. In an early act of rebellion, I decided not to use surnames in greetings or conversation – Smith, Brown, Jones etc. It was always appreciated by my clients, though the officers never used the inmates' Christian names. I gathered they didn't need to be appreciated.

Barry Johnson came blustering in, well-scrubbed and smelling of aftershave. A large medallion swung over his T-shirt, and bulging biceps strained the sleeves. A boxer perhaps? On steroids? I'd been told about the prison gym. I greeted him, 'Good morning, Barry,' extending a hand which he gripped, while I concentrated on positive body language and maintaining eye contact. (Lesson one, first term.) Relieved, when the blood returned to my fingers. So far, so good, I thought. He looked a fraction nervous, a muscleman, rattled at the prospect of an hour's therapy, and I knew that my listening skills were about to be sorely tested.

I introduced myself and explained the aims of counselling, its boundaries and effect, sticking rigidly to its rules and gaining confidence. I smiled. 'Now it's your turn to tell me what bought you to counselling, Barry. Talk as much as you like; or even as little, especially in this first session. The next hour is for you to explore any issues or grievances which may be troubling you.' Putting it like that, I made him sound like an angel with slightly tattered wings. Naturally he was anything but. No lifer was on A Wing for being an angel. And a life sentence allows plenty of time for angst to rise and fester. 'I'm guessing there's a lot that you want to get off your chest. You're in this place, for a start.' I nodded towards him, knowing he was more than ready to talk.

'Whew!' he started, grabbing the chance of an attentive female audience; one fledgling counsellor with L plates just removed. The latter bit he didn't know, and I hoped from observation, wouldn't guess. He leant towards me as if to emphasise what was coming, but he needn't have worried, I got the message. He took a huge breath. It was enough to set his medallion swinging slightly. He also sported a chain bracelet and a clumpy signet ring, with two others alongside, for added gold effect. Another mental note. Do not judge him by his bling; and don't form early opinions.

'This is my story, Kathy. I've told it so often, to my family and the screws too. I want you to hear it. It's true, bloody true. Only they didn't believe me, no-one does, so here I am banged up for fifteen years. I didn't murder Jean but she died that night. There's no denying that. We were arguing – we did a lot of it – and she started screaming, ranting like a fishwife. There we were, parked in the old factory car park – we always used to go there, where Jean's old man couldn't find us. But instead of getting down to business, she started yelling at me. God alone knows what was making her so mad. She wouldn't calm down. Something about another woman. Crazy, she was. She scratched my face and poked me in the eye, as if she'd really lost the plot. No one could rant like Jean. On and on she went. Silly cow, none of her business who I was seeing. I was getting really mad by then and anyway I was hurting, so I lashed out. I hit her. Hard. I caught her on the side of her nose, then her neck, with my ring. This big signet.' Barry paused, and breathed in deeply.

I nodded, attempting empathy, focusing on the size and strength of his hands, which I'd felt in his handshake earlier, and the three heavy gold rings. He was studying them too, spreading his palms wide.

'The ring, Barry. A constant reminder. You're still wearing it. Can you tell me why?'

Barry shivered and looked directly into my face – he wanted acknowledgement, not interruption. 'Are you Ok?' Was I hearing him? he seemed to be asking.

'Yes, I'm hearing you, Barry.' My eyes held his gaze. There's so much more for you to tell, and for me to hear, so please, go on, if you feel able to.'

Barry cleared his throat. 'I was a bodybuilder; you can guess, eh? The ring didn't help - my Grandad's signet. I loved the old boy, promised him I'd always wear it. The bloody ring caught her all wrong. It's heavy. She went limp and I could see she'd fainted. The car looked like a slaughterhouse because my scratches were bleeding and she had cuts on her nose and lip, and her neck. My eye felt like it was popping out. I got a fag out and lit it, thinking she'd come round and anyway, I was in a right old state. I mopped her up with my shirt, and waited half an hour, but she didn't come round. Then I panicked; knew I needed help. The only person I could think of was Greg, my brother. I drove to his house with Jean lying back in the passenger seat, and rang the doorbell. It was two in the morning. He was really pissed off by the time he got downstairs. He took one look at the state of me and nearly passed out.'

'Not too gruesome, is it?' Barry looked at me – anxiously. He'd started sweating a little. Would I be impartial, or appalled, just like the others? I nodded quickly. Yes, I was OK, having decided angelic qualities and piddling problems would be few in this establishment, anyway. This fledgling counsellor was attempting to look as unruffled as possible, although Barry's certainly wasn't an average every-day tale of woe. Nothing like this had come up in our practice sessions.

'It doesn't make easy listening, Barry. But it's even harder for you. You must relive it every time you tell the story. And I know you've got more to offload. Keep going, if you feel able to talk more about that night. Or take a breather, if you want.' I indicated the glass of water I'd put on the table.

No break. This was an outpouring, and he wanted it out. That was a relief actually, for sometimes an interruption can stop an outpouring and I didn't want that to happen. I listened with all my senses, masking my new-girl horror, as the rings dug into his clenched fists and the T shirt expanded over his huge chest. He was off again, in full flow – a lifer's version of the most dramatic event in his already very colourful life.

'I filled my young brother in with some of the detail and showed him Jean's body in the car. He got a shock when he saw the state of the car, I can tell you. Kept on and on shaking his head. He's a different sort of geezer; got a good job, never been inside or nothing. Not sure how we're brothers to tell the honest truth.'

Greg was trying to keep his voice quiet. Neighbours both sides, and all that. He was shaking. 'Christ! Barry, you've killed her, you silly bastard. You've got to go to the police. You'll do time for this. You've really messed up. Oh Jeez. Don't involve me and the wife.'

He was no help at all. My own brother. 'No fear, Greg, not the cops, no way! I'm not going inside for her. The silly cow wasn't worth it.' I thought you'd have a better idea than that. Thought you'd help. I'll take her back to the car park. It was her stupid fault anyway. I hit her in self-defence because she came at me like a mad woman. Thanks for nothing, Bruv.'

'You were running out of options then. You must have been gutted that Greg didn't come up with an idea. Tell me what you thought he would do.' We both needed to take a deep breath at that stage.

Barry clasped his hands tightly, and shook his head in despair.

'Want to take a moment or two?'

'No, I want you to hear the whole story. Want to get it over with. It's pretty gruesome. I'm sorry.' He rocked back and forth in his chair, folded and unfolded his arms in a display of muscles which was far too impressive. His breathing was rapid. He certainly wasn't enjoying recounting events of the dreadful night, though this wasn't the first time he'd gone over it in graphic detail.

'I drove back to the factory and propped her up against a pile of cardboard boxes and lorry tyres. I couldn't think what else to do. Don't suppose it was a clever place to choose, but I wasn't thinking clever at three in the morning. I was angry, still shaking. I had another fag. My next job was the car.

Then the cops came knocking. I suppose I knew they would. Her old man told them who she'd have been with. So here I am, in the nick. My ex wouldn't speak up for me, even though I'd given her the world. Nice house, anything she wanted, her and my little boy, and Jean's kids hated me anyway. The Judge didn't listen and didn't believe me. I loved Jean, that's the truth. And I miss my lovely kid.'

Real sadness now, the love of a father, separated. Barry sat, still and silent, depleted of energy. He'd spent it in the telling. He looked to me; hopefully, quizzically.

And then it was my turn. Gently, slowly, piece by piece.

That's pretty much an account of my first client's story, the beginning anyway. I'm not able to tell you anything of the process, or the progress I made with Barry's subsequent counselling because of the confidentiality boundaries. But I'll tell you one thing. He always came to our sessions promptly, well-scrubbed, and politeness itself. Actually, he was late once. He was put in solitary for making hooch. Once he'd been located, I sat in his cell there for our session. It was bleak and sparse with very little chance to misbehave and not a lot of spare furniture, either. He was proud of the hooch and was making a fair bit on the side, till he got rumbled. Inking tattoos with the sharpened point of a biro was also big business on the wings and yet it seemed to go unpunished. Barry didn't go in for that as his artwork had been done years before.

And then, when I arrived for his eighth session an officer told me that he'd been moved to another prison – for fighting over a debt, and causing trouble in the canteen over a theft. He was unpopular with the inmates anyway, it seemed. It was the prison's policy never to give details of any transfer, especially the date and time of departure, for obvious reasons. I was never to complete my work with Barry, and neither was I told where he'd been moved to. From a counselling point of view, it was disappointing and unsatisfactory, but not uncommon.

All my clients during that interesting and challenging placement were polite and pleasant, clean and respectful. I never had to use my personal alarm and actually felt safe and appreciated in the sessions. The men – some teenagers, some elderly - all insisted they were innocent, (none of them were, of course.) 'On my mother's life,' they all said, looking as angelic as possible. It was clear they loved their mums.

One early client during that placement was just eighteen. He seemed delightfully normal, except for the fact he couldn't read or write. I broke rules by bringing him a roll of wallpaper with the alphabet written on it (it was checked out and X-rayed) and during the sessions I helped him to make words. He seemed to blossom and became so chatty. Working with Daniel was rewarding, until once again I was told he'd been moved on. I imagined that was part of the punishment – to destabilise and prove superiority. Daniel had raided a bank, armed with a gun.

Then there was Arthur, the subject of my Case Study. He was the same age as my son. Writing about Arthur filled many pages, and gained me a top mark. His mother had wanted a girl, so he'd had to wear dresses until he was six. This damaged soul, in for murder, would still be in a prison somewhere, for he refused to accept guilt, and anyway he kept escaping. Not a good career move for an inmate.

During my year there I counselled in the prison hospital, the kitchen, the chapel, visiting room and art centre. I was even shown a pet budgie in a prisoner's cell. The more involved the men were in activities on offer (and there were a lot) the quicker the time would pass for them. Except that most were lifers…

32

Marsh Magic

Riding over the marshes, first on my beautiful Russian thoroughbred, Lady and later on her youngster Gigolo was always a joy. Not many people got the significance of my choice of names for Lady's little foal.

High on horseback, rather than on foot, was an even better way to admire the acres. From the saddle I could see into the delph*, count the moorhen chicks and the cygnets amongst the reeds, ride close to the ditches to inspect them for wildlife, be nearer to the swans as they flew low over the seawall and generally cover more ground in a very pleasant hour or so. Often, I was accompanied by another friend on her horse, but it was just as enjoyable to be on my own, breathing in the solitude and the sanctuary of being down by the Thames.

*The delph is a wide ditch five miles long and fifty meters wide which was dug for its earth. This would be used to rebuild the seawall after the catastrophic flooding of 1953. In that dreadful flood, (there was no warning) when the first seawall was breached, the Macleans lost 3,000 ewes. The poor creatures were heavy in lamb and in wool and therefore couldn't swim to escape. A few were rescued by boat by the five distraught shepherds on several of the farms the two brothers (Ronald and Charles) had at the time. The cattle managed to swim to the safety of higher ground. There was huge loss of life on Canvey Island on the opposite side of the river.

The present robust seawall has withstood all the tides since then, and any potentially high spring tide is now flagged, allowing stock to be moved from danger, should it be deemed necessary.

There are large pockets of marshlands along the lower Thames corridor which span the dry and wet south banks of the Thames Estuary, where the river has marshy edges. Such areas are rare. Many great rivers have developments of concrete and buildings to their water's edge which prevent the formation of habitat and hugely alter the tidal flow. These rare north Kent marshes have, as a result been given international ecological status, and are called Ramsar sites. The scheme was initiated to safeguard the habitat and precious feeding areas for birds and wildlife. Such a scheme has rules. Stocking rates must be low, no fertiliser or spray applications are allowed and there's to be no mowing or topping of grass in the nesting season. Our farm's marshes extend to approximately 900 acres, of which 100 acres are freshwater fleets and dykes. In a normal rainfall year, a further 200 acres are flooded or semi-flooded by fresh water for the winter months.

The unique and eerily beautiful marsh and the river banks provide for the following: migrating and resident wildfowl, notably swans, geese and ducks. These include Brent and Greylag geese, widgeon and teal ducks, as well as mute and Bewick swans - the latter are extremely rare. There are also large numbers of golden plover, black tailed godwits and many other waders. The marsh is a busy place – for birds rather than people. It teems with their activity as they scurry and feed. It is a privilege to be there, on horse, in a farm vehicle or on foot. That such an undisturbed area can be found an hour from London is part of what makes it unique.

The marsh is moody. Low mists sometimes hang just feet from the ground, mystical and magical. From this eerie state the sun can appear in an instant, gleaming on the river. Ships sound their horns when thick fog descends, often rapidly. The only way home from the marsh fields then, when on foot, horseback or in a vehicle, is to hug a fence line or even to first find one. It is very easy to be lost in a marsh fog. And there are ditches to fall into if careless or unlucky.

Cantering along the top of the seawall always proved an excellent vantage point. From that height I could watch the lapping tide, river traffic, or wading birds at low tide, swans ascending, in an eyeball-to-eyeball manoeuvre, or dainty summer swallows following and flitting around for any insects.

In summer the Ramsar site provides nesting grounds for resident ducks, geese and swans, and more importantly for the endangered species - lapwing, redshank and skylark. The reed beds in the many ditches provide nesting sites for marsh harriers, reed bunting, bearded tits and their like.

The freshwater areas are full of fish, notably carp, rudd and eels, as well as common and marsh frogs. These offer up food for the herons and egrets nesting in the neighbouring Northward Hill Reserve. Mammals and reptiles on these marshes include brown hares, water voles, crested newts and grass snakes. The seawall itself is a valuable habitat for rare bumble bees.

Approximately ten miles of footpaths criss-cross the farm and marshes, always proving popular with ramblers and birdwatchers. The walks have been listed in the top ten United Kingdom Walks by the Times Newspaper. We just hope the walkers shut the gates, take their litter home, and keep their dogs on leads.

The north Kent marshes are devoid of population and mostly of people, free of the noise of motorway madness, offering merely the sound of silence. Surprisingly they remain a best kept secret, although the Times Newspaper is doing its best to change that.

From this you might gather that the lower part of the farm – the marsh, somehow 'gets to you' in a way that is hard to explain. It has a peace about it, and as I said, it's moody.

Creeps into your soul, like the favourite place of childhood.

Magical Marshes

33

A New Dawn

Fireworks filled the sky, Big Ben chimed the midnight hour and in the grounds of stately Cobham Hall, once Lord Darnley's home, we gathered in evening dress at an event to welcome the new Millennium. One thousand years of ancient history, and now this one, two thousand years - they were such huge milestones. The significance of the magical numbers was enormous, and we shivered with excitement and anticipation. The new century. What would it bring? Would trips to the moon become commonplace? Or sojourns on the ocean floor? We gazed at our friends, happy yet thoughtful, united and hopeful for continued health and wellbeing.

Even for ultra-rich Lord Darnley in this sumptuous stately pad, few adventurous options were available to him, should he have wished to venture further than a pony and trap could have taken him. Most people in his time were home or island based, unless foolhardy, perhaps intrepid enough to take on the wide blue yonder. In a test of great courage, those few brave souls were forced to rely on a compass and the prevailing wind. There were no guarantees.

With the tempting end goals of the South Pacific Ocean remaining largely undiscovered, the distance and endeavour seemed insurmountable in **1800**. Most wondered if it was worth trying. What unknown destination could be worth risking life and limb for? After all, first reports from explorers Cook and Tasman were mixed, ranging from 'paradise' to a 'certain death trap.' And there was the little matter of 13,000 miles in a small, less than robust wooden ship. But for those who were brave and brimming with adventure, filled with motivation or just plain mad, maybe starving in abject poverty, journeys were indeed made. The majority survived to tell the tale, but their reports – mostly bad – took months to arrive back in their home country. Conditions were primitive and immigrants were unprepared for the hardships awaiting.

Progress in transporting hopeful emigrants to the Antipodes speeded up significantly by the early twentieth century. Many thousands emigrated to new pastures, **sailing** and seasickness going hand in hand for several tiresome months.

Then the changes and improvements became spectacular. Who, way back in **1900** imagined it could be possible in less than one hundred years for four hundred people to cram into an elaborate metal contraption? To **fly** across the world in some degree of comfort in the timespan of just one day? Even to contemplate such a thing was surely absurd.

Flying to the Antipodes from the Sixties onwards involved buckling up, sitting back with a novel or two, zipping through a time zone and disembarking in another hemisphere a day or so later. By **2000** all concerned in this modern-day miracle would be feeling reasonably fresh and happy to step into waiting onward transport, be it train, coach or car. Four generations of Macleans from St. Mary's Hall have enjoyed trips to the Antipodes – by both boat and plane. All undertaken with minimum fuss, maximum enjoyment and much excitement. Perhaps we can pander to our dreams after all, for who knows what will be possible one hundred years from now for our descendants to enjoy, or even take for granted?

Yes, a Millennium eve was certainly a time for reflection and astonishment at the inventive endeavour of the human race. I'm sure every guest gathered in that beautiful garden as Big Ben chimed the midnight hour had a dream to cling to.

Ian and I acquired mobile phones after being urged to 'keep up.' Such devices were unthinkable luxuries not many years previously. Lessons from grandchildren followed. 'A hundred and one things to do with an iPad, Grandad, and don't forget Wordle.' Oh yes, the internet! We've been there, done that! Your Satnav? Why not an electric car? Will it ever end? For us the first decade of that bright new century brought the marriages of our two children and the births of four sweet grandchildren. It brought a farmhouse full of visitors, and endless work and fun. There were many dramas and a few disasters along the way.

The cattle and crops ensured we were never idle. Sloping gently towards the Thames, and within shaking-hands distance from the Essex coast, our land sent us good years and yet it has also spilled out some bad ones. If it all evened out in life's broad scheme, it was all we could have asked for, and it was enough.

Amanda and Johnny, 18th August, 2007

Claire and Spencer, 9th August, 2008

Grandad's little helpers. Sam, Erin, Lily and Amber

34

Victory Dance

Early childhood being a time of magic, monsters and momentous moments, there's something I needed to check out about mine. It's to do with competition, for I think it was programmed out of me, shoved way down the street and around the corner, never to arrive.

There were no glittery certificates on my wall for the neatest joined-up-writing, or perfect Peggy squares; the speediest sums or the finest printing. Not for me the euphoria of having the fattest pumpkin in the show or the best painting of the sun setting over a mountain.

I was better at running, lots better. In fact, on a diet of school milk and endless fruit from the orchard, I ran like the wind. I felt free when my bare feet skimmed over the ground, leaping undulations, not feeling the prickles of short grass, the small stones and indentations. Free, with the breeze in my hair and my skirt whipping up behind. In running I **was** competitive, victorious, and I felt I could do anything, anything at all.

In the wake of that success, I ran all the way to England. No – in truth I sailed – and cooking became a necessity. I discovered how satisfying kneading bread could be, and on discovering ancient flower pots from a century before, baked loaves in them.

A Highly Commended in the Yeast Cookery section followed. There were four entries – so how mean was that judge?

It was the same with flower arranging. To me, it always seemed a shame not to use the entire pile of picked and plucked offerings. As a result, my vases would be crowded and very colourful. The prizes at the Ploughing Matches always went to the minimalist specialists using just three blooms, a solitary twig and a pebble or two. I never seemed to grasp that less is best.

It turned out I wasn't so clever at walking either. Walking, I always assumed was so every-day, so don't-even-think-about-it, it was just not worth the bother of analysis. Until one day it arrived with a big grown-up wallop. There I was in a competition line-up of ladies in shiny black Health and Beauty knickers, at the bi-annual Convention. Lean, lanky, short and stout, from glamorous twenty somethings to post-menopausal hopefuls, all looking resoundly ridiculous in tucked-in tops, tight satin pants, with absolutely nowhere to put their hankies.

'Just walk!' the instruction bellowed across the hall. Aha, I thought, this one's in the bag. What could possibly be easier than this little challenge? So, I walked. But my number wasn't called, nor even short-listed. Apparently, I put my heel down first, and it should have been my toe, or the other way around. I was so shocked to be side-lined, and the heel/toe quandary escapes me still.

But just imagine how surprised I was, when on holiday in Greece, up against a gaggle of sunburnt unfit tourists, to come third in the hotel's Spontaneous Dance Competition with our version of the Quickstep. We'd developed a taste of ouzo, and since the afternoon had been wet, we'd sampled a great deal of it in the beach bar. The dance reminded me of running with the breezes, in bare feet. I kicked off my shoes and felt so free.
'Dance some more,' they said. And, at last, I felt victorious.

35

Lakeside Dining

This story is primarily for English readers so that they might learn of the beauty of a lake such as Taupo - for every Kiwi is well aware of it. It is large and loved by all.

2004

I was back in New Zealand on a brief School Reunion visit and as always happens, hospitality was extended beyond the home front of Havelock North and the wider area of Hawke's Bay. None more so than that offered by my three brothers. I'd driven to Taihape to stay a few days with Spencer and Jenny who had recently retired from the farm in Mangaweka, to a beautiful rural spot on the outskirts of the pretty town of Taihape. As with most farmers, he had retained some acres just to play around with. There was no disputing their far-reaching views. 'Come on,' Spence said, 'hop on the back of the quad bike and I'll take you to the top of the hill.' And it was spectacular up there. Our next jaunt was to visit the site of the second highest bungee jump in New Zealand, over the mighty Rangitikei River. No Brother, not for me!

Back in the Bay, Rod drove me to Napier to explore and exclaim at the Art Deco influence, and re-acquaint me with the Marine Parade. We drove past the orchard house and stopped at Cherry

Grove for a hokey-pokey ice cream. It was all Memory Lane stuff. Then we joined his daughter Jenni to walk up a challenging back-route path to the top of Te Mata Peak. There was no time for sitting around, but that's the way I liked it!

Then Monty said, 'how would you like a few days in Taupo? We'll take the boat up, do some fishing, have a few barbies up there.' My brother Monty had been fishing there for many years, had his top five favourite fishing spots on the Lake, and of course his short list of glorious coves at which to drop anchor. It was an offer I couldn't refuse.

Taupo is the largest and best known of all New Zealand lakes. It was formed thousands of years ago from the eruption of a volcanic crater. Its vast 616 square kilometre expanse is as big as the city of Singapore. The attractions on offer are endless - water sports for the discerning and there's the wonder of almost unparalleled scenery. I use the word 'almost' as New Zealand is surely near the top of the world's scenic tree, and every one of its regions boasts special gems. The Lake is half way between Auckland and Wellington, and makes for an ideal, perhaps obvious stopover for tourists. Locals love it too, and their bustling town on its northern perimeter oozes charm. The Marina is crammed with activity; boats, yachts and small cruisers setting off or returning from their excursions.

Near to the town's centre there are beaches for picnicking and swimming, where everyone can enjoy the clear, cool water. Ducks bob on small rivulets, knowing just where to find the geothermal effect and the resulting comforting warmth as it trickles into the huge expanse awaiting. Children, loving the inviting temperature, take advantage of the shallow pools which form amongst the rocks on the shoreline. And that's possible because the area around Taupo is unique for its underground natural heating. The Lake water is refreshingly cool, even chilly by comparison. Small residential hamlets with their own jetties are nestled in the major bays which are accessible by road. As Taupo has developed in popularity and population, the houses in each of these range from modest cabins to elaborate, eye-popping palatial dwellings - either permanent or holiday homes. It's an Estate Agents' dream. The settlements are few in number as a huge percentage of the outer limits of this vast lake can only be reached by boat. The rewards for the journeys, made over the blue-green and very deep water are delightful, often deserted coves in which to drop anchor. The cliffs are sheer, but not foreboding and the scenery on these remote stretches is usually described as awesome or breathtaking.

The craggy rocks stand guard on the shore line, some with ancient Maori carvings which have stared out, huge and fearsome through the centuries. Navigational skills are essential, for all those watery kilometres guarantee that weather can turn stormy in an instant. It is not a lake for an amateur boatman. The skippers of each craft shout a cheery greeting as they criss-cross en route to their favourite spots, usually with a line out for a rainbow trout or two.

Planning of the picnic baskets and coolly bins for our first lake jaunt began. Sister-in-law Kay's expertise ensured a selection of home-grown salads and flower pot loaves, sausages and steaks in case the trout didn't oblige - or possibly even if they did, for Kiwis eat large. There were a couple of beers: Dominion Bitter and Tui, plus a bottle of Hawkes Bay's famous Te Mata wine. Kay had even prepared a bowl of mussel fritter batter to cook on the fire once it heated up. These delicacies were to be our starter. Mussel gathering in the Bay beaches is something our family have done through the generations. Fritters sizzling over a fire surely take some beating.

With the precious picnic carried aloft to the sand, it was time for a swim. The water was crisp and cool – there was no geothermal warmth in this cove. We splashed around the boat, anchored safely and bobbing gently. There was no-one else around and the cove seemed to be ours exclusively. So clear was the crystal water, it mirrored the beauty of the steep cliffs above. Given the number of boats leaving the Marina, it appeared to me that each was allotted peace and seclusion. How wonderful and how accommodating of the lake.

The beers were opened and the fritters enjoyed. The good news was that the trout had been obliging and they provided the next course, gutted and prepared a la natural. No additions to the fresh, just-caught magic taste were needed. Then it was time to take a breather, with a chilled glass of Chardonnay; time to sit back and breathe in the tranquillity of the scene.

'Listen!' But we'd all heard it. A bell bird's crisp clear ringing call, then another from nearby, in answer. 'There it is, on that manuka bush, half way up the cliff face.' We searched above us for a sign of its mate as the native birds called a greeting, each to the other.

We weren't alone, after all. Then a tui sang its cheerful greeting, and a tiny fantail had spotted our picnic. Its cheeky strutting and demanding demeanour guaranteed some scraps, as it scuttled over the sand, delighting its audience.

Reluctantly, with the last of the picnic enjoyed, and another glass of wine savoured by everyone but the skipper, for we needed to empty the bottle, it was time to leave our cove. The fire was carefully extinguished - there is no ban, except in extreme dry conditions - but fisher-folk are super respectful. We stowed the portable barbecue on board, and packed away the baskets. The two saved trout, fresh and shiny in the chilly bin, were destined for tomorrow's supper.

It was dusk when we set off, and the navigational lights were on. The journey back to the Marina took half an hour; the evening was balmy. To the skipper it was plain sailing, merely a repeat of many such jaunts. The lights of the town twinkled and reflected a welcome. All too soon the boat was being winched onto its trailer, before having a hose-down ready for the homeward journey. There would be another trip out to a cove, to perhaps another of Monty's favourites in a day or two. For this family, like so many others were here on a week's holiday. Fishing and enjoying the lake is a dream pastime for many, and a boat so I'm told, is the best toy a boy could have.

Thank you, Monty. The memory is as vivid as the Lake is vast and from the distance of faraway Kent a memory is all I have to cling to - until the next time I cross the rippling water for mussel fritters by the lakeside.

Fishing on Lake Taupo, NZ

36

Short Listed for Take Off

Twenty years ago, the residents of the Hoo Peninsula were shaking in their shoes, and none more so than those in the small villages of Cliffe, Cooling, High Halstow, St. Mary Hoo and Allhallows. And why, you might well ask? The threat to every resident came in form of Tony Blair's Government proposal for a huge hub airport on their doorstep. It would have rendered the entire area a sea of concrete – be it runway, road or infrastructure.

Naturally passions ran high, while unanimous horror was evident in every quarter. Town and local parish councils, backed by the Royal Society for the Protection of Birds (RSPB) and fuelled by the residents, immediately formed a robust campaign against the preposterous (in their eyes) idea. It went under the heading of 'No Airport at Cliffe' but Cliffe was to be no worse affected than the other villages mentioned. The campaign needed expert research and planning and quickly produced individual leaders and organisers. Their enthusiasm drove hundreds of locals to march in Chatham, Kent and in London, bearing placards and generally making the feelings of the Peninsula residents known. Pages of petitions were delivered to Downing Street, where selected protesters presented a valid case against the idea, but actually merely stating the obvious. It was an absurd idea dreamed up by city big-wigs who had no idea of the diverse value of the marshes they wished to annihilate.

The nightmare threat seemed all too real, given that from four hundred suggested sites, 'ours' fitted snugly and very suddenly into a short list of three. The site, which would cover twenty-five to thirty square miles and cost a staggering nine billion pounds was the most ambitious of all the proposals. It featured four runways with room for a fifth and would therefore be twice the size of Heathrow.

The experts' theories (in favour) were that the area was sparsely populated, it was close to London and take offs and approaches could be made over water, given the nearness to the Thames Estuary and open sea. Air traffic could continue over twenty-four hours; a necessary consideration it was thought, to cater for an expected growth in air travel. Noise to residents from the flight paths would be drastically reduced, compared to the other options being over built-up areas. To the untrained eye, (city dwellers perhaps) the marshes look sparse, forlorn and a wasteland. The Government's arguments gathered pace, while powerful forces added fuel. Their pressure was intense.

It seemed that the very people who had short listed the option had not done their homework. Arguments against, and there were so many, stressed that the proposal would obliterate two nature reserves. This is a Ramsar site – a wetland of international importance. The fertility of the area is unique and it is a perfect habitat for wading birds and wildlife. Many thousands of birds migrate from their Arctic breeding grounds on their journeys further south and use the mudflats as a stopping off and feeding point.

The marshes in question are below sea level and are protected from flooding by a sturdy seawall. Huge swathes of upland would need to have been moved downhill - shaved to considerably raise, by about fifty feet, the enormous area required. An historic church and several Grade II houses would be threatened in St. Mary Hoo alone. Our gentle hamlet on its rise would be all but obliterated, as would much of the charming neighbouring village of High Halstow. In short, remnants of the historic villages which follow the north Kent banks of the River Thames, and which so enchanted Charles Dickens, would be hideously perched on the concrete perimeter of runways.

50,000 new homes would have been needed for workers, motorways would swallow up many more acres, while four (or even five) runways would spread along the river's banks. High speed rail links would rush and roar through the area in links to London and beyond. Peaceful tranquillity, clear air and bird song would be stolen for ever, and the unspoiled landscape of centuries totally desecrated.

Gradually, the relentless efforts of the campaigners and the powerful influence of the RSPB began to undermine the feasibility of the Cliffe Airport option. The Government officials were forced to agree that the huge expense of raising the marsh area and the necessary infrastructure needed was 'possibly' impractical. And significantly, after our Peninsula campaign leaders consulted major airlines, who all stressed the likelihood of predictable bird strike, it was that very factor which played a major part in the argument against an airport in the area. However, it was many nail-biting months before a definitive answer would be forthcoming.

Then, to the delight of everyone on the Hoo Peninsula, champagne corks were popping in 2003 when it was announced that the Government was withdrawing the proposal.

With commendable wisdom, planned procedures, banners and campaign policies were retained 'just in case,' so that in 2008 when Boris Johnson's Estuary Airport idea was put forward, the Peninsula experts were once again at work. It was a tense period of front-page journalism, and again, the Peninsula was in the forefront from the point of view of dire disturbance. With the RSPB's influence, potential bird strikes were forefront in all arguments against this elaborate plan. They stressed that millions of birds have migrated annually for centuries, using the very path of the traffic to and from the proposed Boris Island airport. How would any Government planner be able to divert or stop the historic journeys of our feathered visitors?

In 2014, any thought of an airport in the Estuary was finally put to rest. At least for now. Estimates of expected growth in air travel were found to be widely exaggerated. And who knew that a deadly pandemic would bring some airlines to their knees and reduce numbers of passengers considerably.

37

Flutterings of a Farmer's Wife

The alarm shrilled. I was dragged rudely from my night-time slumber, and an adventurous dream, never to know its ending. 'Why can't these things make a gentler noise?' I mused, peeping out from behind stout old curtains just as daylight emerged. Shafts of grey dappled through sparse sycamores in the copse opposite our bedroom. Only the mighty holm oak shielded dawn's arrival for a few moments more - a fragile scene of muted greens, as yet undisturbed by the morning's endeavour, or tedious wind. And then, in the early softness it became clearer, a kaleidoscope of pinks and golds heralding a new day.

Was it to be just another ordinary day? There was after all, so much to do today – like yesterday, tomorrow and every day which lay ahead, beckoning, impatient. It seemed that life on the farm stretched out in a promise of never ceasing activity and drama, with a regular pattern of animal arrivals or sometimes naturally, market-ready departures. This village farming routine was for me, broken regularly by my counselling clients, open-university lectures, the practicalities of shopping or now and again for a short, much awaited recharging holiday. But today there'd be no time for respite, no time at all for lounging.

Because today was special, you see, Blue Ribbon special. Nothing specific yet, to indicate such an accolade, except a butterfly fluttering in the depths of my stomach. Did I expect a fanfare? Mum always said my imagination was too vivid. You're forever dreaming, she'd say, and I reminded myself of that as I pulled on jogging bottoms and a shirt. How I argued with that memory! No, this was the dawning of a great day. I was convinced of it. This was MY day.

On to breakfast, for dogs and horse too; washing to hang out – all the normal chores to keep me on course, some would say focused. The farmer's shirts fluttered like ships' ensigns – navy-check, white-ish, and frayed blue striped, soaring cheerfully now in the coastal breeze, with merely a peg or two restraining their gleeful freedom. Tea towels, frisky in a semaphore message, line dancing in competition with the bath mats. They all knew to step lively this morning. Socks in pairs, engaged in a military two-step; handkerchiefs gesturing in gentle persuasion. Soon I'd be folding them, smoothing the sun's warmth into the fabrics, ironing little, but for now, for a few moments I watched them billow against the backdrop of a mellow brick wall.

'You wash for England,' a neighbour once said, and it was true, a line full of washing gladdened my heart. I was always at it. Maybe I should get out more, I'd reminded myself, on reflection.

And that was why. Why I'd eventually succumbed to my own lecturing and ventured to the steps of the college. And not just one college. After the first course at Adult Education I was hooked, a mature student with the bit between my teeth. I started tentatively with Flower Arranging and Cooking, but lost patience in the lesson entitled 'There are So Many Things to do With a Mushroom Stalk.' I'd probably just have binned it, but that wasn't a good attitude to adopt, I knew. As for flowers, I'm much too gung-ho to spend hours thinking about style and form. Give me a vase, a dozen flowers, and I'd have them arranged before the rest of the class had picked up their secateurs. Both useful courses, but not my niche, alas. Neither, I discovered was Italian. Not a natural linguist, me. However, I soon postured happily in yoga, though I languished in lampshade making. I was on a roll by now, and I moved onwards and upwards to Word Processing. Getting more confident - having abandoned my trusty electric typewriter - I mastered the mouse, the delete button, and other user-friendly keys. Gathering speed, I journeyed on through Counselling courses, gaining a Diploma and many challenging clients. Introspection and self-awareness became my soul mates. I worked on self-esteem and empathy, kept journals and listened lots. That's what counsellors - years of it, listening, endless empathy, but now … was it time for a new enlightened me? Time for another learning?

I'd always loved words, scribbling them down, jumbling them up…playing with some, discarding others. Yes, that's what I'd do, I would indulge myself, deliciously, selfishly. I burst enthusiastically into an Open University Creative Writing course to practice my skills and learn to let go of clichés. I'm still playing and discarding, still practising, and I will be for ages; forever, most likely. Writing is much more interesting than watching velvet lawns grow, more stimulating than billowing checked shirts on a clothesline; there's always the next challenge, the next chapter, a new plot.

And that is why, three years later, I was so happy.

'Why the smile?' my farmer asked when he nipped in for a coffee, 'you look like the cat that stole the cream.'

'Go and polish your shoes,' I told him, 'Shake out your suit. The children are coming down this afternoon. Tonight, I graduate!'

'Well, I'm blowed.' Or was that my memory playing tricks again? That was what my father always said when he was lost for anything more eloquent to say.

(I gained a Distinction in Creative Writing in 2004)

Graduation Day for me

38

What Price?

What price is life? That's not a difficult one to answer, but one thing is for sure, doctors and crew who attend Air Ambulance emergencies will move heaven and earth to save one. Such was the case one June morning in 2008 when Ian was loading the last bull into his transporter. Eight had gone willingly to the various fields on the marsh, and it was the last, a Charolais, who presented a problem. He was full of testosterone, impatient, and way more feisty than usual. A ton and a half of potential trouble.

Quicker than any farmer could shake a stick, it charged Ian, tossing him across a muddy field entrance where his head connected with brick rubble. This fall caused the first of Ian's injuries - severe lacerations to his scalp. As he lay, dazed in the mud, the bull charged again and began to gore his neck and chest using all its massive head strength. Ian can remember the bull's eyes being centimetres from his own. After fracturing his neck, he then moved to Ian's rib cage, leaving none unbroken and breaking two in two places. For good measure, this last gesture pierced his lungs. Still the bull continued to gore. Only the quick thinking of a stockman, throwing a bucket towards the fracas, distracted the beast long enough for Ian to get to his feet and run to the gate. Amazingly, with the help of adrenalin, he managed to climb this but then dropped to the ground, where his screams attracted some of our neighbours. Several came running and one rang for an ambulance. I was hanging out washing and sprinted across an adjoining field. The situation looked dire as Ian lay on the tailboard of the trailer, with gaping wounds to his scalp. He was becoming colder and less able to breathe with every minute. He was completely covered in mud, and in appalling pain.

The Field Ambulance arrived quickly, but realised immediately they needed further assistance for their patient and that he would need a speedy journey by air ambulance to a major trauma hospital. With the uplands full of standing corn, the only available field for a helicopter to land in was currently being grazed by a neighbour's horses. Our daughter, eight months pregnant, raced to stable these, leaving the space clear. By now, most of the village had gathered, pale and panicking.

Doctor Gunning, ably assisted by his pilot and the crew from the Field Ambulance, treated Ian for an hour before he was stable enough for the journey. They made space in a nearby garden, and gently persuaded the shocked villagers to move while they concentrated and worked on Ian's extensive injuries, in particular the collapsed pleura, where the lower ribs had done so much damage. They needed to ventilate Ian, and with little time to spare they worked as a team, methodically and professionally. This level of expert care continued for the sixteen-minute journey by helicopter to the Royal London Hospital. We had already set off by car to the hospital, not knowing the outcome of the earnest endeavours of the doctors. All we could do was hope, and speed.

Once in Intensive Care, the doctors informed us that Ian was the Royal's first matador. They were unsure which injured part to treat first, and decided to start on the scalp wounds which needed extensive work. Their care was truly amazing. We were kept up to speed with the increasing catalogue of injuries as we sat in a tiny unventilated room on the hottest day of the summer. It was an agonising hour before a doctor told us he would 'most probably' survive. There were eighteen rib fractures in total, a collapsed lung, a broken neck and a lacerated scalp requiring 157 stitches. Quite a tally.

The healing and exemplary care continued and in a surprising five days Ian was home, walking somewhat unsteadily amongst his beloved cattle. In the space of a few weeks, he was able to resume the job he was born to do. They told him at the Royal London that he had the lungs of a twenty-year-old. (He was sixty-three.) Perhaps that was the result of a life in the fresh air, no cigarettes, save for a few crafty puffs at school, and endless exercise. He needed to sleep sitting up for six months, and the scars on his scalp resemble a road map, but he has made a complete recovery. There is no doubt he owes his life to the work of the Air Ambulance team that morning. On one of the many Get Well cards, one of his friends had written… It's amazing what some people will do to get a ride in a helicopter.

39

St. Mary's at Christmas, 2014

I cut my writing teeth on letters home to friends and family at Christmas, never missing a year, even though the postage was horrendous. Once I got hooked up to the internet, pressing a few Send buttons was a whole lot easier. For about 40 years, relations around the world would put the kettle on and catch up with Maclean news. I chose this one randomly from forty or more I've saved over the years. It is fairly typical in length and content.

Christmas! Aha! The bells ring out earlier each year, and the list of uncompleted chores gets ever longer. With Ian driving off to watch England wallop Australia at Twickenham, I have the house peacefully empty, in which to indulge in some writing. Maybe this newsletter won't be the usual slog for you all, as we don't seem to have done anything monumental or breathtaking in 2014, but who knows, once the fingers start tapping there is often no stopping me. As is the case annually, where has the year gone? Naturally, we both hope you and yours have enjoyed a great one, with happy activity and excellent health throughout. Another reason why I would like to get this little number 'sewn up' today is that we are off to Madeira for a week at sparrow's fart on Wednesday and no doubt several dramas will occur before then, and also whilst we are away, for they always, without exception, do.

We are as fit as fleas! For a couple of olds we are often told by our devoted children that we are not normal pensioners, and this is said with shaken heads of despair. Last week I taught Sam how to stand on his head, while Ian loves every opportunity to show off his weightlifting skills in the gym, with the yuppie youngsters gawping on the sidelines. Luckily the stress of a waterlogged farm and falling cattle prices has not dented our enthusiasm for a healthy lifestyle.

The year started with Ian traipsing through deep mud on foot, having given up negotiating the fields with a tractor. The marsh was two parts under water and the cattle had to manage somehow – those that were out of barns and grazing, or attempting to. It was a nightmare for him, and no doubt for them. The ground was badly poached. Now, with one month of this year still to go, it is worrying. We get much of the surface water from neighbouring High Halstow, uphill from our marsh, and we rely on the river board to open our sluice gates to allow the ditch levels to lower into the Thames. Sometimes they forget to do this, and after all, having flooded habitat for the marsh wading birds is all part of our subsidy criteria. While we couldn't survive without the subsidy, we could do with less of the wet and more of the marsh grazing! The weather pattern seems to be for mild, wetter winters these days. We had a boiler split its jacket 3 weeks ago. Since we heat and cook with oil (it was cheap 44 years ago when we installed the system) it took forever to source one. The fitting of it took 3 men a week and the mess of them traipsing up and down into a damp cellar was indescribable. We had no heat and nothing to cook on, rather like camping but without the sun.

In March Ian escaped the mud to ski for a week with his buddies and naturally they had an amazing time. Six middle aged to elderly foolhardy chaps, zooming down the Austrian slopes, then ringing home, feigning exhaustion and proposed early nights, each evening. Yeh, right?

Once home he got cracking on the garden of our newly purchased cottage, putting up a post and rail fence, with necessary rabbit netting, planting up beech hedging in a double row with my help, and laying leaky hose for irrigation. However, we suspect that a lifetime of neglect, and 53 years of tin cans, glass and random rubbish, did nothing to enrich the soil there. We have lost about 100 of the 900 we planted. The grass has taken nicely in the nearly-acre plot and it looks tidy now, with its gentle slope. We have laid a hard area for parking when work starts in earnest next spring or summer. The rabbit netting was essential, as this present garden is all but ruined; a far cry from the Kew Garden effect of Amanda's wedding day. Each morning about 50 bunnies can be seen skipping happily around the lawn, choosing what to nibble next. We have taken down the old horse shelter (lump in the throat whilst watching) which was sagging dangerously, the horse fence which was being held together with our trusty Cyril's handiwork (string and crossed fingers), and the Bull Pen, near the cottage, where Ian had his memorable run in with a Charolais bull. So now our outlook from the south facing windows of Ross Farmhouse will be an uninterrupted landscape of green and trees, plus a sprinkling of the river Medway. Speaking of the cottage, the exciting plans have been submitted for approval, but true to Council form there has been a mix up and they are still pre-Validation. We are none the wiser, after 8 weeks of waiting, for any agreement. We are very practiced at being patient!

Summer was hectic with planned and unplanned activity. As a village we seem to be very social now, and most families hosted a 'do' of some sort. Then we all traipsed down to the beach for the annual barbecue, catching of course the right tide and a sunny late afternoon. Nothing tastes quite as good as a beach cooked sausage! There were about 50 people in all. Children and dogs added to the chaos, with almost as many dogs as kids.

Then it was our turn to host a P&O cruise reunion gathering, so three couples came for the weekend. It was no trouble of course to get the house ready for 6 discerning guests. They loved the tour of the farm, new territory for them all, standing on the seawall looking over at Essex, and all pronounced it a match for the jolly, up and down the Solent, from last year's reunion. But then, Ian has had quite some practice at farm tours.

Come September I escaped the housework for a week's yoga at the Convent retreat in Majorca. Six hours of yoga a day, plus a long walk downhill to the beach for a swim. However, this year there were little fishy blighters in the water. One of our party was bitten. She said being patched up by two muscle-bound hunky Portuguese lifeguards was enough consolation. The nuns in the convent venue looked exactly the same, peaceful and smiling and not yet a word of English.

The four grandchildren are all well. They are now six, five, four and three. Two at school and two at nursery. We see a lot of Amber and Erin as their little cottage is a mere few minutes' walk away; less of Sam and Lily as they live half an hour from here. The cousins are best buddies and love to meet up.

After twenty years, I've managed to extricate myself from facilitating a support group for eating disorder sufferers. It is such a troubling mental illness, and I felt I'd done my bit as a counsellor. Ian grumbles when a 'thin person' (as he calls them) rings up mid activity here. Maybe that will now stop?

Whilst walking Amanda's dog, Tarka this afternoon, I found a pocketful of button mushrooms on the marsh which I'll add to my duck risotto. It's that delicious time of the year when our menus are swelled with the fruits of Ian's labours.

With a win for England over Australia, only two barrow loads of leaves swept, a dog walked and a risotto needing cooking, I think I've rambled on and on long enough.

All that remains is to wish you and yours a very happy Christmas, and a fine, fit New Year.

With love
Ian and Kathy

40

Headway

2012

Walking through the village, passing the Church on our right, we stopped at the corner. 'Here it is,' I told her, 'Our next home.' And I had to admit. It did seem forlorn, having been empty for a couple of years. It was unloved and grey and screamed abandonment. The blackberries and ivy had taken hold, tangling in the gutters. Its pebble-dash exterior was flaking, with patches of damp and glaring orange rust. The garage, made of random pieces of timber, had a serious lean. The hedge had grown so high, it was difficult to see the other half of the semi-detached purchase from the road. To my friend it obviously looked an astonishingly unwise purchase, and her viewing of the inside was still to come.

There was a gasp. 'Good grief, you're both mad! It's such a wilderness. And all these old, ramshackle buildings. Fancy taking on something like this at your age. It'll take you forever to clear this tangle and mess. That's before you start on what's inside.'

'I know that. The garden certainly is in a terrible state, but we can do it. We're both fit,' I reasoned. 'For our age!'

'You'll need to be,' Joy said, shaking her head in bewilderment. 'How big is the plot?'

'I wouldn't know exactly,' I replied. 'Maybe nearly an acre, but it's hard to tell with the trees in such a jumble. Each semi has its own big garden so we've got a double dose of land.'

'What can I say? Good luck! You'll need that too, along with bags of energy.' She was peering into the garage-cum-lean-to and wrinkling her nose. There were skins of things long dead hanging there.

Everybody reacted in the same way when we showed them our project. All this negativity had us doubting our sanity, but we'd battled so hard over the purchase - a pair of small farm cottages on our tenancy, and no longer needed by future farm workers - that we'd dug our toes in and gone for it. There'd been niggling hurdles along the way; convincing the landlords to sell, (the Church of England rarely sell property) and other hiccoughs. Every stage took months, and patience wasn't our virtue. Every delay added to the decline, while the jungle in the garden flourished and grew apace.

It wasn't as if we were going to be reconstructing the houses ourselves – we'd booked the services of very able local builders, Tony and Paul, who were going to turn the two into one. It was our exciting venture, in spite of the many doubters. But we had to admit, the cottages in the state they were in, looked far from an easy challenge. We hoped for a miracle. It was all we could do at that early stage.

Firstly, we needed to tackle the area destined to be our garden. Not personally, by scythe or saw - we knew someone who could work magic with his 360 Hymac - that's an earth-moving machine to the laymen amongst you. Defiantly, after years of neglect, an impenetrable mass presented its challenge.

On the day Norman arrived, half the village turned up to watch. They'd been told (and it was true) that he could pick up an egg with the blades of his digger. Completely unfazed, he made a start. Elderly conifers, cast-offs planted after umpteen Yuletides were broken and slanting, having fought and lost against howling westerlies. Blackberry fronds snaked in every direction, grabbing and scratching. Enough elderberries to start a brewery restricted daylight; ivy choked wherever it could gain purchase, and in a forlorn row, spindly apple trees fought for survival. The out-of-control hedge hid some of the sorry sight within, while tangled amongst the hedging was a mass of wire netting, rusted, broken, jagged and protruding in places. The entire site had lost its battle against any order years before. It was obvious nothing in this landscape was worth saving. But we knew Norman loved a challenge, with or without an audience.

His grim work was spectacularly successful – all it took was a day and a half. Apples and pine cones, branches, berries and brambles, plus the raggedy hedge all landed randomly. The various heaps of assorted debris grew skyward.

Successful demolishing of the derelict outbuildings surrounding the cottages proved just as effective with the trusty miracle machine. Norman was in his workaday element. A tumbledown garage with its perilous lean-to toppled. There was a lean-to tacked onto the first one which was full of one-time treasures and tins; an abandoned Flintstone-like ferret house, the rabbit hutches, and the large chicken coop were all chucked. The deserted driftwood dog kennels and garden hidey-holes - and let's not forget a worse-for-wear large caravan - all of it needed to be disposed of. Dust, cobwebs and junk from years back added to the task. Spiders from yesteryear scurried for freedom. Twenty giant trailer loads were carted to an untimely end, a large crater on the farm, affectionately named 'the Dead Hole.' When full, it would be covered over, and normal pasture would reinstate in time.

Then there was a shout from Norman. 'I've found a hole. A well I think, and it looks deep.' With reluctance, that piece of history was filled in, when a pebble took anxious seconds to reach the bottom.

I'd asked Norman to create a gentle slope to add interest. Then in deep shock, we stood back to admire a blank canvas. It looked vast, and very empty. But there was work to be done and bucketfuls of broken glass, wire, cans and assorted hazards needed to be picked up from our new wide-open space. We found no artefacts, treasures or anything of value, save for an old New Zealand penny. We took that to be an omen.

Our village is in a Conservation Area and this presented strict rules and restrictions which needed to be adhered to. Though these rules caused delays in starting the build, we knew they made sense. We were required to state the trees we chose to plant, and where (with a diagram) and what our hedging should comprise of. Too late, alas. It was the first task we undertook, and we chose and planted beech. I think it's called jumping the gun. They wanted to know the colour of paint we'd use externally and where we would site any sheds. Extensions needed to be within certain parameters. Plans were submitted and re-submitted until all parties were satisfied. The delays were lengthy. However, we used the time to good effect, worked on clearing the land, levelling the ground where needed, and sowing grass seed. We needed to placate the council in our hedging choice, but eventually they agreed to allow us to leave hundreds of young beech trees where they were settling in nicely around the boundary fences. Such is their power, we half expected we'd be required to pull them up.

We knew the last occupant of one of the cottages was fond of the bottle and that he brewed concoctions in the big old caravan from everything he grew. He and his friends sampled his work enthusiastically, sometimes tossing empties amongst the trees below. The glass was a hazard for many weeks, along with cans, wire and strange sharp objects of little use.

The lawn is wide and green now, and the surrounding beech hedge is well established. We have a new copse of lovingly tended shrubs which is a delight to behold.

Our able builders have started on the cottage. Progress there is ongoing and exciting.

We're making headway.

Footnote 2015: This was the state of the gardens to Numbers 1 and 2 Ross Cottages which we purchased in 2012, in an ambitious plan to convert the two cottages into one. We will call our new home Ross Farmhouse. In days gone by there was a farm of that name with cottages on the site.

41

The Move

St. Mary's Hall, August 2016

It was the least we could do. We needed to celebrate the long tenure of four Maclean families in this remarkable house, oozing with history, drama, fun and laughter. And here and there, a little bit of sadness. We threw a party! There had been so many happy parties at The Hall over the years. One hundred friends and extended family arrived to farewell the house in style, to enjoy food and drink on a balmy summer evening, and admire my handiwork in the garden. We weren't the only ones fond of the place it seemed.

Ian and three others at a previous party, while inebriated, had decided to purchase a marquee - so that was erected for dancing. A neighbour provided a sound system. Balloons and bunting helped to set the scene.

It seemed the future of St. Mary's Hall was unclear, although ideas were plentiful. Would it be sold off; or would it be rented again? Meanwhile, our move across the field was imminent. Big cardboard boxes were piling in a bleakly empty room downstairs. There was no disputing now, the Macleans were vacating the place.

September

What does one do with 57 recipe books, 217 coat hangers, five extra-large saucepans, some with lids missing, and 330 well-loved books? Or the lofty silver cup won by Grandfather Maclean for his prize-winning field of turnips?

We have thrown away shed loads of tat, skip-loads of junk, wardrobes full of unwanted clothes, followed swiftly by the ancient wardrobes they'd been crammed into. We put all of it in a very large pile and made a spectacular blaze of the lot. We can do this you see, because we live on a farm in the middle of nowhere, and the smoke from this blaze and the four that followed it, troubled nobody. But still the sorting continued. It was endless, lasting into the night and starting again with the first light of day.

As if the farmhouse, circa 1736 (bits of it are 14th century) and the immediate barns surrounding it, were not enough of a task to clear, I knew the garden I'd beavered over for 45 years would be a heartbreaker to leave behind, so I more-or-less cleared that too. These random horticultural loads were taken by wheelbarrow through our tiny village – little shrubs and large ones, clumps of flowers, bulbs, roses and perennials, all scheduled to restart life in well prepared and very new beds around the corner, past the pond and church and further on a bit. Locals grew used to me trundling well-rotted farmyard manure, affectionately called FYM, in dozens of not so fragrant earth-improving trips, ever onward to our new place. Then there were assorted garden treasures, varied and heavy, like terracotta pots and small statues, their concrete make-up turned greenish with age. No gnomes to speak of, but a couple of cherubs holding bird baths, and a gentlewoman, who I swear looks more serene in her new surroundings, in spite of her mouldy exterior. My biceps became the envy of the yoga classes, as I rippled my way across the gym floor, and my weight dropped too, which was another bonus.

Not to be outdone, the man of the house heaved the big kitchen table and its chairs onto the back of his truck for the short journey.

With the success of the inaugural flight, an assortment of chests of drawers, nests of tables, bookcases, beds, mattresses and general flotsam faced a similar means of transport. The days of to-and-froing were never ending, but we were able to dispense with the need of a removal company and the expense and pressure of the middle man. I wish I could say the stress had been minimal, but it had merely been of our own doing. Clearly, we would never have coped with a move in a single day.

We became overwhelmed with options, and bamboozled by decision-making. The latter needed arriving at with regularity and the former left much to ponder. Our eyes were continually crossed with myriad colour charts, but in the end, charm and wise-enough choices won the day.

There were endless visits to charity shops. The Medway towns comprise, it seems, of so many shops where all and sundry buy - well, all and sundry. I'd take my boxes and bags through their doors, and be met by varying degrees of enthusiasm, though never a lot. I mourned just a little that they now had responsibility for 50 of the 57 recipe books, and some of the saucepans, to say nothing of cast-off coats and dresses of dubious vintage. How dare they not be just a little bit thrilled by my generosity? I couldn't however, impart my second-string sewing machine onto any of them. It seems that not many people sew these days, not even a curtain or a hem.

'How will you feel leaving the old place?' We were asked that question on a daily basis, until we'd reply rather snappily, something along the lines of, 'It can't come quickly enough.' And then we'd go on a guilt trip because we wondered how one is meant to feel about leaving a large, lumbering, inconvenient, leaking but very lovely old home which had done us proud over generations; a happy place where our two children grew up in harmony, and where three previous generations of the family had also enjoyed (or is it endured) decades of farming's fickle fortunes. On the one hand, we felt so protective of its foibles, forgiving of its faults, but gradually, and certainly with a delightful replacement taking shape so very close by, we began an early, necessary process of weaning, or separation. And we managed ultimately not to shed a tear, for we were so busy packing saucepans, negotiating with the charity shops, starting fires, and trundling wheelbarrows to allow emotion to creep into the equation. Sadly, the old house remains empty, and it has lost its soul completely.

We left Ischgl* the cat until last, thinking he'd be traumatised at worst, confused at least, but actually he coped to the manner born, for he knows when he is onto a good thing. The old Hall cat flap remained in place if he'd needed a bolt hole, but when the time came, he followed me over the field, through the back gate, and into a warm heaven of draught-less comfort.

*I *called him Ischgl as he arrived as a rescue while Ian was away skiing there. (Ian having said, never another cat, but he quickly learned to love him.)*

Ross Farmhouse, December 2016

We've been here two months now and it is wonderful. This lovely new place doesn't leak, it is warm and cosy, while everything which needs to open and shut does so without the need of a kick, push or expletive. It's a sociable house too, right on a bend and not able to be missed, where the village residents drive or stroll past, smile and admire its newness, wave and generally pop in for a chat. There are windows everywhere, and the views from these are endless. From one aspect we can see the mighty Thames, whilst from the other side of the landing it's the river Medway we can spot, charting its course through the towns and onto its estuary. It will merge with the Thames, also making its entry into the sea, off the Isle of Grain.

I gaze out of my office window for inspiration as I type, and see the flower beds I planted three years ago, when the house was vacated and begging to be transformed. I thought then if I could make a start on the garden, at least some order would be restored. From first dream to moving in, the process has taken six years, and many discussions regarding risks and/or our sanity. It has been expensive, hugely stressful, but so worthwhile.

Our dream project was to purchase two semi-detached farm cottages and turn them into one house. There were seemingly insurmountable problems from the outset, with the first and most major being the fact that a widow of a previous worker was living in each and they needed to be found alternative properties. Both ladies admitted it was time to go. The west winds were lifting their carpets and their meagre means of heating weren't proving sufficient. Neither lady drove and the village was isolated. This dilemma was finally resolved after three years of negotiations, all of them complicated, until finally they were vacated and we were able to move to the next hiccough. Our charming village is in a Conservation Area, which basically means that any change to a property, in planning, design or construction had to be channelled through a select committee. These ogres, we were warned, will agree with nothing you request. The scary stage was approached with caution, but we breathed our way through, and the expert plans were finally approved.

The cottages stood untouched for a while longer, waiting for our busy builders to begin the transformation. And what a job the gang faced. They had to first demolish the three chimney breasts. This was a time of crossed fingers, aching backs and foul language. Something along the lines of 'they knew how to build houses in 1930' was uttered on an hourly basis. But come down they did, leaving forty percent more room inside each house. (Waiting on permission to take down the huge internal chimneys was the cause of weeks of delay.) Inside walls went the way of the stacks, then the floor was excavated to allow for insulation. At this stage our sanity was certainly in question. On and on the work went, nail biting at the beginning, until gradually a shape emerged and we knew that it would all work, and beautifully.

The original doors and handles were kept and stored for stripping. The building timbers of 1930 were re-used, as they were superior in quality to any available today. Conservation officers had decreed that the windows must stay the same shape, though the houses they said, could be extended, but not by more than 25 per cent. Their department worked with the architect over time – we learned to be very patient – and their decisions in the end proved to be the right ones. I busied myself sanding and waxing both sides of the 18 stripped 1930s doors and sanding my favourite pieces of furniture, all stained in a garish pre-war dark varnish. These I painted in delicate New Gardenia, a Dulux cream. Early twentieth century doors and furniture, we knew, would add character and be in keeping with the cottage.

Eventually we looked on in delight as the shape and interior of the house grew into something so handsome it was difficult to reconcile it with the sad, grey semis, hidden by years of neglected outbuildings and near-forest. We were warned by our loyal builders that there would be periods where we wouldn't notice much progress, but we knew that in time the chrysalis would reveal its treasure.

We have our beautiful home at last and the settling in process is under way. It has been far easier than we thought it would be. Ducks to water comes to mind, though it **has** been six years with periods of panic along the way.

And the cat now has his fine flap – actually it is more of a tunnel – It took nearly a day to fashion. A cat-sized hole had to be drilled through fourteen inches of outside concrete wall. I told Ischy he was not to get run over after that expense. Like us, he has adjusted well. Life is good.

42

On Reflection

---◇◇◇◇◇---

People have lived and loved, been born and passed on within the confines of St. Mary Hoo for many centuries – nine could be an accurate estimation. That is a very long time for memories to have been made and stories to emerge. They're sometimes gruesome, often amusing, but usually interesting. One thing is certain, those who visit the village for the first time always comment positively. All around is farmland where crops are drilled, harvested and carted in a never-ending cycle, year on year. That activity, though ongoing, is gentle, methodical and that's what gives the place its charm. There are so many adjectives which describe the tiny village where I have lived for more than half a century. Yes, it's tiny – there's no disputing that. And I've already spoken of its quaint and tranquil qualities. If I add warm, bonded, and friendly to the mix, that is surely enough for the moment.

Passing by the Church wall, The Street is bordered on one side with a high hedge of hawthorn trees. Spring rains have sent the nettles waist high. The cow parsley seems more prolific than usual and the scent is pungent. Growth is what this place is all about and right now it's nearly harvest time. The thousand acres of oil seed rape are like a vivid yellow forest. When the rape seed is harvested, and the nettles die back, some Good Samaritan might trim the hedges, then yes, the little place is fit for the accolade of quaint and charming.

Each evening and early morning a 'Watership Down' of rabbits scurry around, criss-crossing the road playing kamikaze with any traffic, before searching for a tender morsel – usually in our gardens. There are badger sets in a small area adjacent to the Church, gifted to the parish by the daughter of Henry Pye. Foxes come and go regularly, and we welcome several families of swallows who miraculously return to last year's nests. This is exactly the type of village where we ask one another, 'Did you hear the cuckoo last night? 'Whose was that white van that came in late?' Or, 'There's another brood of moorhen chicks on the pond. There won't be room in the duck house if she carries on at that rate.' Ian is the resident Mr. Fixit, usually on hand to help. 'Can he come and look at my chicken, it seems poorly?' 'The dog has a tick! It takes a farmer to deal with a tick, or a farmer to share out his big pile of farmyard manure, when requested. These are not the conversations of an uptown street.

During Covid's lockdown, if we were relatively unknown before, then the village came alive over the two-year period. St. Mary Hoo became a pleasant two-mile destination for a morning's stroll from our considerably larger neighbouring village, High Halstow. The route took the admiring visitors along a track which meandered through fields of onions, rape and wheat. Pedestrians by the dozen wandered over here, walking on the ancient footpaths. They'd suddenly discovered an adventurous streak hitherto unexploited. Many exclaimed, as if they had no idea St. Mary Hoo existed, just how pretty it was. We found it amusing rather than invasive. Friendly chats took place over the hedges or fences. With Ross Farmhouse in the middle of the village, and on a junction, our hedge was a popular barrier for these 'distanced' chats, or perhaps we talked over the garden gate at the corner. It's where new dogs were introduced, gardens were admired and advice on how best to prune roses was gratefully received. Quite by chance as a welcome, a huge display of wild poppies which had mutated into myriad glorious shades, had displayed themselves conveniently on a field bank. Cameras were evident then amongst the visitors.

Very gradually, machines and progress have begun to threaten the precious tranquillity of our little village. It started subtly, but the lorries are getting longer and can no longer turn easily at the pond. The drivers are in a hurry, their trips are multiple and we are noticing it more. We might get a bypass as a result of this impact; in fact, it has been scheduled in. A few hundred yards of high street from pond to corner is feeling the effects of the trundle of heavy wheels. After all, The Street was designed for pony and trap and is narrow as a result. Whoever was farming in 1750 would never have imagined that a monster in the form of a tractor or combine harvester would be invading their space. For centuries, until the inventive twentieth century, horses and manpower provided the workforce on the land. Just like our forebears, we cling to the old (our old) but gradually the need to allow the new creeps in. It may override our peaceful place and our hold on it. How will that feel, I wonder?

Part Two

Characters of The Hundred of Hoo

Selected Tales of Times Past

1

Introduction

My characters are tough, just as their forebears needed to be. Those who lived on the Hoo Peninsula were often sick, and those who arrived, didn't live long. The Hundred of Hoo forms a large part of the Peninsula, that crooked thumb-shaped projection jutting out eastwards from the Gravesend-Strood area of North-West Kent. Way back in those earlier centuries it was dismal, desolate and sparsely populated, and generally considered to be an unappealing, unpleasant place. Alongside the river Thames, the Anopheles mosquito thrived in the stagnant water of the marshes and filled the graveyards with its victims. The ague, or marsh fever as it was also known, was a grim deterrent to any settling.

And then, in the mid-1800s, along came a farmer called Henry Pye, with his innovative ideas for improvement, his quinine supplies and his philanthropic gestures. His concern for the frequent deaths, especially those of children, concerned him greatly and he vowed to do all he could. Two of his children succumbed as tiny babies, and this propelled him to improve the health of local families by eradicating the mosquito and draining the marshy swamps. Only then would life improve and farming could begin in earnest. For in the 19th century, it was predominantly an area of agriculture, though life was hard for anyone working the land.

In Part Two I have written a whole chapter about Henry Pye and the important part he played in farming technology, in Kent and far beyond it. He farmed land from High Halstow to Grain, in acres which were divided into twelve small lots; small farms with names which remain to this day although they have been incorporated into larger holdings. His workers were numerous and some of their descendants can still be found on the Peninsula land today.

St. Mary Hoo is one of a number of small villages, all on higher ground, allowing fine views sloping down to the Thames. The area and that which surrounds it is teeming with history and intrigue, and was home to the dear, departed characters on which I based Part Two of my book. Without their courage and my curiosity there would be no story-telling.

Most of them knew the area as farmland - as they **were** farmers, farm workers or maybe merely resilient residents of a quiet, rural idyll, recently freed of mosquitos. I wonder what they'd have thought of the developers' building blocks and paving slabs, fields being swallowed up, or the traffic lights, dual carriageways and container lorries? My stories relating to almost all of them, concentrate on the time before these present-day changes, some of which trundle and thunder nearby. I hope I did my characters justice. For often they shaped the land, or were legends, and they left memories for the generations to come.

Some of my subjects I knew, others I merely knew of, but all of them played a part in the legacy of the villages, these wonderful villages we must cherish. We have much to be thankful for. I have written their stories as the memories occurred to me, in a wonderful, colourful, random fashion. There are many Characters I have surely omitted, for everyone is extraordinary in their own way.

In writing Part Two I would like to acknowledge those who have helped me with extra detail, to ensure facts are accurate – descendants, friends, and information derived from reading the relevant chapters of the books of Ralph Arnold and Brian Matthews.

Just occasionally, my subjects were of a rascally nature, but I feel they too made for a worthy story. To the best of my ability my writing is factual. However, I could not resist writing some fictional tales - in keeping with the theme, whilst offering additional relevant information. After all, my university tutors stressed that I employ differing genres as part of the writing journey.

I am often asked the significance of the word Hoo, which forms part of the name of this and another nearby Peninsula village. Hoo is a Saxon word, and means 'on the spur of a hill.' Aptly named, St. Mary Hoo does indeed perch on a high point between two major rivers, the Thames and the Medway. And as a nod to his importance, Henry Pye was known as the King of the Hundred – Hundred being another Saxon term, for a unit amassed by several of the Peninsula settlements; an area of local government and taxation, which survived into the 19th century. Originally, in medieval times, it referred to a group of 100 hides (units of land to support a peasant family.) Though rarely used today, I think referring to this special area as The Hundred of Hoo has a pleasantly appealing ring to it, and is the reason I have chosen to name Part Two in honour of bygone times.

The readers of Charles Dickens' novels will be aware of north Kent's stark beauty and the perceived mystery of the marshes, especially when the great man found mists hanging low and the cold eerie light of day arriving late and limply. Dickens wandered for hours over the marshes on the river banks below Higham, Cliffe, Cooling, High Halstow, St. Mary Hoo and Allhallows, all the while gathering ideas and inspiration for his writing. Some scenes of the film Great Expectations, starring John Mills, were filmed on St. Mary's marshes and featured our very own draft horses, their grooms and a village boy, one Douglas Packman. Those were indeed halcyon days. WWII was over, the Anopheles mosquito was ancient history, the land was fertile and producing well once again. Farming was making money. The people who lived here in St. Mary Hoo were, on the whole, contented with their lot.

Apart alas, from the fickle fortunes of farming, little has changed for fifty years, and unlikely to in The Street. Here, by the Church, we are protected from development by being enclosed in a Conservation Area. Nevertheless, we watch with alarm while new housing estates appear a mere few miles away, with still more scheduled even closer. Larger and noisier farm machinery is inevitably forever evident.

This farm, two thousand acres of tenanted land, is owned by the Church Commissioners of England, and forms a large part of their Rochester Agricultural Estate. They own many thousands of rural acres all over the country and therefore have many tenant farmers acting as caretakers on their land. Henry Pye, soon after moving to the St. Mary's Hall in 1851, became a Church Commission tenant on twelve small local farms.

Local Agents act on the Landlord's behalf, dealing with issues from housing to rents and everything in between. Very occasionally a visit from a small delegation of eminent Church Commissioners is scheduled, when much dusting, polishing, sweeping of barns and strimming of ditches takes place. They meet farm workers and sometimes, as part of the tenancy visit, check the state of their houses. The Church's immense property portfolio also includes huge swathes of the city of London and other major towns.

The farmland bordering the Thames is low lying – acres of it are below sea level - and other marsh acres are prone to flooding from winter rain. The seawall was raised and strengthened after the catastrophic flooding of 1953. It has not been breached since that time. Then there are tidal saltings, home to many species of wading birds, making this and neighbouring farms a unique habitat and an area of special interest to bird watchers strolling on the high seawall or on designated public footpaths. Whatever the tide, whatever the season, there is something of interest to spot.

The population of the Hoo Peninsula has risen to approximately 35,000 with a huge surge in building in the last few years. All it seems, is set to change further, yet there is still only one road onto the area and the same road off. In many ways it feels remote, even though it is close enough to London. As such it is an anomaly. It is possible to see both rivers from several high vantage points. Our house is one such place.

Our nearest city is Rochester. That historic town is on the river Medway, and thus forms part of what are known as The Medway Towns; five cities joined without space between them. The town of Hoo St. Werburgh is three miles away from our village, and many a confused visitor to our home has driven there first, but it is known as merely 'Hoo.' Huge housing developments are taking place in Hoo where, just fifty years ago, the area was almost exclusively farmland.

So now that I have set the scene, and given a backdrop to the unique and historic area we live in – off we go, into the magic which is north Kent. This is where my feisty, fabulous Characters laboured, loved and lived their interesting and mostly long lives.

2

The Legacy

The people who came, populated and passed on, through death or onward journeys, left a legacy of loveliness in the shape of a tiny village community - my village community - which hasn't grown much at all. If anything, the population has shrunk considerably, though the loveliness remains. Our present neighbours live happily and quietly, making few waves, and never those of discontent. Nothing damning or dastardly ever happens and the tiny population of less than 250 live in harmony, in four small 'pockets' of housing. I will concentrate for now on the oldest of all, the little pocket by the church.

The dear departed souls made many waves. They created, invented and toiled, forging a life, which depending on circumstances of chance or choice, ranged from poverty and strife to high-ranking aristocracy. Each had a part to play, and collectively created an historical place where stories abound and yet where so many adventures and colourful tales remain buried in the sands of time.

Our village lies uphill, one and a half miles south of the mighty river Thames, near to its estuary, and goes by the quaint name of St. Mary Hoo – previously known as St. Mary's Hoo, or Hoo St. Mary's. Someone in their wisdom in recent years dropped the apostrophe, and though this caused confusion, it is now mostly settled and agreed. From their lofty spur-of-hill positions, each one overlooking respective coastal banks of the Peninsula, the local Hoo St. Mary and Hoo St. Werburgh villages look down onto the Thames and Medway rivers.

Before the St. Mary's marshes were drained, this village was considerably closer to the water, with inlets filling on each high tide and snaking their way from the busy Thames waterway. They were known as creeks. The widest of these, though none were vast, provided access by small boats to the point where the land began to slope. The inlets headed towards St. Mary Hoo, several meandered inland from Egypt Bay, and one or two pointed to Cooling where there is a Castle, built in the 1380's. In fact, the marshes could be accessed at many points. At Cliffe, a wharf existed prior to the erection of a seawall. It was busy, if primitive. The entire area of marsh, from the estuary to Cliffe and beyond was bleak and malarial, often referred to then as a mist-shrouded swamp. It provided a perfect and secluded setting for smuggling contraband, which came into the Thames on larger vessels, to be unloaded onto smaller boats at high tide. Many law-abiding travellers would also choose this method of arrival. When the inlets petered out, they'd walk uphill for a couple of miles to civilisation to one of the hamlets on the spur - to St. Mary Hoo perhaps, such as it then was. To greet them was a church, built around 1300, a manor house and workers' dwellings from around that time. The hamlet boasted a blacksmith and wheel right. The farm workers, travellers and labourers found respite in the Inn, and later they were able to fraternise in a second hostelry. And a street was formed. But always there was the threat of the marsh ague, and the terrible toll of those who succumbed.

St. Mary's Hall is thought to be one of the earliest dwellings, and has been altered and added to each century, possibly since the 16th century. Some suggest earlier than that time. A Rectory was built in the 18th century; a fine house which affords a sweeping panorama of the marsh, the Thames and the Essex coastline. It looks directly over the five miles of water towards Leigh on Sea and Canvey Island, with Southend on Sea to the right.

But that is now, what of centuries ago, when the Essex coastline was clear of oil storage tanks and a city with its very long pier? What of the Vicar in his grand Rectory, able to gaze out on a wondrous view, totally unspoiled? Robert Burt, Rector of the village until he died in 1791 was able to purchase the livings of two insignificant and remote parishes – St. Mary Hoo and High Halstow - after agreeing to illegally marry the Prince of Wales (later to become George IV) to a beautiful Catholic divorcee, Maria Fitzherbert. The year was 1785. The prince rescued the unfortunate Burt from a Debtors' Prison by paying his debts of £500 and considerably more. In the eyes of the Church of England such a marriage would be void, and by law any officiating clergyman performing such a ceremony could face transportation to Australia, or worse punishment. However, since the prince was hopelessly in love and Robert Burt had little to lose, languishing as he was in Fleet Prison, he was freed on the promise of secrecy, in order that he conduct the service. Robert Burt's son, another Robert, eventually succeeded his father in the pastoral care of the parish and remained there for 53 years. During that period, he opened a village school and congenial fellow that he was, was seen daily visiting friends and worshippers in his pony and trap.

Further back now, to the 16th century. One historic journey from the London docks, down-river, carried Good Queen Bess, daughter of the ill-fated Anne Boleyn. Transferred to a smaller boat which then moored at Swigshole – a desolate enough spot - her courtiers carried her through the sloping farmland upwards and onwards to higher ground. The path her helpers scrambled through is still known as Bessie's Lane. Transferring to something more comfortable, a trap perhaps, she no doubt passed through St. Mary Hoo for sustenance at the Inn on her way to Cobham Hall, a grand and sumptuous place. (After the considerable damage to the much closer Cooling Castle by the Duke of Norfolk's cannon, the Castle was virtually un-repairable, and deemed not fit to entertain a discerning monarch.) The year of the Queen's visit was 1559.

Though deaths and sickness from malaria or consumption were prevalent in the district, it did not deter the visitors who came to investigate, remembering of course, that the Thames was a major access route. For those who stayed it took immense courage and challenging toil to establish a community and sustain a good living. A closeness to Rochester, Canterbury and London would have been a draw card. The Chancellor of the Exchequer lived in a grand house here in the 18th century, and within a few miles are five additional listed buildings, all of them centuries old. Clearly, the area attracted those of noble birth to add to the rich tapestry of its formation.

In the garden of one listed building, St. Mary's Hall - in the grape arbour by the high brick wall of the neighbouring church - a young man of 36 years of age reputedly shot himself. It is reported that he was spurned by a young lady, and unable to pay a dowry to her family, he took his life. The year was 1828, the month August. That summer garden, a place of peace and giving, was my garden and as I tended it, I thought of poor Robert Gunning from time to time.

It is impossible not to imagine intrepid souls, arriving, labouring and living right here in such remoteness – relying on transport by horse and cart or merely on foot, and by necessity, being totally self-sufficient. Were there highwaymen, was there a brothel? Who meted out the punishments? What of the Innkeeper, and the Clergymen, as there were many over the years? Nevertheless, the village grew rapidly, the living made easier by a seam of fertile ground which ran along the spur.

Along the river adjacent to our marshes, are several small bays where bigger boats would anchor off-shore to be loaded with sheep and cattle, packed onto rafts for the short journey to the larger vessels. Coombe Point was just such a loading venue. After the seawall was built, and with no easy access to the river any more for loading cattle, they were driven from the farms of the

Peninsula, along the main road to Rochester Market. This method was still in place until the early 20th century. Some of the stockmen were our stockmen, walking for miles behind their charges. What traffic there was at that time had to heed them and give way to the sheep and cattle. It was the responsibility of those living along the route, residents and shopkeepers alike, to protect their properties from the livestock, and not the other way around. I'm told that sheep careered into Woolworths on one occasion. What an amazing recollection! After a station was built at Sharnal Street, nearby to the local farms, livestock was transported from, or arrived there, which was a much easier alternative. This practice continued until the middle of last century. Cattle, purchased in Ireland by my father-in-law, arrived safely at Sharnal Street after a sea crossing and a rail journey from Holyhead, to be then driven along the Ratcliffe Highway to their new home. A hundred of them!

In the late 1800s a seawall was built along the Thames which protected the North Kent marshes all the way to the estuary. This enabled many more acres of marshes to drain, though saltings remain, rich in bird life, near to the river. Once recovered from their salty beginnings, the land was ploughed and grassed for grazing. The soil was rich and farming through the years continued profitably. One farmer in particular is remembered for his many pioneering ideas. I write about this man, Henry Pye, whose house became our house, in a subsequent chapter. While Elizabeth I might well have walked our village street, The Chancellor too; probably whores, highwaymen and many other colourful characters, it is this man, Henry Pye to whom I feel most empathy.

We mustn't forget these early settlers, the stockmen, the gamekeepers, the children of yesteryear, who often struggled against a legacy of poor health, and whose environment inspired Charles Dickens to write his most famous story, Great Expectations. This area is the backdrop to his story and the local villages, churches and churchyards are where he researched, pondered and wrote his notes.

As I wander through the village, and if I pause and ponder, I imagine those who have been hereabouts before me. I can feel the history in gentle waves, and I'm full of admiration. This street (there is only one) is where for me, the legacy is strongest.

Ian's Grandfather, Lachlan Maclean
Born Tiree, Scotland, 1873. Tenant of St. Mary's Hall from 1921

3

A Tempting Trade

(A mixture of fact and fiction)

1790

At the Three Daws Inn, one of Gravesend's oldest drinking establishments, business was brisk. The rotund landlord was almost as round as he was high, with wispy hair and a badly trimmed ginger beard. Edward Jakes, known as Mister Ted to his regulars, had learned to keep his head down and his mouth shut. For this Inn at the river's edge was the epicentre of a brisk smuggling scene. It was best, he knew, to merely serve the men their ales and not get involved in what was happening around him. His inn boasted three tunnels which made hasty escapes possible, and even the Pilots' House behind was reputed to have seven staircases. Money changed hands at an alarming rate, but Mister Ted just carried on as usual. He missed little, and said naught.

For the most part, the currency of the illegal trade in those early days of the eighteenth century was wool. Every garment to be made in England and abroad, required its uniqueness, and its strength and warmth. The fleeces were keenly sought after just as soon as they were off the sheep's back, and dry. Continentals craved the quality and the softness and money changed hands as rapidly as the customers could do their dealing. In this black-market way, the deals in pubs and back alleys were free of the duty which would have been levied when the wool was traded legally in the larger cities' markets.

Egypt Bay, eastward and down river towards the wide estuary of the Thames, was an ideal landing point for contraband goods, such as tea or liquor, or a place of deliverance for the bales of new fleeces. Just a few miles down well-trodden tracks from Gravesend, the ponies, sure footed in the dark, tripped along with their handlers - all of them hardened smugglers and part of well-rehearsed inland gangs. On the return journeys these trained men filled their carts with items landed from the ships coming up river. Before the exchange of goods there would have been a signal from the shore in the form of a flash or flicker, or a flag which would indicate that it was safe to land or anchor a craft, and for several crew to make for the shore in a laden rowboat. These had been loaded with all manner of tempting Continental delicacies, worth a small fortune, and bound for the London markets.

Except that half of their cargos did not make it to the city of London. The black-market goods would find their way to Rochester, Gravesend, Canterbury, Maidstone and places in between. Once at Egypt Bay, wide and sandy and an easy place for the ships to anchor on the Thames tide, smaller boats would then travel up the tidal creeks with their precious cargo, towards the waiting ponies and carts. That initial process was called landing. If they were intercepted at any stage, the marshes had many inlets and deep ditches where it was easy for the inland gangs to hide and wait until the coast cleared. Smuggling was such big business, and those who operated and organised the gangs were always moneyed, influential and given to bribing. Arrests were not common, because everyone seemed to benefit from the flourishing trade, and especially those at the very top. Spirits of all kinds, tea and tobacco were in high demand by those organising the gangs, and in this way the contraband was devoid of astonishingly high duty. Large amounts of money could be made by the gang leaders. Hundreds of men were involved in the trade all along the Kent coast, as far away as Margate and beyond. Some of the ships used for this trade were blackened, making them virtually invisible on a dark night. If a flicker of light to herald a safe rendezvous was not forthcoming, then a ship would move on to the next waiting bay and its inland gang. Other ships were often camouflaged by two-tone paint – green below with a white top to resemble seawater.

Egypt Bay was a perfect choice for smuggled goods to arrive as it was a desolate enough spot, prone to mist and fog and it had an additional detraction in the form of marsh ague, or malaria. The Anopheles mosquito, peculiar to the damp, muddy and tidal conditions of the marshes, caused an alarming spread of malaria in the eighteenth and early nineteenth centuries. There were few inhabitants nearby, save for the very poor, because not many people wanted to live there. It was an excellent location for clandestine ventures. Knowledge was necessary, as negotiating the saltings and the creeks was dangerous to any other than those with a business to consider.

Shade's House was in the middle of a marshy field and just big enough to allow a smuggler to rest up and sort or store packs of ill-gotten loot. It was a mere mile from Egypt Bay and a stone's throw from Cooling Castle where a smuggling family was reported to reside in considerable safety and wealth, further away from the dreaded marshes.

It was to the vicinity of Egypt Bay that Elivina Took and Allen Dayes were due to travel. Their gang leader had given them instructions whilst in the Three Daws Inn. They were to meet an inland gang member, name of Paynter and each take from him a large pouch. One containing tea, destined for Maidstone, the other to Canterbury containing rum. Somehow, but perhaps because of - as Elivina and Allen were half frozen by the time they arrived at the secluded Shade's House - they'd consumed a fair quantity of the rum as they waited. The pouches were mixed. At the Chequer's

Tavern in Maidstone where the gang boss expected his tea consignment, the pouch when eventually opened, was nearly full of small bottles of rum. In the fracas, fisticuffs were exchanged and Elivina was handcuffed and charged with an affray.

Occasionally when apprehended, and merely in an attempt to paint a picture of a law-abiding society, any poor detained individual was hung, or imprisoned in a hulk moored at Grain. These hulks were considered a worse punishment than death. Another option for any beleaguered soul was transportation in a convict ship to Australia; a dreadful punishment also, but with the chance of a new life eventually, if the ship ever made it to the other side of the world - freedom being granted only after serving a term of imprisonment there.

Although loathe to implicate his fellow gang members, Elivina knew that his chances were few and he prayed for transportation as his destiny. The other options were far worse. He was in a right pickle. It was enough to put him off rum for the rest of his life, should he still have a life. Such was the perilous existence of those who lived and attempted to carve a living in the poverty stricken south east of England in the eighteenth century. Crime was rife and life was impossibly hard for those in filthy overcrowded town tenements. After supplying the names of the gang, Elvina was reprieved from a gallows death, and instead spent eight tortuous months mostly chained below decks in a convict transportation to Port Philips, New South Wales. By the time the men and women arrived, it was questionable which punishment would have been the most severe. To Elvina's dismay, the primitive settlement was plagued with mosquitos which descended while they were put to work for long, hot gruelling hours. It was an ironic reminder of the little creeks at Egypt Bay.

When the marshes along the river were drained and the malaria carrying mosquito eradicated, life improved for everyone and the population grew in all the towns which were, after all, so close to the French coast. Trade improved between the two countries but smuggling continued until about 1830. Those little bays along the coast were so very secluded and just too tempting.

4

In Memory of Robert Gunning

who died in the garden of St. Mary's Hall, August 6th, 1828

———⋄⋄⋄⋄⋄———

Weep no more Robert, for she has gone
Forsaken, you took your leave.
In this spot where I stand now,
you ended life, without her.
Unveiled tears flowed free for weeks.
From another's arms
she observes you, now at peace.

How could you, Robert
So gallant, in your prime?
Swept away by eyes so fine
Is it true that love is blind?
Her beauty was a mere skin deep -
Real love with her you did not find.

Your mother Robert, how she wailed
Your siblings and your father paled.
Shame and blame you could not face
For the rumour offered up
It was so unlike you, Robert
Did you steal the silver cup?

Though the high brick walls remain
Only the children and the seasons change.
Five families have lived their lives
Midst joy and laughter within these walls
Just as before – before you fell in love.
Do you regret it now?

5

Mary Prouse

Springtime, 1828

She was a country maiden of seventeen summers, with tumbling curls and skin so fine; the first blush of spring lifting the colour of her cheeks to palest pink. Mary Prouse was her mother's joy and her father's pride. Sir John guarded her carefully. Suitors were few, not for lack of effort, but from the fierceness of his protection.

A precious daughter, born after four sons, Mary provided a novel feminine distraction in a mainly masculine household. She was indulged by adoring parents and brothers, though the patience of many a governess had been sorely tested by her wilful streak. Since this was an endearing quality in her father's eyes, the protesting ladies were dismissed, along with the occasional maid, foolhardy enough to disagree with the child's upbringing. In spite of this pampered existence, Mary had a sweet temperament and an outgoing nature. She loved being outdoors and had a natural affinity with animals, in particular horses. She spent hours as a toddler fine-tuning her skills on the rocking horse in the elegant drawing room. Eventually, at three she begged to sit on a 'real' horse, having proved to her father she was ready for a small pony. All four brothers squabbled to lead her around on little Minty.

Within weeks she was independent, though restricted to the manor garden. When Mary reached her eighth birthday, she begged her brothers to allow her to ride their larger ponies, and eventually their hunters and thoroughbreds. In a mere two years, she became as accomplished in the saddle as they were. Although Sir John Prouse viewed this progression with pride, the parental restrictions for the wilful beauty remained in place, as she alighted like a chrysalis upon her teenage years. He dressed her in the finest Saville Row riding habit; always enjoying the compliments regarding his comely daughter.

Whenever she could, she rode her thoroughbred without escort, across the fields from the manor house where her family had lived for generations. On these occasions she felt freedom and excitement, alone on the North Kent marshes, and away from the closeted strictness of her home. It was familiar country to her and she felt exhilarated by the changing patterns of weather, and contrasts of the seasons. The marshes were a haven for birdlife, and sometimes the happy teenager would position her horse quietly, witnessing the different species flying overhead, or swooping to fish in the creeks of the river Thames, close to her home. With London so near, it amazed Mary how still and quiet it could be on these marshes. She felt so at peace there.

On a crystal-bright spring morning, during one of these outings, she spotted a horse in the distance. She could tell the rider was male from his headgear, and that he had a dog at foot. By then she had trotted and cantered for several miles from the village of Cooling and had reached the neighbouring marshes of St. Mary's Hoo. She reigned in and settled for a more sedate pace, along a bridle path below the rise of the land. She could see the church tower about a mile uphill. Eventually horse and rider came close. The stranger was about thirty she supposed, handsome of face, with long slim limbs astride his sturdy hunter.

The horses were abreast now and Mary allowed Bounty to greet the hunter with her customary whinny. Robert raised his top hat, and marvelled at the girl's vibrant beauty, remembering the pretty child from their previous meeting and how charming the transformation, in a mere three years.

Mary was also eager to make the stranger's acquaintance. 'Good morning, Sir, I'm Mary Prouse of Cooling Manor. You can't be from around here, I'm sure. I ride nearly every day, and I've not yet seen you!' She extended her gloved hand to Robert. Her curls were framed by a fetching hat and the ribbon tie to secure it was the height of equestrian fashion. Robert noted her confidence and easy manner as she sat side-saddle on the exquisite mare. She was a picture of elegance. So healthy, he thought, after the wan faces of the city girls who had offered female company until now.

Robert obligingly explained who he was and why he had not been spotted until today. 'This is our boundary path, Miss Prouse. It's Gunning land. You've come a fair distance this morning. And we have met before, actually. It was during a hunt three years ago.'

Bounty tugged to reach a drinking trough. 'I'll dismount, if you'll kindly assist.' She looked at him beguilingly.

Nimbly, Robert leapt from his saddle. The pretty young rider kicked free her stirrup irons and reached down to place her hands on Robert's shoulders. He gripped her trim waist and eased her to the ground. His effort was minimal as she was so lithe. They smiled shyly at each other. She was about five feet three inches tall, and he noted with approval, her firm breasts were barely restrained in the quality brown habit.

The horses drank at the trough and nibbled the grass adjacent to it. Nipper, the lurcher licked Mary's fingers in approval, giving Robert time to compose himself.

'Perhaps I could ride over to visit you one day soon, Miss Prouse?' he asked tentatively. He'd heard of her father's attitude. The Prouses were a grand family, to be held in awe he supposed, but Robert was already smitten, and not ready to relinquish this fine chance. Even at this first meeting he was determined to soon attempt another.

Mary giggled charmingly. 'Why yes, Mister Gunning, I'd like that. Please, do come.'

What she didn't explain, for she felt no need, was that her brother Ben – next to her in age – had furtively introduced her to one of his friends from his school days at Eton. The eligible Simon Young, now twenty-three, was possibly another reason for the flush to her cheeks, but he was miles away and Mary was frustrated by his long absence. She was also not yet versed in loyalty, having discovered her ability to flirt years before. Here was a young lady who was well aware of her effect on the opposite sex. But from this brief observation, she liked Samuel Gunning's son, and sensed his attraction to her. And there was one distinct advantage; he was living nearby.

'I must be getting back to Cooling now. I'm very pleased that we've become acquainted. Please could you help me into the saddle?'

Robert obliged willingly, arranging her habit as best he could, then summoning courage to ask, 'May I visit on Saturday afternoon, Miss Prouse?'

Mary thanked him and smiled in agreement, 'I bid you farewell then, Mister Gunning.'

He watched her canter away. Robert mounted and rode home as if on air. He handed Jasper back to Ted who would wipe him down and gave him hay. During the next days he attended to all the chores expected of him; efficiently completing account books and budgets; overseeing the feeding of the Hereford herd, and the shepherds' tasks in the lambing fields; the wagoners and their two teams of four draught horses, plus the spring planting. There was a constant rhythm – the never-ending pattern of rural life. The workmen respected 'young Mister Gunning' who had effortlessly, it seemed to them, slotted into his new life away from the city. But Robert had found adjusting difficult, and he also felt the restrictions of his family circle. There was pressure from his mother who fondly reminded him weekly of his advancing years, and single status.

Robert rode over to Cooling Manor the very next weekend, taking in his saddlebag, some tiny spring flowers from his mother's garden. He'd chosen hyacinth, narcissus, miniature daffodils and japonica. He'd wrapped them carefully and tied them with ribbon. He was as excited as a teenager. Mary was delighted to see him, and they walked, chaperoned, in the garden, later having tea in the summerhouse. Sir John and Lady Anne were welcoming enough, considering their lofty reputation. Sir John was impressed with Robert, and yet knowing his daughter's flirtatious nature, felt a degree of unease.

The Gunning's farm was extensive. John Prouse had often admired Samuel's fat cattle, for they were renowned breeders. Sir John also farmed, but his herd was small. His wealth was inherited and he lived a life of the privileged gentry. Robert began to relax as they all chatted happily, discovering shared interests. At half past five he reluctantly realised it was time to ride home to St. Mary's.

For Mary's eighteenth birthday, Squire John planned a grand coming-of-age party at Cooling Manor, his family seat. He sent his head groom with invitations to neighbouring parishes, where offspring of farming gentry were to open the buff envelopes with gathering excitement. Her party became the talk of the district. The Gunning brothers each received an invitation and eagerly awaited the gathering, to include the young and privileged of the district.

At the Manor all was bustle; the stables were made ready for liveries and carriages, lanterns were hung, and the house and marquee festooned with blooms from the walled garden. No-one was more excited than Mary, who knew that most of her childhood restrictions could be lifted now. The eager butterfly would emerge from her chrysalis and conquer north Kent, although it was on London, she set her sights. Violins played amongst the guests as they gathered in the garden, enjoying the canapés that a team of chefs had prepared in the Manor kitchen. Mary, quite used to being the centre of attention, greeted everyone with a warmth and maturity beyond her years. With a radiant smile, she offered her hand to Robert and all the young male guests. A delighted Robert claimed Mary for a waltz, knowing it was a dance he'd perfected while in London. He hoped his nerves would hold. Her dance card was soon full and there wouldn't be another chance for him to hold her tight. Not that night, at any rate.

Sir Miles and Lady Anne's hearts burst with pride as they surveyed the early evening scene in the carefully landscaped garden. The young ladies from surrounding hamlets danced or strolled in billowing gowns of style and colour, while attentive sons of local gentry vied for their attention. After the waltz, which was a triumph, and an opportunity to hold Mary for a few precious minutes, Robert was even more determined than he'd been previously. She'd gazed into his eyes, smiled adoringly, but could he court and win her?

The weekly visits continued into the summer. Mostly it was Robert who rode to the Manor. He became friendly with Mary's brothers and more at ease with her parents. Occasionally Mary rode to St. Mary's Hall and took tea with the Gunning family. They found her charming and of course pretty, though Robert's mother thought her a little forward for her years. In the garden of The Hall, Robert proclaimed his feelings for her and she allowed him to steal a kiss. He was so in love. There was a hesitancy about Mary – though she was sweet and kind to him. He sensed her feelings were guarded, but undaunted, he put that down to her inexperience.

'I'll propose marriage before the year is out,' he declared to his family that evening. 'I adore her.' They felt his happiness and were delighted for him.

The pair talked for hours in the summerhouse at Cooling Manor, often about their shared passion of the outdoors. Mary also spoke of her love of shopping and journeying to London, until now with her father. Robert longed to take her there, to show his new trophy to his banking friends. But until then, they would enjoy their respective homes as the romance nurtured, then blossomed.

'I'm going to be away for the month of August,' Mary said, towards the end of July. 'Mama, Ben and I are going to the Midlands. Goodbye until I return, my dear Mister Gunning.' She held his hand, and gazed up at him with shining sapphire eyes.

Robert was appalled. 'What will I do without you?' he whispered, but she didn't answer, in truth she couldn't.

He missed Mary terribly, was totally at a loss, wandering around the estate without purpose. Towards the end of the very first week of August, the letter came. He stared into the whiteness of the page until his eyes could comprehend the message. It was brief and it was clear. Mary was in love, but not alas, with him.

'... I'm sorry my dear, dear Mister Gunning, so very sorry.'

Closing the hall cabinet, he walked slowly into the garden and down the path to the grape arbour. There, where he had tasted the sweetness of Mary's kiss, he put the pistol to his head. It was the sixth day of August, 1828.

6

Robert Gunning

---

*The **Gunning** family were farmers in Kent for generations during the 18th and 19th centuries. They were highly regarded, diligent and honest. Apart from the tragic demise of Robert on that summer evening, and the vague story of a theft, other aspects of the story are fictional.*

The Gunnings were wealthy, hard-working farmers living right here in St. Mary's Hall. Their farm, just as now, stretched gently down to the Thames, at its estuary. The marshes weren't drained then so the river, at high tide, came half way up the farm as we know it these days. Robert was the first-born of four sons. The family thrived on a healthy life of honest toil, all except Robert that is, who lived the life of an academic in London. He was not cut out for farming and was the least robust of the brothers. He loved riding however, and became a competent horseman. It was on one of his early outings with the hunt that he'd first set eyes on the vision that was Mary Prouse.

Robert's chosen career of banking soon took him away from the village of St. Mary Hoo. He was to excel in the city, earnestly working his ledgers at his carved oak desk. Articulate, genial, frock-coated Robert socialised easily with his banking colleagues. He regularly attended Covent Garden as an opera lover, promenaded in the parks of London with well-bred daughters of society, and naturally he learned to dance with elegance.

Robert had recently been summoned home to oversee the family farm at St. Mary Hoo after his father's health problems worsened. It had been a complete culture shock after city life, and a learning of new skills. Without question, being the first-born son and loyal, he'd made the move back to his roots.

Now in his early thirties, he was pressured regularly by his parents to settle to matrimony. They could never understand that the young ladies he socialised with in London would find the smells, the isolation and his tasks in the tiny hamlet hysterical and alien. He busied himself with the responsibilities of staff and livestock by day, and yet became ever more lonely. The only respite from his melancholy were the rides he took over the marshes, when he checked the Gunning's pedigree cattle. He thought constantly of seeing the lovely vision he'd dreamed of for several years trotting by on her thoroughbred mare. And occasionally they did meet, each flushed and excited. Mary flirted with him deliciously. He was optimistic, if a little too hopeful perhaps.

Maybe, just maybe, this embossed invitation held the key to his future. It was an invitation to Mary's 18th birthday party at Cooling Manor. Naturally Robert accepted with great pleasure and escalating excitement.

Amongst the elegance, the musicians, the violins and canapes, Robert was able to claim Mary for a waltz. He held the exquisite girl in his arms and for the first time in his life he felt sure this was love. Mary was radiant and her sapphire eyes sparkled.

Once back in St. Mary's Hoo, he wrote Mary a tender letter, outlining his admiration for her and his hopes of a formal courtship in the chaste, proper way of the 19th century – with permission and chaperoning at the outset, and riding, picnics and dancing as the romance gathered strength. He wished it could commence that very summer, just as soon as he could visit and speak with Sir John. Mary did not discourage him. She refrained from telling Robert that she had another new love interest, in London, though temporarily in Europe.

Sir John welcomed Robert, and his visits to Cooling were joyful. He ventured there when his farming duties allowed. His family were overjoyed at Robert's good fortune, for Mary Prouse was not only beautiful and well versed in country ways, her family's estate – in the nearby village – was considerable. Her indulgent father was eminently wealthy. Robert was so helplessly in love and dreamed constantly of the time when Mary could be his wife. Yet at the same time he was confused and anxious, for he was daunted by his lack of material assets and the difference in their ages. Flirtatious Mary meanwhile, whilst Robert was busy with livestock or staff problems at St. Mary's Hoo, was not entirely faithful.

Robert, determined to succeed, hatched a plan which would improve his status. It involved a major image change, and that in turn required funds, which frankly he was aware, after two poor seasons, the Gunning family were short of. Their house and estate, though large, did not remotely equal the vast fortunes of the Prouse dynasty. Robert needed to increase his expendable income without involving his father, whose health was a major concern. Using his contacts in the world of banking – remember, he'd been a successful academic – Robert travelled to London, and with arranged invitations to a variety of high-level functions in sumptuous venues, he was able to discreetly smuggle small gold and silver pieces into his frock coat pockets. The sleight-of-hand was so easy, he was euphoric, and his trinket pile mounted. To think he'd soon be competing with the debonair style of any rival – once he'd laundered the bounty. Robert dreamed of being able to court his lady with panache.

Then he set about cashing in his trophies. But it didn't quite go to plan. Robert was rumbled by an observant pawnbroker who'd been offered a handsome reward for the return of some of the most valuable items. Two miniature silver candlesticks and a small silver cup in particular were what clinched his downfall. He scurried back to St. Mary's Hoo, on bail but with a court case pending. Rumours abounded in the district. Naturally the Gunning family were appalled by the notoriety. Poor Robert could hardly bear the thought of his honest and loving parents seeing him in handcuffs. He knew that the Prouse household would also be buzzing with news of his misdemeanours and that not only broke his heart, but also his spirit. Knowing that he had lost his very first chance of finding true love, and feeling nothing but shame, Robert realised there were no options, no avenues now. It was early evening in the grape arbour, and the sun was dipping low in the sky. The day was drawing to a close. It seemed apt.

The characters in this story are fictitious, apart from Robert Gunning and his family, who lived in St. Mary's Hall.

7

Robert Gascoigne Burt

Robert Burt Junior was never to know his father, the Rector of St. Mary Hoo, for he was born six months after Robert Senior's unexpected and premature death in 1791. Few people knew the significance of his father's famous place in history, as secrecy was an important factor in him agreeing to marry the Prince of Wales (Prinny) to the beautiful Catholic widow, Maria Fitzherbert. In the eyes of the Church of England, it was an illegal marriage and dreadful punishment awaited any clergyman, should they agree to perform the ceremony. But with his confinement in a debtors' prison over a deficit of £500, Robert Burt Snr. had little to lose and much to gain. The marriage took place privately in the front room of the bride's home in December, 1785. Robert's debt was paid, and in addition he received a large cash inducement. He was also handsomely rewarded with a Domestic Chaplaincy to the Prince and presented to the living at Twickenham. More tempting promises were alleged to have been made, once the Prince became King George IV, so besotted was the Prince with his intended.

Feeling vulnerable, but now having the means at his disposal, Robert Snr. was able in 1786 to purchase the living of two villages, both of them remote and insignificant enough that no questions would be asked; namely St. Mary Hoo and High Halstow. It would be 114 years before the name of the officiating clergyman of the illegal ceremony was officially made public, though it is inconceivable that some local residents of these small villages were not aware of his importance. That the participation of their past Rector in such a ceremony should largely remain a secret for so long is remarkable. Robert Burt Snr. and his wife built a fine rectory, surrounded it with trees and settled into a quiet rural life. Alas, Robert Snr. died aged 35 and was never to set eyes on his only child, born to his grieving widow six months after his death. His premature passing came before the Prince of Wales became King, and with it any chance was lost to him of a hoped-for Canonry or any other ecclesiastical limelight.

The child, also called Robert, was brought up in the village by his mother in a somewhat isolated fashion, though the house was pleasant and they lived in considerable comfort. His mother died in 1845, by which time Robert had long since married. No children were born to the marriage. Robert's career was marked out from his birth – that he should follow his father into the church. Elderly vicars were appointed to the parishes, assuming they would provide a stopgap before the young hopeful would be presented – but there were five before Robert Gascoigne was inducted to St. Mary's Church in 1816. He was 24 years old, and remarkably, remained in the post for fifty-nine years. He became Rector of High Halstow in 1824 and remained as Rector of both parishes for a further fifty-one years.

He loved the seclusion of his beloved Rectory, which he had extended considerably. Though Robert Gascoigne appreciated living in the village of St. Mary Hoo and exploring the area of the Hundred of Hoo, nevertheless for three months out of every twelve he could be found at Twickenham, where he owned a house. He kept his clerical duties to a minimum, and services lapsed completely while he was annually absent at Twickenham. He imported sermons in such quantity that he never had a need to compose one and he even installed a curate at High Halstow and built a house for him there, so he needn't be responsible for matins in that parish. It did not seem as if he was overworked.

Worshippers were segregated – men on one side of the church and women on the other. Children were herded into the chancel and order was maintained with the aid of a stout stick. Music was supplied by a barrel organ, purchased second-hand from Cliffe Church. It played six tunes. Church collections were spasmodic, but instead he would frequently hand out half crowns to the children.

Robert Gascoigne was a generous man and kind. (The stout stick was wielded by another.) Apart from Sundays, and for baptisms, weddings and funerals, he wore a dress suit and top hat, and on fine afternoons he drove out in his carriage pulled by a pair of grey horses. He subscribed lavishly to parish funds and left a considerable amount on his death to local causes. In 1868 his wife opened a village school to cater for farm workers' children in its one classroom. He was a Christian gentleman, a perfect example of a sheltered Victorian existence, not making waves and merely existing quietly from Sunday to Sunday. All of it was made possible by ample private means – the legacy of his father's important part in history.

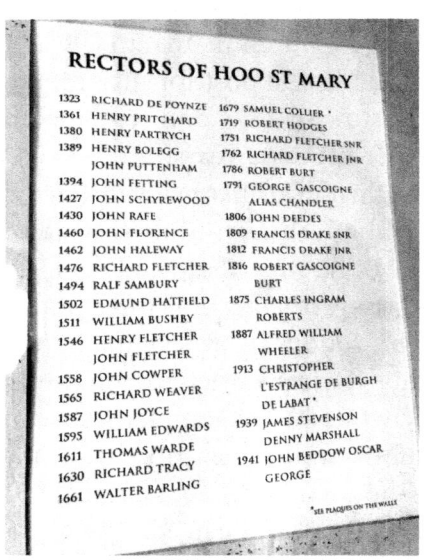

Rectors of St. Mary's Hoo through the ages

8

Henry Pye

1824-1909

It is impossible to read a book on the history of the Hoo Peninsula without frequent mentions of Henry Pye. He was in fact, its saviour, turning it from a soggy place of unwholesome air, best avoided, into a place of fertile opportunity. Henry was born in Court Lodge, Cuxton, in a fine farmhouse, where his well-to-do parents raised eleven children. They were one of the best-known farming families in the county. His mother, descended from Henry Hudson the explorer and navigator, instilled in her children a pioneering spirit and the will to branch out on their own. Henry in particular, also inherited from his eminent parents an attitude to succeed, and a zest for life, for work and for sport. He arrived in St. Mary Hoo in 1850 as a tenant of the Dean and Chapter of Rochester Cathedral. Many were to question his choice, for at the time the Hundred of Hoo (a large portion of the Peninsula) was an unkempt area with disgraceful roads, rampant malaria, and undrained marshes. Agriculture was at a low ebb. The land was heavy and yielded little. But Henry, young, progressive, opinionated and confident was also a passionate farmer. He quickly made the advances which had previously not been attempted and soon he was setting an example to his neighbours and to farmers further afield.

Many acres of Peninsula farmland subsequently became the property of the Church, managed by the Church Commissioners of England. Henry became their tenant on eleven local farms which went by the names (and still do) of St. Mary's Hall Farm, Moat Farm, Swigshole, Ross Farm, Hoppers Farm, Turkey Hall Farm, New Barn Farm and Malmaynes Farm. He owned only one, which was Clinch Street. His brother James held the tenancy of Coombe Farm, which was the closest to the more enterprising Henry. All of the farms were adjoining so that his land stretched from High Halstow to Grain.

Shortly after settling into St. Mary's Hall, he married Elizabeth Guy. They had six children. Tragically, their first child, son Henry died after a week and their second, a daughter Elizabeth, at just nine months. Their deaths were followed by the births of another Henry, and daughters Emmeline, Marian and Edith. Henry Jnr. and two daughters remained local to the area and never married. Edith married twice and later became a magistrate. I was told on good authority that she, reputed to be very stern, booked Uncle Charles Maclean for speeding through Rochester in his sports car. Emmeline, who settled in Hoo St. Werburgh and later in Sharnal Street, died at 95, apparently looking, though it sounds unkind, rather like Miss Havisham.

Henry Pye is particularly remembered for his innovative ideas. This venerable man whose house, St. Mary's Hall, eventually became our house was appalled with the incidence of infantile deaths. Having lost two precious babies, he set about attempting to lessen the fear and foreboding of life hereabouts at the time. The north Kent marshes then were bleak and inhospitable, with stagnant water caused by the blocked ditches providing a perfect breeding ground for the Anopheles mosquito. This lack of draining over decades had created heavy, unyielding grazing ground. Henry could see the potential; he understood the source of the problem, and was keen to rectify it. Others had not been prepared to invest time and effort, nor of course, did they have the means to do so. Henry, though still a young man, had the backing of an extended and wealthy Kent family.

Tiny graves were commonplace in the churchyards. It's reputed that the sight of thirteen small graves in Cooling churchyard, from one family, was the inspiration for Charles Dickens to write Great Expectations. All of this evidence spurred Henry to act quickly. He filled a huge cupboard in The Hall with quinine which immediately helped to save the lives of the residing children of the village and beyond. He instructed his workers to dig ditches. These were then lined with plentiful cockle shells from St. Mary's Bay. This simple drainage method proved so effective it was used on all local farms adjoining the river. It also explains why shells are still found a mile uphill from the river. He also sprayed ditches, creeks and saltings to stop the spread of the marsh ague. Generous by nature with his time and advice, always eager to help, and a natural mediator in any dispute - under Henry's guidance, The Hundred of Hoo gradually became a healthier, happier place. With its potential discovered, it began producing. And his own acres at last became fertile for the varied crops he chose to grow and for the livestock he grazed near the Thames.

Henry is mostly famously remembered for his farming techniques, which were revolutionary. Working tirelessly, he became one of the most respected and forward-thinking farmers in the country. He applied chalk to the land, while his method of ploughing provided a template for others to follow. He was the first farmer in the land to use his friend Thomas Aveling's steam plough. It was Aveling, the designer of the steam roller, who was responsible more than anyone else for improved surfaces on roads, not only in the Hundred but eventually, almost everywhere else in the world. Henry bought three of Thomas' steam engines, three steam ploughs and threshers, all of which were in great demand in the district. As a result, wheat production on a large scale proved successful. All the while he was happy to help other farmers inside the Hundred by offering his time or his machines.

Not surprisingly, as a nod to his importance, Henry Pye was known as the King of the Hundred.

He was reputed to be kind and fair to his workers, and there would have been a large number of them. They were as well paid as any, in the clear divisions between the rich and poor of the time. And he was hugely respected by his staff. Henry found time to host the Hunt over his farms, and he rode his thoroughbreds whenever possible. He played cricket and enjoyed watching local cricket teams. He chaired many local committees and was on the Boards of others. He was also a Justice of the Peace. The family holidayed extravagantly, with many adventures in this country and abroad. But for the most part, he loved being at the helm of his farms and was an icon, a pillar of the community, a Church Warden and devout Christian.

Henry grew hops at Turkey Hall, early potatoes for the London market, and fruit on other farms. His wheat was the highest quality. He soon set about establishing seed growing as an industry – particularly radish, pea and wurzel - which formed the backbone of the Peninsula's farming economy at the time. And he grazed sheep, cows and bullocks on his newly drained marshes. Because he was so progressive, and knowing there was a seam of rich, fertile land on the Peninsula, he encouraged others in the production of potatoes, hops, fruit and agriculture.

He was instrumental in persuading the powers-that-be of the need for a railway link from Hoo Junction to Sharnal Street to transport the harvests of these plantings to the ready markets of London and the larger towns in Kent. Henry was eventually successful in this venture and Sharnal Street Station was opened to a busy trade in 1882. Thanks to this new rail system which also included a single line track to Grain, produce from The Hundred of Hoo was shortly being enjoyed in major cities.

The Royal Family chose to use the station at Grain, which became known as Port Victoria. Queen Victoria particularly enjoyed leaving from the newly opened port, when she visited her daughters in Germany.

From a place of foul air and stagnant water, from its unhealthy residents and the dread of the Anopheles mosquito, the Peninsula began to transform. While Elizabeth I might well have walked our village street, the Chancellor too, and whores, highwaymen and other colourful characters, it is this man, Henry Pye, to whom I feel most empathy. After all, I've climbed the stairs he climbed, gazed from the same windows. The marshes he part-drained with shells from the beach we've both ridden over, he and I, every inch of them. Remarkably, he lived in St. Mary's Hall for sixty years. I was there for a mere forty-seven. This man was known as King of the Hundred for all the right reasons.

Henry passed away in 1909 and his death is marked with a headstone at St. Nicholas Cemetery, Rochester. His children are buried in the churchyard in St. Mary Hoo. Emmeline Pye played the organ in St. Mary's Church each Sunday until she left the village in 1921, while Henry Jnr. attended every service in all weathers. The eleven Pye siblings of Henry Snr. have ensured the legacy of the name lives on. There are a number of descendants scattered worldwide, though many are based in Kent. Soon after Henry's death, a diligent editor asked for family contributions towards a *'Ye Family Pye'* diary. This resulted in at least three heavy, bound volumes, with illustrations. They cleverly contain valuable information of births, deaths and marriages over a period during WWI until way after the War ended. There are also descriptive letters from family members enjoying exotic, adventurous holidays, and other news - local and farming - and anything worthy of interest. Sometimes, not surprisingly, mentions of brave family members losing their lives in combat were also chronicled. These precious, expertly edited diaries are stored in the Medway Archives. This was an extended family which was as enterprising as it was wealthy.

After Henry's death in 1909 his children remained for a decade, until the tenancy passed into the capable hands of the Maclean family; one I became part of when I journeyed from New Zealand to be married in 1968. And it is to New Zealand where I am reminded of a parallel with Henry Pye – that of another intrepid young man, one Donald Maclean, who arrived from his barren Scottish island of Tiree, to become well known and even knighted for his remarkable work as Government Land Purchaser. He worked tirelessly with the Maori people, showing great skill and empathy in their land deals with the early settlers. But in transforming his own coveted huge acreage of Hawke's Bay tussock, swamp and scrub into renowned, hugely admired farmland, he provides that parallel. He was passionate and confident, so like Henry Pye. (Except that unlike Henry, he travelled on horseback through bush and rugged terrain, fording rivers, or on foot, and he arrived in New Zealand penniless.) Donald and Henry were exactly the same age, and their ground-breaking work, 13,000 miles apart, took place in the mid-19th century.

The stations mentioned – Sharnal Street, and Port Victoria (Grain) closed, due to dwindling customer numbers, and in the case of Port Victoria, structural decay. Sharnal Street Station remained open until 1961.
A station was opened at Allhallows in 1932, as it was thought to be a potential delightful answer to those who wanted a seaside resort close to London. A return ticket from Charing Cross was 5s6d. It was initially popular, a pub was built, and a fun fair established. There was also a promise of a huge number of houses in a proposed new community. That never materialised at the time. Numbers dwindled after the war, and the station was closed in 1961. The attraction of Brighton was too great.

Henry Pye

St Mary's Hall, circa 1890
Elizabeth Pye and daughter in doorway

9

Justice For George

1914

George Phelps was a local lad, just a normal naughty kid, the youngest of three boys born to Joseph, a retired grocer and keen gardener, and his wife Meg. They lived a happy, uncomplicated life in the countryside on the outskirts of the village of Hoo St. Werburgh, in North Kent. George messed around like kids do in the wide open spaces surrounding his home. He didn't much like school and absconded rather too often, preferring to help his father on the family allotment, or getting up to mischief with his mates. Sometimes he tagged along after his two older brothers, although they were six and seven years his senior and up to their own mischief. By nature, he was helpful and kind-hearted, popular too, and definitely his mother's favourite.

The family were not well off, but Margaret Phelps did her best to keep her brood clean and well turned out in whatever clothes she could rustle up. She was a practical cook; providing tasty, wholesome meals for her menfolk wasn't a chore in her eyes. There were always eggs from the chickens clucking away at the bottom of the garden or hearty soups produced from the vegetables Joseph tended so carefully. It was George, rather than his bulky brothers who caught eels in the creeks of the marsh and he regularly presented his mother with a rabbit for the pot. They fared all right.

The years passed uneventfully, until the outbreak of war in 1914. The announcement shocked everybody, especially families with young, fit sons deemed suitable for combat. Only boys beneath the threshold of eighteen years of age or those with flat feet, poor eyesight, or ill health were ruled out of the enlisting process. Teachers, clergymen, or conscientious objectors at the time were also exempt. The upper age limit for single males was forty and married men were not required to enlist, though this was to change as the war raged on and on. There was also a lower height restriction of five foot three. To start with, this call to arms was voluntary. Young men and youths answered in a rush, keen for the chance to 'do their bit' for King and Country. The queues formed along pavements, around corners and way beyond. The menfolk placed the thought of being killed way below the idea of the great adventure that would surely materialise. These queues were themselves providing huge motivation to further swell the ranks. On one day alone 33,000 men enlisted. Soon three quarters of a million men and boys from every walk of life had answered Lord Kitchener's plea. *'Your Country Needs You'* propaganda posters were hugely visible on every vantage point, and proved a magnet.

George, at seventeen was insistent. 'I am going to sign up, mother. We have to beat those rat-bag Germans. John and Harold have already enlisted. I'm going to follow them.'

'George. No, please no! You're a mere boy, you're my baby, and you're way too young. You must stay behind. Let your brothers do the fighting. God forbid, I don't want them to go either. Speak some sense to the boy, Joseph.' Margaret, terrified, turned to her husband.

'Look George, the army won't accept you. You're below the age limit for conscription. Don't volunteer, son. Please have some sense. Just look at the state of your mother.' But Joseph knew his son, and he'd seen that determined look many times. There was little they could do over the next few days to change George's mind, although they tried. Oh, how they tried.

With a cheerful 'We'll all be home by Christmas,' George and his pal Frank Morgan set off for Chatham town, waving from the bus, slightly embarrassed that both their mothers were crying. It was a balmy September morning and the sun gleamed on the river Medway with its busy mix of shipping manoeuvring to and from the Dockyard. Their stomachs churned in anticipation. The boys had little idea what lay ahead - surely a training of sorts, and learning how to shoot? Death and deprivation had barely entered the heads of these two young recruits. Though they felt apprehension, there was also a large measure of excitement.

Not everyone had birth certificates at the time so George easily managed to persuade the enlisting officer that he was eligible and indeed 'of age.' Various health checks followed and the two robust country boys sailed through these. Both were well over five foot six, each had fine arches, their eyesight was adequate, so they were bundled towards the next process. This involved being measured and kitted out for uniforms and boots. Once these had been issued, George and Frank were off, again by bus to a training camp. It had all happened very quickly, before they could have a change of heart, if they had wanted to. But they hadn't, not for a moment, and resplendent in khaki they eyed each other with something resembling awe.

They joined the ever swelling ranks of the Royal West Kent Regiment and were drafted into the 11th Battalion of men from the Medway area. The extensive, exhausting training lasted for three months. George and Frank were pleased that they were able to stay together. In charge was a young officer, recruited from Oxford University, and a mere nineteen years old.

'He looks a right wimp, Frank,' George whispered. But they'd have to obey their superiors, whatever opinions they might form in their lowly rank, and they knew it.

After weeks of bayonet training - thrusting into sacks filled with straw, and running through obstacle courses whilst carrying heavy loads, George had thrown off the shackles of youth. He and Frank learnt to use and maintain their rifles. With endless target practice they became proficient and accurate shots. They marched, carrying full kitbags, until they all but dropped with fatigue. They were instructed in map reading and they dug trenches. They learnt the importance of being part of a team and looking out for each other. Occasionally George had home leave, as did his brothers, and Margaret's heart nearly burst with pride at the sight of her burly soldier sons. Only when they returned to their tented training barracks did she let the tears fall. Would they come safely home? The risks were becoming apparent as sobering reports were posted daily. But still the queues formed and volunteers by their thousands offered to join up.

Troops filled the trains to Dover, training was over and the soldiers were smiling and eager. The wailing continued on the platforms as their womenfolk bade farewell. 'We'll be home by Christmas' was the universal cry as they waved goodbye to mothers and girlfriends. There was a war to be won and off they went with purpose.

Christmas came and went. Word of huge casualties filtered back to England. Mothers received letters of sympathy, fathers despaired, nothing was ever going to be the same. The months dragged on and the dreadful toll of young lives continued. George and Frank were still together, attempting to stay alive, just one day at a time. Their trenches were hell holes and death and disease raged. They lost three of their Battalion to cholera over the first winter and more were slaughtered in the carnage of battle. Their clothes were sodden and infested with lice. Almost all the soldiers suffered with trench foot from the inescapable filthy water. The bodies of comrades lay mutilated in the mud, alongside horses killed by machine guns and exploding shells. The stench of decomposing flesh was ever present in the trenches and near the front.

George received a letter in Forces Mail. It was from his mother telling him that Harold was missing, presumed dead. It ended with her plea, 'Keep safe son, remember, you're my baby.' George cried. He despaired of ever seeing the family again. And now they'd lost Harold.

'We'll be lucky to get out of this bloody lot, Frank,' he yelled to his chum as the fighting raged around them. He'd never told anyone that his eighteenth birthday was still a few months away, Frank knew, but George wasn't the only youngster in his Battalion. It made little difference when squatting in the wet trenches; tasks and terror were the same, whether underage or not.

'We'll need more than luck, mate. A miracle might do it, and I don't see one of those coming any time soon.' Frank's feet were raw in his wet boots, and he had become worryingly thin. At least they were still together, but their resolve was at rock bottom.

More and more men were drafted in to fight on the Western front. Restrictions were lifted back in Blighty and now, countrywide, young wives bade their men farewell. The Objectors needed to prove by Appeal their reasons for abstaining from battle. There was huge stigma attached to those who stuck by their beliefs, won their Appeals, and remained at home. And all who failed to convince a committee would be made to fight like every other soldier. If, at any point in the conflict, any recruited man wanted out, a Court Martial awaited.

Each soldier took his turn on guard duty at night, and since times were increasingly dire, and allied man power weaker than the opposition, night duty frequently followed a full day of cross fire, or crawling through the putrid mud. George took his extra turn often enough. In the small hours of one such night, fighting exhaustion all the while, and during a lull in activity, his eyelids drooped over his sallow young cheeks. George drifted into a dream-wracked sleep. It was in this state he was found by a senior officer, and immediately instructed to attend a field Court Martial. George knew the outcome would be bleak and was not surprised to be handed his sentence. Death by Firing Squad, to take place the following morning.

'I did a dreadful thing, Frank. I fell asleep, and I'm sorry. Please tell my mum I did my best and that I loved her.' He hugged his best mate, and gave him a brief letter for his parents. He said his goodbyes and was put in solitary confinement to await his fate.

His courage surprised his comrades, but George was so tired and despairing, this punishment seemed to him a way out of the cruel, stinking ordeal of combat. Where was it all going to end, anyway? With the dawn execution a mere few hours away, an urgent message had to be taken to Headquarters. The British troops on the Western front were surrounded by the Germans and help was needed. George, on hearing of the danger, volunteered to deliver this plea for assistance. The task seemed impossible, but after all, he had little to lose. He successfully achieved the task, stooping low in the darkness, stealthily crawling through mud all the way, finding strength from heaven knew where. His exceptional gallantry was noted.

For his efforts he received a pardon. It was a hollow sort of justice, because his war wasn't over. He was still only seventeen. He was soon back with Frank and the others, scrambling through the filthy mud, enduring the trenches, fighting off lice, disease and picking off as many Germans as humanly possible. Although he couldn't comprehend how, he made it through until the end of the war. Frank, his best ever friend, did not. Mustard gas was Frank's undoing, along with so many others. Wicked and cruel, and not even swift as it descended, choking and blinding Frank as he screamed his farewell to his best mate.

With a heavy heart, and almost totally broken by his experiences and the sheer length of the Great War, George was finally shipped home. He grieved for Frank and his comrades with an acute pain, etched deep. He came home to Hoo, to his depleted family, a broken stuttering wreck. He had no accurate tally of the men he had slain, but the vision of death on their young faces was real enough, fixed forever somewhere in his distorted, despairing mind. There was no fanfare, not a huge welcome, and little help offered to the troubled men and boys, fresh from battle and so scarred by it. They had to 'make do,' join the ranks of the unemployed, and recover to the best of their ability. Or, in many cases, not at all.

His mother Meg had her 'baby' back, and it was to take her all her skill and love to retrieve something of the jovial boy who had skipped off to Chatham to sign up. He slept fitfully, screaming through his memories. George was never to lose his stutter, but very gradually he started to embrace the life he had left behind. He took once again to gardening, fishing, and walking in the countryside. But he would never be the same person, that mischievous, carefree teenager, circa 1914.

In time he purchased a small house in the hamlet of St. Mary's Hoo, in the roadside corner of a farmer's field. He set up a business selling fruit and vegetables, paraffin, cigarettes and groceries in the two tiny downstairs rooms. He lived above the shop, which made him a modest living. There was a little picket fence and he arranged advertising placards along the front. The shop was on the main road leading into the villages of St. Mary's Hoo, Stoke, Allhallows and Grain. George was able to benefit from passing traffic. He delivered orders by bicycle, always wearing a shiny blue suit and bicycle clips. He was well respected, being a local and also a hero, of course. Parents chided their offspring if they teased George about his dreadful stutter, or his face, which was a little crooked - a legacy of a stray tracer bullet and the lingering wound. It all added to painful conversations and tiresome social situations. Often his bike was propped up outside the Fenn Bell Pub where he would meet his friends. They were accepting of his problems, and there George could relax. He eventually employed a local farm worker's wife to help him in the shop. She and her family became his closest friends, protecting and assisting. The years rolled by and George's shop was forever busy. He never married, and was by nature reclusive and melancholy. In many ways he remained another victim of war; outwardly seeming to function but messed up on the inside.

'Let there be no other war,' he used to say. 'Such a bloody waste.'

But his hopes were unfounded and in 1939 conflict raged once again. George, the shop, and the small hamlet somehow survived it. George remained, doling out the paraffin and cigarettes, delivering orders by bicycle, until the late forties. These days, save for one of his admirers from before WW2, a dear man called Douglas, about whom I have also written in Part Two, no-one remembers George or his courage. The shop changed hands several times and was eventually demolished. A house was built on the site.

When you read this story, please spare a thought for the brave young soldiers of the Great War. Youngsters like George, and the million others like his friend Frank who never came home.

10

Douglas Packman

Douglas came to St. Mary Hoo as a two-year-old in 1927. His father had delivered sheep to Lachlan Maclean in the Packman family's Model 'T' truck. Sheep and driver made such a good impression, Lachlan offered Douglas' dad a job as Chauffeur/Groom. It came with a small farm cottage and a wage of 28 shillings a week. The Model 'T' was called into action again to deliver the Packman's worldly goods to Pond Cottage (now Pudding Cottage.) They had little to unload. Money was tight for this young couple after the General Strike of 1926. Everything they owned fitted easily into Pond Cottage, even though there were only two rooms downstairs and two up.

Every new man and family employed by Lachlan Maclean (Ian's grandfather) were given a welcoming meal in the servants' kitchen at St. Mary's Hall. Their tiny cottage was spotless and their coal shed was full of coal on arrival. Lachlan was a kind boss and believed in keeping his workers warm and well fed. However, the cottage had no electricity, lighting was from oil lamps and candles, and their toilet was down the garden. There was no shop for miles, and no bus service; all things which made it difficult for Douglas' mother with a small child to care for. 1927 was a harsh winter. Ponds froze solid and even the Thames had icy patches. Douglas nearly died with pneumonia mid-winter and the local doctor was called. He prepared Lucy Packman for the worst, suggesting a trip to town next day would most likely be to collect the little boy's death certificate. Thankfully, Douglas pulled through after mother Lucy used her grandmother's wonderful powers, her alternative folklore cure – which was placing several of the child's hairs in a sandwich, prior to feeding it to a dog! Similar cures were known and practiced by the hop pickers who came annually to Kent.

Douglas' adventures as a child were just as numerous and exciting as any young person lucky enough to grow up on a farm. He explored the sea shore and the marshes, scrumped apples, caught rabbits, climbed the stacks and walked on the beams of the old farm buildings to discover owls' nests. He often found the name H. Pye burned into the wood. Mr. Pye was so well known of course. Scenes of the 1946 classic, 'Great Expectations' were filmed on St. Mary's marshes. Douglas featured, wearing a long coat and leading Biddy the draft horse through a gate. He was delighted with his few minutes of acclaim, and even more so to be paid handsomely.

One weekend when Douglas was thirteen, he was checking his rabbit snares on the farm in thick fog, when he heard the putt, putt of an engine, and then silence. He climbed through a fence and to his amazement made out the rear end of an aeroplane. The pilot calmly pushed back his canopy, climbed down from his cockpit and helped his passenger out. Douglas knew the plane was a Gladiator from the boyhood knowledge his father had taught him. The pilot produced a map. 'Where are we?' he asked Douglas, who pointed to the village of St. Mary's. 'Good gracious!' he replied, 'I know this place. I was billeted at the Rectory during the last war.'

They all walked up the farm and had a cup of tea with the Vicar, quite forgetting the rabbits in the excitement. The plane had been on a training exercise and had become lost in the fog while on its way to the RAF airport on the Isle of Sheppey. It had made a forced landing in a field, having just missed a fence and a row of large elm trees. The next day it took off from the hilly meadow, expertly missing the trees with just feet to spare. Douglas had played truant from school to watch, but was in worse trouble for forgetting the rabbits from the previous day.

After a fire at Pond Cottage, the family moved next door to the Red House, which was considerably larger. The Red House, like most of the cottages in The Street had an interesting history from centuries ago. It had been a Poorhouse in days gone by. In the garden were the toilets for the school just across the road. It also doubled as the children's playground.

Most of the village's cottages were part of the farm tenancy. Two pairs of unstable semi-detached cottages at the end of the street were demolished in the 30s. Douglas told a tale of a tenant in one of these old cottages emptying a chamber pot out of his window with disastrous results, and a falling out with his now damp neighbour. They were replaced by two new buildings in 1936 to house a growing staff. The new cottages had toilets which flushed. This caused much envy amongst the workers.

While very young, Douglas learnt engineering and mechanics from his father, who also taught him how to box and how to drive. He owned and fired guns from the age of ten, shot duck and game, and trapped rabbits to help out with their meagre budget. Although he attended the village school just yards from the family's front door, he was not academic, preferring always to be outdoors, or tinkering with engines. He was given extra schooling from the Rev. Oscar George who lived in the beautiful eighteenth century rectory. Unlike his non-progress with Miss Henry, the battle-axe teacher in the little village schoolroom, he was mastering Latin and enjoying the learning provided in the big house across the field. His father paid for the tutoring by servicing the Vicar's car. By the time he left school, just before his fourteenth birthday, war had been declared. He became a telegraph boy, and more often than not, delivered bad news to young wives or mothers. He remembers one young wife, now a widow, collapsing into his arms and knocking his slight teenage frame to the ground.

Like so many teenagers before him, Douglas yearned to join the RAF, thinking he would rather fly to war than march and fight in the trenches. He wanted to give Hitler a bloody nose. But annoyingly, he would need to wait until he was eighteen. On his sixteenth birthday his driving licence arrived in the post. Charles Maclean (son of Lachlan) had applied for it for Douglas, who was already skilled at driving the farm vehicles and the Maclean family car, a Packard. As there was a war on, no driving test was required. He had already begun work on the farm and had joined the Home Guard alongside his father. His Dad had been unable to enlist because he had lost the sight in one eye. Most of the Platoon worked on the farm. In the Home Guard he learned un-armed combat, weaponry and was given a fine pair of British soldier's army boots, an army type gas mask, plus a uniform. Douglas cherished his boots! The men were protecting an important area, namely the seawall, the Estuary, the villages close by, due to their closeness to the river Thames and London. It was valuable training for the boy. All the while, with the help of Rev. George, he studied hard towards entry into the RAF. But not as a pilot, for he knew he wanted to become a Flight Engineer.

At 18 years and 2 months he was on his way towards flying in the wonderful Avro Lancaster, and yes, as a Flight Engineer. Training first while stationed at Syerston, Nottinghamshire and shortly after, when nearly ready for war, he was sent to 630 Squadron, East Kirkby, Lincolnshire. With his training complete, he made his first flight in May, 1944.

There were many dangerous operations for the crew. On a raid in Holland he witnessed, flying right next to them, a Lancaster receive a direct hit, killing all on board. And en route to Paris they were hit by the dreaded Schrage Musik. On fire and in a spin, Douglas somehow managed to climb to the front of the plane (he said it was like climbing a mountain) and help the pilot pull the control column back. He never knew how it had missed the tops of the houses, or how it had managed to get back to base. The next day the crew were off again in a borrowed plane and reached another French target. He was just nineteen.

The crew completed 34 operations before World War II came to an end in May, 1945. Douglas missed the comradeship of the Lancaster crew, and said they were the brothers he never had. Many of his RAF friends never came back. He had no idea how his crew survived the terrors and the dangers, but he put it down to the ministrations of a guardian angel. At the end of the war, he flew into Berlin. He never forgot the dreadful sight which greeted the crew. He was at last able to spit on the grave of Hitler by bribing the Military guard with cigarettes.

After the war Douglas moved to 44 Squadron doing runs to bring POWs back from Italy. He was still flying, and still busy and made several more nostalgic flights in his beloved KM-N Lancaster. One in particular he remembered fondly. As a special favour his pilot flew him down to Kent, to fly low over St. Mary Hoo so that he could wave to his mum and dad. That they narrowly missed the Church tower and the chimney pots of the Red House, is also well remembered. Next day they flew to Pomigliano, Italy before returning to base at Mildenhall.

Two weeks later they took off on 'Operation Sinkum' to get rid of bombs no longer required for war. They dropped them in Cardigan Bay off the Welsh coast. 'Take her back home, Doug, she's all yours.' Another favour from pilot John. Douglas, of course, had a smile from ear to ear.

Along with three others (one was a Russian Corporal, unusually serving in the RAF) Douglas travelled to Uxbridge with his Class B release demobilization papers. They were handed rail tickets and sent on their way. There was little fuss or recognition, he remembered sadly.

Arriving at the Demob Centre in Uxbridge was like entering a junk shop for throw-outs. There were no pockets in the dreadful suits, just flaps to look like pockets. Shirts were in some horrible, scratchy material. The raincoat would not have been out of place on a scarecrow and was not waterproof, while the shoes must have been rejects from a factory. Hard hats and bowlers were for Officers only. Other ranks, the likes of Douglas, were to choose between flat caps or trilbies. When Douglas arrived at Strood Station his father fell about laughing and said he resembled a drowned rat with his trilby sunk low around his ears. Once home, he demanded he rush upstairs and change before his mother had a heart attack. Returning to Kent and the life he'd left proved very hard. He was unsettled, unhappy and badly paid. He was forced to stop on the farm until 1954, as a condition of his release from the RAF, earning just £3.50 a week.

Later, it was while he was working for C & A Bowers of Knockholt as a horsebox driver, he lost his council house, his wife and his job within the space of a few days. Showing true grit whilst grieving, he then became a steward with P&O. While travelling 44,000 miles that year, he met his second wife. They remained happily married for 45 years before he was once again widowed. There were no children from either marriage.

Finances picked up when he started work for the American company Huyck as a product development specialist, travelling often to Europe. Douglas naturally kept his log books safe, and from these he wrote copious accounts of his wartime adventures. He gave talks locally and enthralled his many friends with his endless reminiscing. He was outgoing and great company. When he retired, he had more time for writing and recollecting. After researching his notes, I have enjoyed putting some of the information into my story. I therefore know it to be accurate. We met Douglas many times as he loved to revisit the village of his childhood days.

As a little chap he was loved by Grandfather Lachlan and Madge Maclean. They tended to spoil him. Along with his friend Dorothy, who was a maid at The Hall, (and about whom I have also written) Douglas was able to relate many a tale about his days in the village. He was a remarkable man, a cut above many. While laying a wreath in our village, he spoke of remembering two men in particular. One was his best friend and fellow Lancaster Flight Engineer, John Mannion, who perished somewhere over Europe.

John was never to see his twentieth birthday. The other was George Phelps, who didn't die, but he may well have done.

The next time Douglas had a chance to take the controls of a Lancaster was 49 years after WWII ended, flying in a tribute over London. This time it was 'The City of London', taking part in the Battle of Britain Memorial Flight. The pilot that day was Mike Chatterton, the son of his original dear friend, pilot John.

Douglas retired at 58 and so was able to devote hours to his new hobbies and adventures. He spent many hours at the Greenwich Observatory, learning and researching. All of his considerable knowledge and his varied and lifelong adventures made excellent material for the talks he was frequently asked to give. Always immaculately dressed, standing proudly at well over six feet, Douglas made a huge impression on everyone he met. Audiences large or small, were captivated. One could say, his was a life lived to the full.

He passed away, surrounded by loving friends, aged 95.

11

The First Born

Though this story is fictional, I feel certain that it would accurately describe the heartache of separation forced upon loved ones at the start of WWII. It could depict a young couple in any rural county of the British Isles although I have placed Dan and Claire near to our own farm.

1939

The colours. Oh my! The colours. Claire has been in this field often, gazing at the wondrous view, but today the vibrancy of hues seems even more glorious. The landscape is so strikingly clear in the September sun, she is catching her breath before her emotions take hold. It's as if John Constable has painted the idyllic scene, and not Mother Nature herself. The harvest has been safely gathered; golden, ripened wheat stems stripped of their bounty of corn. Bales of straw are stacked in piles waiting for the trailer to arrive. But that will be tomorrow, for this afternoon Daniel is with her, taking a time off from his toil.

Daniel's father has one of the first machines for baling straw in the county. The tedious job is easier now, following the invention of the baler a few years ago. The field of golden stubble, clear now save for the stacks, is ringed with gracious elms and ancient oaks. Beyond lie sloping pastures and here the Friesian cows and calves of the breeding herd are grazing. The little ones are adolescent, having been born in March. Soon they'll be weaned from their mums, who are already in calf again. Claire hates the bawling, protesting noise they all make. She sees the shine on their black and white coats, even from this distance, and remembers that it's partly the clover, carefully managed which results in the healthy gleam. She is constantly being fed this information, as if Dan is teaching her. *I hope it will always be so*, she muses.

The fenced boundaries of the grazing pastures display hedges of hawthorn, with occasional pesky blackberry bushes vying for dominance. Claire knows which are the most yielding of these, as she sometimes picks the berries amongst the tangles while Dan is working. She stays at the farm most weekends, and always when he is so busy with harvest. Her visits have spanned two years now, and she feels part of this caring, hard-working family. In the field to the left there's a tractor pulling a plough. She knows that's old Tom, whose knowledge of the farm goes back way further than Dan's. Behind the plough a flock of gulls swoop low, squawking and squabbling over the spoils of grains and worms. They surround the tractor, soar and then do the same, all over again. Tom ploughs on, up and down, all day long, and perhaps will do the same tomorrow. This farm has been his life for forty years; observing the seasons and the circle of things, and slotting into the tasks. He has his dog Floss on his lap – Claire has been told of his love of Border Collies. When Floss was young, she would run all day, faithfully following, chasing the gulls, but now she watches proceedings from inside the cab. She is his fifth Collie dog.

'Here we are, love,' Dan says, putting down the picnic basket on a fresh patch of pasture. Downhill, Claire looks at the river. It's mighty, magnificent and the tide is high. As always, there's something happening on the five-mile stretch which borders Kent with Essex. There's a small cruiser heading out from Tilbury, and a tug pulling a clumsy coaster up-river. It seems a juxtaposition of old and modern to her. There are a few small yachts, keeping well out of the way of the shipping, whilst making full use of the tide and the breeze. The river is a clear greyish-blue today and compliments the sky's clarity. With this peaceful scene played out in the south-east, whoever would believe that those reported evils might be occurring just across the channel? It can't be true, this scare of war. No, more like this promise of it. Not now, not with things so perfect. Claire shivers and reaches for Dan's hand. Thank God he is a first-born son of a farmer and will be spared the call up. The thought comforts her.

They sit on the brown tartan rug and watch a large butterfly attempt to gain purchase right in the middle of it. Laughing, Dan gently removes it. 'No, you don't, my beauty! I have plans for this rug.'

'Naughty boy!' Claire giggles and melts into Dan's welcome arms. She couldn't feel happier than she does this afternoon, with Dan extra thoughtful and loving; when there seems an inkling of something in the air. Will this be the day he'll propose? She hums a tune – a happy ditty and a song they love to dance to. Daniel smiles, aware of her pleasure. Claire arranges the food and the salad. She has made a quiche – cheese and asparagus, and knows that it's a favourite of his. Dan pours a glass of wine for each of them.

'To us.' And Dan stares ahead, at his life, the farm, the view, his future and eventually at Claire, his first and only girlfriend. 'Come on sweetie-pie, the food can wait,' he says, pulling her to her feet. 'Let's dance!' And they sway to the tune they know off by heart, their bodies close and loving. Then as passion overcomes them, they lay entwined on the rug, oblivious to the gulls, the cows and the picnic spread.

Dan sits up, clearing his throat with a strange cough. He struggles for words. Claire's eyes are wide and waiting. 'Claire, darling girl, there's something I want to say. Something so difficult I'm not sure where to start. For, for ...' He stops, stammers, and Claire gasps.

'I've signed up. I'm going to train with the RAF. Peter and Tom will run the farm while I'm away. I love you more than is possible, but this is something I must do. The war will be short, surely? I've OK'd it with Dad and Mum. Please don't cry, Claire, please. Say it's alright, that I have your blessing. I'll think of you every chance I get, and there'll be leave to come home now and again.' He gazes at his girl, sobbing and clutching her knees to her chest. 'Oh God, Claire, please understand. Remember that Dad paid for me to get my pilot's licence for a 21st birthday present? Well, they told me then that I'm a natural and that the RAF would snap me up. But there was always the farm and I couldn't entertain it. I absolutely love flying and want to join the Fleet Air Arm after a bit more training. They're desperately short of volunteers for that. I was lucky to be selected I guess, and it's more or less settled. Thank God I've got a brother to help out here, because farm or no farm, I'm going.'

Dan brushes her cheek. It's white with shock, wet with tears. 'When it's over, we can get married. That's if you'll have me.'

Claire can tell that nothing she'd say will make Dan change his mind. The war effort is larger than the love they share, that much is clear. Dan's proposal has come, but not in the way she dreamt it would. Everything was in place this afternoon, but the pallor of her face tells a story. Eventually she will tell Dan she is so very proud, but she can't yet mouth the words. He waits nervously for her response.

When it comes, her heart is as heavy as lead. 'Yes Dan, I will marry you. When it's all over.'

12

Game-keeper George

(Written from Ian's point of view - when a young boy)

'Can he have Christmas lunch with us?'

'Who, dear?'

'The old chap, George Osborne.'

'Of course not. He'd hate it.'

'Why on earth would he hate it, Mum? Christmas is a special day, and he hasn't any family. None who care about him, at any rate.'

He didn't come, not that Christmas, nor any others. Mum said that was what he wanted – to be completely on his own. She talked about a deal, made five years earlier, that Mr George could stay in his modest little cottage, in complete isolation at the bottom of the farm (he called it blissful solitude) in return for the position of game-keeper. He'd knocked on the Moat Farm House door and made the request to Dad. He actually seemed, when the idea was agreed, very happy with the arrangement. My father was happy too – for soon there wasn't a rook, crow, fox or magpie to be seen over the wide acreage.

I could never understand why he wanted to live like that, all alone. It didn't seem normal to me. There was no point challenging the way my parents accepted the situation. They just left him to it, with little effort on their part. On the occasional sightings of George walking purposefully from field to field, trap to trap, or to wherever his agenda directed him that day, my father would nod his thanks, chat briefly and move on. There was never a need for supervising George. They always rated his work as excellent. And there was little point taking him biscuits or food packages, as he seemed to have sufficient supplies in his tiny larder. Naturally he ate rabbit, duck, pheasant and partridge, offering any surplus to the marsh shepherds, Bill Higgins and Fred Brunger. He cooked what looked like tasty meals on a strange black range, which burnt the wood he was able to gather from fallen trees. He was a long way from being thin. In fact, he looked like the country gentleman he was, standing upright, quite stout and smart in a tightly buttoned waistcoat, breeches, and expensive boots.

George's early career was in the Army, my parents told me. He'd served with distinction in Malaya, but the price he had to pay for that were the recurring bouts of malaria which put him to bed for several days at a time. He would then be visited by the local doctor, directed to his lonely cottage by my father. Occasionally he was taken into hospital to recuperate further. He never complained, but it was concern enough for shepherd Bill to check on him most days. Bill's wife Dorothy had a soft spot for the eccentric gentleman and supplied him with a roast dinner once a week. The couple were two of his few friends and showed him loads of kindness. They also fetched medicine when it was needed, and groceries from the local Jack Parker Store in High Halstow. Before long he was calling Dorothy, Dolly, in a rare show of informality, but then both the Higgins' definitely cared more than most.

'Come in, Bill,' he'd say. 'I've a cup of tea on the boil.' Trouble was, with no electricity and therefore no refrigerator, George's method of a cooling system was a bucket of cold water. The milk was always a little (or a lot) sour as a result. No, he didn't have many visitors, but neither did he want any.

My mother had explained to us about his moneyed childhood, his private school education, and his lack of family connections, apart from two nephews who never saw him from one year's end to the next, and a son who despaired of his father's decision to be a hermit, albeit a clean-ish one, yet hadn't provided an alternative future for him.

It always puzzled me, especially that people mostly just left him alone. Whenever I asked, I got the same answer. 'George was married once, but his wife died ten years ago. Now I think he wants to be able to quietly remember his life with her by being down there, away from people. So that's your answer, Ian, and Swigshole is George's answer.'

'That's so sad, Mum. Swigshole is a lonely place and I reckon it's a peculiar choice for an old chap.'

But for George, it was perfect. Around his tiny cottage he planted plum, apple and pear trees, and even grew his own tobacco plants, drying the leaves in the nearby barn. When strolling around the marsh he was never without his pipe, and the cottage always smelt strongly of tobacco too. His garden, neat with vegetables, was edged with a row of lilac and laburnum trees. The pretty mix of mauve and yellow grew quickly to cheer him up on bleak spring days in his marshy home. And in winter the frost glistened from the branches until the weak sun dripped them bare. His neat picket fence had a gate for the visitors, but they didn't often call. George never had a car while at Swigshole, so Bill and Dolly brought his mail from the village store. Not many postmen would want to drive down that winding hill. I knew all of this because my brother and I visited him one summer day, walking to the extreme southern boundary of the farm. We were too young to pick up on any eccentricities or anything else come to that. We found him friendly, especially when he fed us fancy biscuits from a china plate, and when he formally shook our hands, like our headmaster. There was a parental element of trust at the time, and children then were allowed more freedom. And boarding school was a training for who to avoid. Instinctively, Robert and I felt safe with George. He talked a lot about the marshes and his work on the marshes. He said he was really happy there.

On our next visit he explained the workings of his very special Navy telescope. It was a heavy, expensive thing, which he had set up in his porch. From that vantage point he could see over the seawall and all the way over the river to the houses and buildings on the Essex coast. It was so powerful that he could see through the windows. We knew that was a distance of six miles. 'But I'll only let you look through it for thirty seconds, boys. It's too strong to use it for longer than that or it could damage your young eyes.' It was the most marvellous thing, and we were excited to see so far.

Immediately we were astounded on that first visit by George's knowledge of birds, and his books on the subject. In the winter months, he read by gaslight, or merely sat contentedly surveying the night sky. He knew every inch of the marsh and was thrilled to share his delight in the astonishing array of birds this habitat offered; his habitat now. We were country boys aged eight and ten, and the interest in birds and wildlife was mutual. And a unique friendship began. He was such a good teacher.

In the school holidays, before our muscles could cope with the weight of hay bales and straw cart, and before we were old enough to drive tractors, my brother and I, and our cousin Duncan too, pestered Mr George as he liked to be called, to teach us how to tie fishing hooks and set traps for stoats, rabbits and weasels. We learnt how to skin rabbits and pluck the birds from the game shoots. And always there would be a running commentary on the method we were using, which to us made perfect sense. We never tired of these lessons and quickly became juvenile experts dealing with the hooks, traps and the carcases.

Mr George's day started early with a brisk sluice from the cool waters of the spring – this clear, pure spring water cascaded down the hill to the stream which gurgled alongside his garden. He used it for cooking and laundry also. After dressing smartly in one of his shooting suits – breeches and jacket - tying one of his assorted ties, donning walking boots, and long socks to the knees, he routinely met up with the shepherd who lived closest. As Fred Brunger finished milking the house cow, George attempted as always, to engage Fred in conversation. After five years of trying, a few sentences were pleasantly exchanged. A daily jug of fresh milk was also part of Mr George's deal with the farming partners - my father and uncle. All parties were happy and no money changed hands. The farm employed three shepherds. Fred Brunger was one, and like his friend Bill Higgins, their allotted 'patches' were the extensive marshes, nearly 1,000 acres of them. Another shepherd tended the sheep on the uplands.

Fred had no problem with solitude, just like his near neighbour, George. His life was nicely mapped out; shepherding was enough, the marsh environment his paradise. Wages were spent on a Friday evening in the village pub and perhaps a little at Parker's store.

In the school holidays I sometimes got to watch Fred milk Daphne. With his head comfortably nestled in her flank, it was never necessary for Fred to tie Daphne up. George always admired this process too, listening to the milk spurting into the bucket, forming froth. I had a go at milking Daphne a few times, and Fred said I wasn't too bad. The bucket didn't tip over and the cow didn't kick, at any rate.

Trying as always to be friendly, on one of his morning visits, George commented that the autumn nights were drawing in. He asked Fred how he spent them. 'Are you a reader?'

'Not me, George,' he'd replied. 'Never learned to read, more's the pity. Would have liked to, but I left school at twelve. Never took to lessons, and that was that. I don't mind winter, though it's long, I grant you. I just sit there.'

'Not all night, Fred, surely?'

'Well, sometimes I sit and think. I listen to the night and it talks back to me.'

George knew what he meant. He'd left the old chap to walk back to the cottage and make his porridge with some of the still warm milk. Mr George told us the next weekend that they'd had quite a chat.

One day, soon after that, we biked down the hill to see him. He welcomed us with fancy chocolate biscuits and gave each of us a home-made lemon drink. We settled down at his kitchen table to study yet another manual of British birds. He always seemed a natural teacher, but then he had a receptive class of three. The meeting was interrupted by the arrival of a Rolls Royce at his gate. It looked so completely out of place, and could barely fit the confines of the lane. It was his son paying a rare visit. He greeted his father, and they chatted happily.

'I'm going up to London, boys. Staying until tomorrow. I've got some shopping to do.'

We watched while he settled himself into the wide seat. With a wave through the elegant window, the huge car turned around, ready to retrace the journey back up the winding hill.

Apparently, his mission on this occasion was very different. He visited a bookshop, and with the help of an assistant, armed himself with several lined exercise books, manuals and picture books, a fountain pen, ink and a ruler. Not books about birds, but reading books for beginners.

This kind old gentleman stayed in his cottage for years, diligently keeping the marshes clear of vermin, chatting to the shepherds, lending Fred something to read, and enjoying Dolly's roasts. He was never paid, and was always welcoming to the three of us whenever we were on our holidays from school. Those early lessons stood us in good stead.

As the years disappeared, and we were sent back to boarding school, to sports fixtures and a social life, we visited him less and less. We were now old enough to be useful on the tractors during the holidays and were too busy to sit and chat over chocolate biscuits and fizzy lemon. I guess we forgot about Mr George to a certain extent.

One day when the summer term was over, we were driving home with our trunks in the back, thinking of the long weeks ahead, and Mum suddenly said, 'He's dead.'

'Who?' I asked.

'George Osborne, dear. The poor man went into hospital with malaria and this time he never came out.'

Sixty years later, his lilacs remain, battling with blackberry bushes. The stream still gurgles and his plums grow wild. The marshes are overrun with marauding magpies, and the foxes eat the young partridges. There's a plague of rabbits, but not a Rolls Royce in sight. In fact, there hasn't been one, not since 1960.

13

Stan The Man

Stan Crayford

There are postmen and there are treasures. And there was a postman when we were first married who **was** a treasure. I doubt there's ever been another postie in the Rochester district who has been as well known or as well-loved as Stan Crayford. The mention of Stan never fails to bring a smile to the faces of Hoo Peninsula residents of a certain age.

Ian told me that he was also the family's postman when he was growing up on the farm, so by the time I met him, he'd been driving his red van up the Hall Road for years. In those earlier days, postmen stayed ages on the same patch, the same doctor stayed put for four decades or more, and our one village bobby kept excellent law and order in the district, giving errant youths a clip around the ears, for twenty years. The Bourne and Hillier milkman never missed a day and life chugged along pretty much without change. Stan was nearly due for his long service medal in 1968 when we returned from New Zealand.

Apart from cheering everyone for miles around with his morning visits, he had at least one other claim to fame. Stan had a natural talent as a comedian, and appeared at venues locally. He could sing and hold an audience with his banter and his natural charm. It was obvious when two farming families, the Filmers and the Macleans, were about to celebrate the country weddings of their offspring and planned a joint pre-wedding party for all their farm workers, that it should be Stan who could provide the entertainment. It was a riot. Everybody in the district knew him anyway, but he wasn't fazed by that pressure. Instead, he was even more outrageous and the evening was a riot. Our tractor drivers became legless with laughter, and many were fairly legless from other sources. I met a heap of happy people that evening and thought that maybe I'd be OK living amongst them, after all.

Although Stan had a huge area as his allotted patch, and a peninsula full of needy but nice customers all with their personal problems and foibles, he seemed to find time in his daily round to cheer and chuckle at every door. He had no need to practice his jokes, but we heard them anyway. Ever cheerful, was Stan. He'd often arrive wearing a cowboy hat or a sombrero, to the delight of the children. And he'd try out a song on the doorstep, always getting a good reception, mail or not, for that seemed incidental.

He realised in the early days of my marriage that I was homesick. And he had also picked up on the fact that my busy mother was not a regular communicator. I would meet him at the door, hoping for a blue airmail letter and he would see the look of disappointment on my face. This must have troubled him. When letters did eventually arrive with those colourful exotic stamps, he would put them in a bottle and say with great ceremony, they'd washed up at Allhallows. (He was their postman too and I think he had a good source of bottles.) No other postman who followed him could compete in the popularity stakes, in spite of them bringing biscuits for the various dogs. Stan knew all the names of dogs, cats and customers and enquired after the health of everyone on a daily basis. There was something very special about Stan. He was a real tonic – so good for our health and he became a part of our day – or certainly a cheerful start to each one.

Soon, when my days consisted of bottles for two babies and/or sock lambs, sleepless nights and too many terry-towel nappies to count, he willingly did a bit of shopping for me, to ease the burden. Roy Stopps, the local butcher regularly gave him our meat order to return to us, and he took parcels into the depot to weigh, with money stuffed in his pocket to be sorted out later. Sometimes the parcels were destined for New Zealand, but he coped with international stuff too, having met some of the recipients over the years. They don't make 'em like Stan any more. And really, should we expect the little red vans of today to be stocked with milk and sausages, or 'to-do' lists. Of course not.

Our postmen – sorry post people – these days are all very obliging, but it seems as soon as they bond with the village they disappear on to another Medway round. Stan stayed with us for years. He became part of our day and part of the village history. He was born and lived locally all his life. I was told by our village war hero, Douglas Packman, that Stan's father, 2nd Lt. Crayford was Field Marshal Viscount Montgomery's colour sergeant, when they were together as young men in France in WW1. Monty came to inspect the Hoo Battalion of the Home Guard at High Halstow, recognised his colour sergeant from years before, and told the gathering he was a first-class man.

Before we were all seduced by social media – to send and receive emails, there was so much more snail mail for Stan to deliver. There were piles of it, all shapes and sizes, every day. He was needed, and we were grateful.

When life got too crazy-busy and waiting for letters in bottles or by any other source became less important, I regret to admit that when Stan was moved on, we were too occupied with the new internet invention to wonder where the cheerful chap in the red van had gone. Emails seemed the way forward. Life's rapid routine got in the way.

Perhaps Stan made a fortune on the comedy circuit – he could well have done, but he was too modest to let us know.

14

Dear Dorothy

Loyal Maid to Lachlan and Madge Maclean

2010

Today, a photograph of you with another young woman fell from the album, an old brown leather thing which had lain at the back of the dresser drawer for all the time we have lived here. The photos in it were yellowed, small and a reminder of farming times which were infinitely grander than they are now.

You and the other maid are sitting in the courtyard of The Hall with a sheepdog lying contentedly at your feet. I remember, much later, when you were very elderly and I would visit you – that you told me the farmer was tough on his dogs and you sneaked them all out, one by one, to give them a pat and a touch of human kindness. How I loved you for that.

You both look bizarre in your maid's outfits. You're wearing belted smocks which go right down to your laced boots, and funny little hats. I am left wondering how cumbersome such apparel must have been while doing chores, such as dusting low down, and vacuuming under beds. But actually, did the family in the big house have a vacuum way back in the mid-1930s? I wish I'd asked you more about what was on offer to make your lives easier. There can't have been too many gadgets to help you, but out of loyalty you never dished the dirt, well not a lot of it, anyway.

The lady of the house was a right madam. I know that from other sources, and it must have been tricky for you when constantly striving to please her. She and the farmer entertained frequently so I've been told, and you and Maud, your fellow maid were kept on your toes cooking, cleaning, and washing for a continuous stream of guests. There were often visitors from New Zealand, from places you could never pronounce. 'Maori names, and they talked with an accent just like yours,' you told me. Without a washing machine, Dorothy, I hope you had help with all that laundry and carrying it outside to the lines to dry. There were long clothes lines spread out in a criss-cross in the bottom garden. You said the sight of all that bedding blowing in the summer breeze gladdened the heart. Your heart probably, for I wonder if her ladyship noticed, or appreciated your endeavours. You had a reprieve each winter, for the sheets and towels went off every week to the Rochester Laundry in a huge wicker basket. We came across that basket years later, covered in cobwebs in a barn.

The mistress Margaret was forever occupied in her favourite occupation – shopping. You told me she would return from London, having been collected from the station by the chauffeur, with several hat boxes and bags of dresses. There would be a fair amount of shouting and slamming of doors while she justified her purchases to Grandfather Lachlan. Apparently, all the aggravation was short-lived for the couple would regularly disappear to Scotland fishing, or to the Home Counties visiting similarly wealthy farming friends. Occasionally they would sail to New Zealand to visit relations there. Then they'd be away for several months at a time, and that of course was when you all came out to play.

The gardeners slackened off their frenetic mowing and edging, and no doubt you all squabbled over the grapes from the arbour. The chauffeur had nothing much to do, and the boy who cleaned the shoes was positively unemployed. The farm manager tried to keep things running efficiently, so the farm work would continue as always. Mr Lachlan was merely the overseer, never out of collar and tie, so any manual work did not fall his way anyhow, though when at the coal face, he did give the orders. The stable block where the handsome team of draft horses rested up after their labours, was as pristine as ever, cobblestones scrubbed clean. These gentle giants were like children to their grooms. The cowman milked the house cow and milk and cream were delivered to the kitchen door. The gardener brought vegetables of your choice from his patch, and you'd cook up something special for you, Maud and the others.

What fun it was when Madge (your pet name for her) and Mr Lachlan were away and you were all left to your own devices. Certainly, you and Maud were able to relax a little. For a start you could take off those silly hats. When you were on duty there can't have been any time for relaxing. You told me that you'd be summoned by the bell system in the scullery to put another log on the fire in the morning room. And this when Mr Lachlan would be sitting a metre from it. Oh dear, I cringe at the thought. I am as smug as you would be, to know that the bell system ceased to work a few years ago after the ministrations of my dear Ian.

How I gasped to hear tales of the two little boys being sent off to boarding school, trying hard not to cry as their trunks were stacked into the back of the big old Packard car. They would not see their home again until the end of term. But for you Dorothy, we wouldn't have known that father-in-law had braces on his teeth. Now we know who to blame for all the orthodontic work of later generations. You had us in hysterics with the story of catching Uncle Charlie out -when he crept in late and tripped over the cotton Maud had stretched across the landing.

Then there was a gap in your story-telling, down to the fact that you married, and became Dorothy Mortley. War came along to haunt and disrupt; and soon you had your own two children to raise. Your first house, owned by Emmeline Pye, was in Fenn

Street. You and Bill were very happy, but there was one snag. The toilet door was inclined to stick, and with there being no window, it was a dark space. When Miss Pye came to collect her rent, you asked if you could have a new door, and perhaps a window for light.

'Nonsense, no!' you were told. 'Just leave the door ajar.' It seems Emmeline was not as benevolent as her father.

Luckily you were able, in a Government assisted scheme, to secure a council house in a terrace of twelve at the bottom of our road. It boasted a large garden, and you were comfortable there.

Eventually, you returned to work at the Hall, this time as a married woman, and not a live-in maid. Great Grandad Maclean eventually passed away, in the blue room you said, and the rambling place was deemed much too big for his widow. She was packed off to a fine house in a nearby village, away from the hurly burly and sniffy livestock commotion of the countryside. With her went the faithful Maud, whose life in service was the only one she knew. It was all a time of change, but you began work with the new family in the big house. How loyal you were, Dorothy. It was now the abode of Charlie, being the elder brother of Ronnie, and Charlie's wife, another Margaret. The marriage didn't last, alas and Charles was so appreciative of you, Dorothy as you brought in toys, books and cuddles to his two children. When his new partner, a mother with three children moved in, household order was restored. They married several years later.

Life in the big house became so very busy. You left to become a domestic to a family in the next village. You were happily there for 25 years and yet the three-mile cycle ride in all weathers gave you dreadful arthritis. That seemed a cruel legacy after years of willing graft.

Charles left the partnership of the farm at St. Mary Hoo, and moved to another farm near Gravesend. St. Mary's Hall was then empty, providing a rather large home for a third generation Maclean. The excited new residents were Ian and I, who moved in after our marriage in the village church next door.

A few years later you, dear lady, saw me waiting outside your neighbour's house week on week whilst Amanda, our little daughter, had her half hour piano lesson. You invited me in and our friendship began. For the half hour, with the scales tinkering through the wall of the semi-detached, we chatted over a cup of tea on a weekly basis. From these visits I learned so much about the Maclean family, the village and your time and role in St. Mary's Hall. I was so grateful for all of this detail; informative snippets from your crystal-clear store of memories.

When you left your council house to move to sheltered accommodation nearby, you gave us three pieces of furniture to help fill some of the still near-empty rooms, now that we were the latest custodians of The Hall. I think you'd be so happy to know that the furniture you and your soldier husband bought with your meagre post war means, is being put to good use. The sturdy wardrobe and chests of drawers were all painted then in the heavy black varnish which was the fashion in the first half of the 20th century. I sanded that off to reveal the lovely oak grain. I would later paint them in New Gardenia, a gentle, subtle shade which shows the charm of the pieces perfectly – in readiness for our next move.

I salute you Dorothy, for your diligence, your loyalty and for the part you played in the jigsaw of life in St. Mary's Hall. Over the years I have thought of you often, along with others from the village who have passed on. You all deserve recognition for years of loyal work and for your dedication.

15

Edie Hassell

In a family of modest means, there was little alternative for the young girl. Edie was pressured towards going into service in her mid-teens, for times were tough and money was tight. Tears were shed and hands were wrung until a position was found with a wealthy family in a large house on the outskirts of Tunbridge Wells. She was to be a junior housemaid, living in and expected to work hard, be diligent, obedient and well-behaved. Hours were long, wages were low, but she would be 'kept' – with three meals a day and a warm bed in a shared attic room. Her employers were kind enough to her but she was expected to quickly adapt to the routine and never be late for her duties. These included clearing the many fires, re-laying them and polishing the grates. Each bedroom had a fire, which involved carrying coals and kindling upstairs and bringing down the ash from the day before. Not a drop of ash was allowed to show after the grate was polished. When that was done, once in a clean smock, Edie needed to be ready to serve breakfast to the Major, his wife and four spoilt children. Little notice was taken that Edie, at fifteen, was also still a child. There were constant dinner parties comprising Army personnel and guests enjoying the hospitality of the Major and his wife. When Edie wasn't changing bed linen or helping the cook, she was ironing, dusting, sweeping or polishing. The work was relentless.

Knowing that her employment was necessary to help the family's finances and that her parents were happy, (for she was expected to contribute) Edie persevered and eventually settled, over-coming her homesickness and actually beginning to enjoy the house, the large garden and the company of the other maid, Jocelyn. Jocelyn was seventeen and way more confident. They shared the attic room, lots of gossip and girly dreams. Both girls looked bonny on the nourishing food fed to the staff in the scullery. Edie often felt guilty when describing the family's meals to her own less fortunate household. The large gulf between rich and poor was something very apparent at the time, but it was accepted by maids like Edie and Jocelyn.

Several hard-working years passed and Edie, at eighteen had acquired enough confidence to venture out socially. She went to functions in the town on her day off which was usually Saturday, but only after she had attended to the fireplaces. She had grown into a pretty lass with dark curls, a fair skin and slim figure. In the town of Tunbridge Wells, while at a Church social she met Ivor Hassell. He was a twenty-year-old farm worker. He could dance, and he had motorbike! Edie was smitten and they began courting. Riding pillion on the back of the bike was thrilling. The shackles of childhood and service could be left behind for a few hours as the wind swept her dark curls flying. She clung tightly to Ivor as they explored the city surrounds. Edie would have prepared a picnic which they'd packed in the saddlebags. Ivor was able to arrange his day off to coincide with his new girlfriend's free time. The routine of motorbike riding, picnics and occasional dances continued, until permission was given by Edie's father for the couple to marry. By then she was 21.

The Major was sorry to lose his loyal maid, but gave her a tempting bonus for a wedding present. The couple moved to St. Mary Hoo where Ivor obtained work on one of the Batchelor farms, in Sharnal Street. At about that time he became known as

'Sonny' and this name remained for the rest of his days. They had two children early in their marriage, Rod and Margaret, who were to remain local and caring to their parents.

Never one to sit around for long, Edie purchased two Nissan huts which she cleverly transformed into a roadside café, attracting passing motorists en route to Allhallows or those who just wanted to relax over her wonderful fare. She was a natural, excellent cook, quick and proficient. In no time her breakfasts, cakes and sandwiches were legendry. The little place was often packed. Sonny helped at weekends but mostly it would be Edie who cooked, served, kept order and generally ran the place with expertise which seemed to come naturally. I'm sure she must have had staff to help her, because alongside the work of the café, there was a petrol pump (with a handle to turn) and a tiny Post Office. It's questionable that there were only 24 hours in Edie's day. Her smile of welcome was just as broad at the day's end as it was for her first customer of the morning, greeting them by name when that was possible. And it usually was.

Teenagers on bikes and scooters were delighted when she installed a jukebox and then the place really rocked. This was in the fifties – the time of the jukebox. On good authority I learnt that it was definitely the place to go, and be seen. Ian remembers biking there often for a bottle of Tizer, and taking empties back for threepence. No-one made hot chocolate like Edie. Ian enjoyed the jukebox too – aged ten at the time.

Eventually it was time for the couple to take life a little easier. When they retired, the café, the Post Office and the petrol pump were taken over by Lofty Fuller and his wife. Edie and Sonny moved a little further nearer town, to West Willows, a pretty semi-detached house with a long, sweeping garden. Here Edie was able to nurture her other passion. She developed an attractive garden and was often entertaining large parties of members from the Gardening Club or the Women's Institute, who made use of the space with stalls, games and competitions. Naturally, her wonderful cakes were centre stage on these occasions. Edie would have organised a raffle and I'm sure she donated profits to her favourite charities. She had Sonny, she had her friends and she had her garden. She didn't need much else, she told me.

When the two-acre plot became too much, the couple moved to Hoo. I used to visit them regularly and they loved to talk about the old days; Edie's time in service in Tunbridge Wells, the café days, and so much else. Neighbours dropped in continually, but that was just how she liked it. There was always a tempting cake in the kitchen cupboard. She and Sonny positioned their armchairs so they could watch birds feeding from overflowing bowls in the little garden. But that was when they weren't talking about old times.

With such a wealth of memories, it's a shame Edie hadn't kept diaries, or written about her interesting life. There were so many chapters to her eventful lifelong story. Though she spoke kindly about the Major who insisted on sparkling fireplaces, I felt sorry for the child he failed to acknowledge at the time. But Edie was accepting, even grateful of the humble start in his fine house.

'It was all part of my journey,' she said, 'and that was how it was if you weren't born to riches.'

16

Doctor Mac

R.P.C. Macdonald

Of all the characters I have chosen to write about in Part Two, perhaps the biggest outpouring of affection would surround the memory of Bob Macdonald, or Doctor Mac, as he was known to his patients. In the early fifties he joined Doctor Tilley in his practice on the Hoo Peninsula, where Doctor Tilley was already happily settled and married to Bob's sister, Marjorie. The practice was hugely successful. Both doctors were admired and in demand. They dispensed and treated for many years, one mostly in the Elms Surgery in Hoo, and likewise Doctor Mac in Brook House, Lower Stoke. They also held surgeries in what had been a Chapel in Grain. Their patient list was vast, as was the area the surgeries covered. Then there were countless home calls, which were miraculously fitted in. They filled the eminent shoes of Doctor Wall, and all three men were legends in their time.

My personal memories of Doctor Mac are of a kindly listener, a family friend; an approachable man of the people, and one who was never judgemental. In his long tenure at Brook House, where his patients attended surgery in a custom-built extension of their lovely home, many thousands of troubled, hurting locals would have visited, myself included. He would have helped, dispensed and calmed each of them. Sometimes, a shoulder to cry on was all that was required, and his shoulders were broad. When homesick for New Zealand, I was to welcome that approach several times. I never needed pills or potions, for Bob knew that a soothing chat would suffice.

To enrich my tribute to him, I was delighted to have assistance from his children; five clever offspring, who were forced to share their dad with half the population of the Peninsula, or certainly the Hundred of Hoo. This sharing was sometimes evident during the night, and neither was he spared on Christmas Day.

Doctor Mac was born in Gravesend in 1923 to Scottish parents. He had a happy childhood, along with his siblings, and attended the local Grammar School, which in the 1930's cost the princely sum of £4 a term. Traditionally, the elder son of their family – in this case, Arthur - was expected to become a doctor and the younger, by seven years, a minister. This plan was not to Bob's liking, as he also yearned to go to medical school. It was considered beyond his capabilities, and especially so – when he was thought to be asleep – he overheard his parents discussing his future, along the lines of 'what are we going to do with young Bob?' This proved to be a spur and he worked hard towards selection. At the beginning of the war, Bob achieved his dream, training at Guy's Hospital and later qualifying as a doctor on his 22nd birthday, in 1945.

He then followed his doctor brother, Arthur into the Navy; one brother leaving, the younger arriving. He wore Arthur's uniform with pride, joining the officers on *HMS Warren*, and settled into his life at sea. From Doctor Mac's endless stories of that time - some unprintable, involving roving eyes and randy sailors – it was obvious his days were full and varied. Bizarrely at one stage, he was put in charge of 600 Wrens, confessing to be terrified at the prospect. As the resident doctor on board the naval ship, he found himself invited to many elite functions, but he thinks that honour might have had something to do with his initials, R.P.C. In Navy jargon that transcribes to Respect the Pleasure of Your Company, and indeed Bob's Christian names were Robert Park Cumming. But he went along to them all, mixing with the great and good, and no doubt charming them in the process.

Occasionally, Bob (as a family, he was always Bob to us) covered surgeries for the elderly Doctor Wall while that hugely charismatic medical man was still practicing. These took place in the Cock Inn, (later to become the Cat and Cracker) in Grain. However, with whiskey on tap, and the pub landlord convivial, this was perhaps not the best idea for either of them, especially when the patients each arrived with an additional wee dram in their pockets. Bob had some explaining to do when he went home for lunch after the morning's appointments. Prescribed medicine then was one shilling a bottle, whiskey a little more.

Fond stories from his Peninsula patients came thick and fast, and many from Bob himself, for he was a great story-teller and one with excellent recall. He loved nothing better than an audience, and their attention was always guaranteed.

One evening surgery, the young doctor was faced with a slim and most attractive patient who was distraught and threatening suicide. On enquiring what had brought her to this unhappy state, she said she had been dumped by her boyfriend and her life was no longer worth living. Doctor Mac, confronted with a potential suicide for the first time, and initially flummoxed, used his built-in soothing skills to the best of his ability, assuring her there were plenty more fish in the sea and that she would soon forget him, mentioning also her obvious attributes. Eventually, the girl stood up, seemingly recovered. She smiled coyly and asked, 'Are you married, Doctor?'

One Christmas Day a resident of the caravan park in Allhallows was in an advanced stage of labour. The snow had filled the country lanes to the point they were impassable and panic had set it. Under the Macdonald Christmas tree was an unopened sledge, destined for No. 2 son. Doctor Mac used that to carry his medical bag, and set off on foot through the snow, a distance of two miles. He arrived exhausted, to find the anxious mother-to-be in bed but very relieved to see him. 'You'll have to get up, Anne,' he told her.

'Why?' she replied, through gritted teeth.

'Well, I need to get in there to thaw out.'

Baby Ruth made her appearance soon afterwards and Bob was able to trudge homeward, having given Alistair's sledge an excellent trial.

There is an adult in Grain who owes their life to a quick-thinking Doctor Mac. He was called to a very sick tiny baby, and quickly realising that an ambulance would never reach Grain and make the return journey into the nearest hospital in time, he scooped up the child, and carrying it close to his chest, drove with one hand into town. This saved considerable time, and the baby survived. It would not have done so but for the speed of Bob's decision and subsequent action. Nowadays, it would be illegal for a doctor to take such a risk, and of course, even then the risk was enormous, but one Bob chose instinctively to take. Luckily, it proved to be a brave and wise decision.

No. 1 son, Iain loves the story of one of Bob's disastrous shooting expeditions. Although he was a brilliant doctor, Bob couldn't hit a barn door at twenty paces, but that didn't stop him from trying. Joining his friends now and again, duck shooting on the fleets of the marshes, was a hobby he enjoyed. This particular September, with water levels low and smelly ooze in the bottom of the ditches, Bob slipped off a narrow plank into the Stoke Creek and descended up to his waist in glue-like mud. There was nothing for it, but he had to strip off, before sitting minus trousers and socks, and smelling incredibly bad, for the short drive back to Brook House. He had no duck to boast about, and though he'd held his gun nearly out of harm's way, his boots were somewhere in the creek's bottom, and his pants were destined for the bin. Surely no-one would see him? But just around the only bend in the road, the village bobby and Willy Hurst, the vicar were attending a minor accident. Tug Wilson put his hand up to stop Bob. In those days, the local bobby was as well-known as the local doctor.

'Sorry Tug, I've got to get home. And he drove on, feeling ridiculous and guilty. After a rapid shower and a hasty new set of clothes, he returned to the scene, applied a bandage to the bleeding knee, a compression to the head wound, and was able to add the story to a gathering tally.

When a sweet little boy needed an injection, he sat impressively, without flinching. No tears at all from this child.

'How old are you, David? You're being very brave.' Doctor Mac asked.

'I'm four.'

'My, you're so brave, I thought you must be five.'

'Well, I've already been five.' That story came from Geoffrey, a local chiropodist. So many people remember him with fondness and have their own memories.

Bob was naturally able to relate to children. He had plenty of practice, after all, having five of his own. Every summer, the family holidayed in France, taking the caravan which was pulled by a long wheelbase Land Rover. It had a safari roof, and fully loaded was a heavy beast. Their first trip was a test run. After the crossing, they decided to have lunch in the middle of a corn stubble. The caravan soon sank to axle level. Bob wasn't fazed, insisting he could save the situation. The result was a burnt-out clutch, 2 days camping, a large bill and additional help from the farmer and his tractor, with subsequent negotiation.

Obviously never one to underestimate his own DIY skills, Bob bought a JCB to work on an additional plot he'd purchased. In his first adventure with this wondrous new toy, he fractured a gas pipe. He also bought a dumper truck, but that's another story. His 'can do' attitude just had to be admired.

It was 'Hero Bob' in the mid-nineties. London wanted to dump all their rubbish at a site in Grain, claiming there used to be two hills in the area and another hump surely wouldn't hurt. After all, they reasoned, it was a desolate enough area to start with. The waste disposal boffins, who had clearly not done their homework, arranged a hearing and hired a barrister, at huge expense. Bob rocked up to the meeting with his historic pictures showing no hills whatsoever. He had also collected a mound of information about the Anopheles mosquito and how the marshes locally would be re-infected if the plan went ahead. (The Peninsula being one of the last places in England to have cases of malaria.) London argued, amidst angry exchanges, but they lost the case. Never underestimate a loyal local.

And something which clearly illustrates how interested Bob was in local history was his research into the courage of an illustrious Lower Stoke resident. Doctor Mac's daughter, Lindsay, and son Peter alerted me to the information surrounding the Naval career of Jim Prett. He was a true war hero, serving on more Royal Navy ships, experiencing more combat trauma than most human beings could ever contemplate. He was shipwrecked six times, miraculously living through the horror of all of it. On one occasion, he and the crew found themselves in the China Sea with sea snakes surrounding them. Jim, who really deserves an entire story to record this herculean tenacity, returned to Lower Stoke after the war, living quietly in Shepherd's Way. He had served his country well, and was happy in retirement to mentor and advise a young Peter Macdonald before he was selected to join the Royal Marines. Jim embodied all the qualities of patriotism in abundance.

When a flu epidemic swept through the district, the doctors and surgery nurses succumbed, all except Bob, who, rushed and exhausted, attended to all the home visits. He lost count of the times he needed to explain that his flushed face and sweaty demeanour were merely signs of exhaustion and not flu.

There can't have been many angry patients visiting the practice, but one obviously was, for in a rare fracas, Bob was shot in the lip by a patient who then turned on the village policeman with a knife.

Bob and his lovely wife, Daphne were stalwarts of the community. They were extremely sociable and so hospitable that their parties in the rambling house which adjoined the surgery are still talked about. Bob was never prouder than when Daphne became Mayor of Medway for a term. Both of them multi-tasked to perfection. All five children were, and still are, high achievers in the varying fields they chose to work in, at home and abroad. The family loved to travel and Bob recalled many memorable incidents, and far-flung holidays, including singing karaoke at a function in Japan, whilst wearing his kilt. He felt at home in his Macdonald kilt and wore it regularly to select functions. He and Daphne loved their Scottish dancing sessions, which seemed very sociable occasions. Friends were sometimes invited to dances where the haggis made an appearance as a piper welcomed it into the gathering.

One of his twin sons played the bagpipes perfectly, and was piper in a mournful farewell at each of his beloved parents' funerals. Hundreds paid their respects to this much-loved couple.

Each Christmas Eve the hot ticket was definitely a Drinks and Kiddies' party at Brook House. Bob was disguised (quite well) as Father Christmas and each excited child received a gift. It was always a very happy, boisterous night. When we had all returned to our various homes, Doug Bradford would arrive on the Brook House doorstep with a bottle of whiskey to share with Santa. That tradition lasted for many years. It was the favourite tipple of both local Characters.

Another regular party was held early each January. Three local farmers, (Ian Maclean included) shared Bob's birthday and naturally that was cause for celebration. Bob never failed to liven these Birthday Boys' proceedings with his recollections. He had a knack of being completely at ease in any age group, and in this case, a twenty plus year difference. This was when his raunchy recollections from his Navy days were aired and countless other stories would emerge throughout the evening.

For 64 years we had the benefit of his wisdom and he, an avenue for his medical expertise, before he hung up his stethoscope for good. Bob called it being devalidated. Many doctors have come and gone since we farewelled Bob, all trying to administer to the rocketing population of Hoo and surrounding villages. The task for them is enormous, though Bob managed it so well back then, when a village was, well, just a smaller version of today's sprawl. I doubt any of his successors offer a broad shoulder to cry on or the comfort of a soothing chat. There just isn't time in this fast-paced world.

Doctor MacDonald

17

Doug Bradford, Snr.

The Bradford Family Garage is a thriving business with a very interesting history. Three generations have sweated and strained under the cars of loyal local customers, with their mechanical knowledge in great demand. Petrol pumps have increased, from a solitary couple to a sophisticated double row, offering all the options of modern-day motoring.

In 1921, Francis Ralph Bradford purchased a Chapel at St. Mary Hoo. It wasn't that Frank was overly religious, or that he wished to become ordained into the ministry; but showing considerable foresight, he was interested in the ground it stood on. The Chapel was demolished and in its place a Garage emerged. Francis began to serve petrol from his shiny new pumps and the rest is history.

I think the Maclean family were likely to be one of the first customers of the newly opened Garage, as the date of their new tenancy of the farm, and the Garage opening coincided. I imagine the farm's custom was valued, given the vehicles required to manage the acres.

Francis, who decided to become known as Frank, chose his site wisely, for it is in a prime, impossible to miss position, to the left of the busy road leading residents of Grain, Allhallows, Stoke and St. Mary Hoo off the Isle of Grain. To one side of Frank's Garage in those early days, lived the Mortley family, and nearby was a small roadside shop, run by Miss Lodge. On the other side of the Garage lived the Overall family who boosted their income by selling fruit, vegetables and plants. The roadside shop of Miss Lodge was previously owned by George Phelps, the war veteran – one of my previous Characters, who returned from WWI with what would now be described at PTSD.

Two sons and a daughter were born to Frank and his wife in the decade from the mid 1920's; sons Douglas and Keith and their sister, Sue. The elder son, Doug Snr. surely merits a place in my Character section. He worked alongside his father, picking up all the skills and more, necessary to become an excellent mechanic. The Garage was in good hands by the time he took over from Frank, after the hard-working, enterprising gentleman passed away. They had already established a thriving local business with a reputation for successful, speedy repairs.

Ian remembers hearing the story of when Doug Snr. applied for his M.O.T. testing qualification. A car was delivered to him, not obviously displaying fifteen faults. The test was to find them. Doug Snr. found seventeen. These mechanical skills were not limited to Doug Snr. for there was also a family Garage established in Hoo, run by another of Frank's sons, Keith.

Doug Snr. acquired a Morris Bren Gun Carrier (ex WWII) which he turned into a tow-truck. It boasted a turret and had an enormous hook on the back to cope with frequent call-out emergencies. On one occasion, it pulled a trailer load of farmer Arthur Muggeridge's spring greens out of a ditch, but he was known to do many favours for the farming fraternity. In fact, any friend in need. The next working vehicle happened to be a two-door Ford 8 with a large wicker suitcase attached at the back. When Baby Mortley was due next door, Doug Snr. was summoned to fetch a Silver Cross pram from Sharnal Street station. He tried, but failed to fit it in the car, or in the wicker case, so the elegant pram was towed back, very slowly, using its very own fancy rear wheels.

The Garage was open seven days a week, and the hours were always an impressive 7am – 9pm. Super petrol then was 19/6d for four gallons. Five shillings would half-fill a Reliant Robin. The family of Doug Snr. chose to live in Sharnal Street, St. Mary Hoo and young members still reside there.

Doug Snr. and Delia had four children, two daughters, and twin boys, Douglas and Dave. The postman (Stan Crayford) would have had a problem as all their names began with a 'D'. Nowadays the Garage is run by the twins, and to save confusion I have referred to my cheerful Character as Doug Snr. For cheerful he most certainly was, and along with his brother, Keith, was a natural trickster. They were both in the Hoo Platoon of the Home Guard which no doubt gave them many chances of getting up to mischief. When they weren't busy protecting the great and good of the Hoo Peninsula, they were dreaming up tricks to play on their Sergeant. The Platoon met up in their hall, which stood then, near the Scouts Hall in Hoo.

During the dreadful winter of 1962/63, the roads around High Halstow were blocked with snow. All bread, milk and urgent supplies were delivered to the Garage, and Bill Rayner, from Hill Farm in Christmas Lane, trailed across the fields to collect them and deliver by tractor to the hungry villagers. The Garage became a hub and a necessary base for emergencies at the time.

Doug Snr. upgraded his office from a little shed, to an average sized modest caravan. Housekeeping was not his forte, not in the caravan at least. We would pop in to sign our tab and Doug, warm and welcoming, would be up for a chat. At Christmas, or more often if the occasion warranted, a bottle of whiskey would come out of the top drawer of the filing cabinet. Two glasses were squirreled out from behind some obstruction or other. Doug loved to share his growing good fortune, and the top drawer was specifically opened for these occasions. That the glasses never saw the benefit of Fairy liquid from one Christmas to the next did not apparently bother any of us.

One of his mates, whose twins made an appearance at exactly the same time as the Bradford pair, was Doctor Macdonald. They would polish off a bottle of malt every Christmas Eve, while Daphne stuffed the turkey and the hubbub of Brook House went on around the mellow pair.

Doug Snr. would be amazed, delighted and humbled that the garage these days is so very organised and especially that it is always busy, often with queues snaking out onto the Ratcliffe Highway. The little shed and the not-so-posh caravan have been replaced with a large shop, where customers pay or sign their tabs, and where they are enticed to buy sweets, cigarettes and groceries from ridiculously tidy shelves – all stacked efficiently in a tempting, grown-up way. There's not a bottle of whiskey to be seen, no time at all for cosy chats, but so much else is on offer, especially the personal service.

It is one of the few garages with attendants to fill customers' vehicles in a personal way. There is currently no self-service option at Bradford's. In that way, a friendly touch was easily established, with most drivers emerging to pay, after this service, with a handshake or a cheerful greeting.

Perhaps the most pleasing aspect of all is that another generation is working alongside his father, Doug Jnr. having taken his grandfather's middle name and clearly, his work ethic. Enter Ralph Bradford. He has big shoes to fill.

18

Percy's Perks

When it wasn't the lambing season, or the time of year for shearing, when the fleeces weighed heavily on the ewes, our shepherd Percy found ways to occupy his time, for he did love to be busy. He potted and planted, dug and dispatched from a vegetable patch in his cottage garden. It was full of every variety of veg our contrary climate could grow with ease. And even some other gardeners found difficult. The produce he harvested daily would have won prizes anywhere. He was proud of course, but mostly he just loved gardening. The success he enjoyed was partly because he covered every row in copious amounts of agricultural substances and this potent brew helped the process along nicely.

He was a Jack of all trades, master of many. Any carpenter would envy the wooden frames he rustled up for his climbing beans and berries, while the local garden centre took orders for his rustic benches, arches and bird tables. As if that wasn't enough, he plucked ducks and game, skinned foxes, rabbits and anything else with a need to be minus a coat. Strange objects would be hanging up to dry from trees and poles, causing walkers to gasp, or at the very least, blink.

Percy's giant poppies and roses were legendary and on show in the summer. His cottage was bang in the middle of the village and if his barking dogs didn't startle you, the fragrance of the roses did.

The years-old bushes were tended with Percy's care, ancient remedies ensuring that no crawling or flying insects ventured near them. In between all of these random tasks he tended his, or rather the farmer's sheep.

But it was the perks which were of most interest and value to him. A shepherd is entitled (so says an ancient law) to any mushrooms which grow - in his case, on the marsh - and any eels which frequent the shallows of the Thames. This was very fortuitous for Percy, as we farm on the banks of the Thames and the marshy part of our farm measures a whopping 950 acres. Percy made the most of these freebies when he had a moment, and was sometimes known to make moments when he really shouldn't have. He sent his mushrooms up to the London markets and the eels went to Billingsgate. It certainly subsidized his farm wages.

When checking his eel traps one day, soon after dawn, he spotted some shiny plastic packages floating on the high-water mark as the tide slowly receded - depositing as it always did, seaweed and the spoils of the river. Though it was not unusual to find random objects discarded by the estuary tides, nothing, save for a tortoise we called Ronnie, was ever of much value or even interest. Think old shoes, just one of a pair, bottles, bits and pieces of driftwood, and endless seaweed, laced with torn plastic debris, the odd dead cat and you'd be near the mark.

It was the shiny plastic wrappers on the packages which attracted Percy on this early morning visit. They were brick sized, all of them uniform and very carefully sealed. He split one of them open with his pocket knife. Percy, not known for his worldly wisdom, was nonetheless the father of three teenagers and he was sufficiently intrigued to toss three of the bricks into his tractor cab, alongside the eel catch, to consult his children, or perhaps Dave Wallace, the local copper.

'That's cocaine, Dad,' said Glynis. 'I'm absolutely certain. You'd better report it.'

His wife Kathleen (another Kath in in the village!) sniffed the stuff. 'Ugh!' She grimaced. 'How strange.'

'Careful, Mum, we don't want you getting hooked.'

And then Dave, friend to all in the Peninsula villagers, appeared. 'That's quite a coup, Perce. Beats a trug full of mushrooms any day. We've gotta report it.' He then supplied the number to contact to help speed the process.

'How many packages have you got hold of, Mr. Boakes?' the telephonist asked.

'Well, there's these three and another half dozen down on the beach lying near where the others were. I guess I'd better go and collect them before the next tide?'

'My goodness, yes. Please do that. Washed up, you say? Mmm, that's fairly unusual. Must have been tossed overboard.'

Soon he was speaking to someone higher up the pecking order. A Drug Squad Officer. 'If the packages prove to be cocaine, as your daughter and the village constable suggest, the street value would be colossal. It could be a very important find. Well spotted, Mr. Boakes. I'll drive down to Kent this afternoon to speak to you. And of course, I'll collect the bundles.'

Percy gave the Officer directions to the village and to his cottage, and set off down the tracks in his red Massey Ferguson to gather the six plastic packages still on the sand. The beach was deserted as usual, as at weekends it attracted merely a few walkers along the seawall, or friends of the farmers. They would have needed permission to drive sturdy vehicles through the fields to the river to reach its little beaches and bays. As expected, the bundles were there, scattered within a few yards of shore, gleaming in the morning sunshine. And there was a seventh, as a bonus, under some seaweed.

'This is shaping up to be a very interesting day, Kath. Best make some scones, love. We've got a visitor coming down from London. He's from the Drug Squad.'

After a large mug of tea, scones with home-made gooseberry jam, and a great deal of chat - some involving the drug, now identified - Officer Brent was taken on a tour of the rose garden, the vegetable patch, and the Boakes' menagerie. There were the four ferrets, reasonably tame, except for the one, assorted bantams and chickens, two sheepdogs, three cats, and two ten-year-old sheep, raised from bottle-fed lambs to very demanding, overweight pets. For a city dweller, this was a lot to take on board, although he was extremely heartened by this tiny taste of cosy village life. For a breather they sat on Percy's rustic bench to enjoy the late afternoon sun.

'You've saved a lot of grief for a great many people. Hideous drug, that cocaine. There must have been a tip-off. This lot would have been thrown off a ship before it was searched at Tilbury or the London docks. The Thames is a busy river, that's for sure, so someone might have seen something suspicious. Or perhaps a police launch was spotted, coming to intercept it before it docked. They do that sometimes. Whatever the reason, we've got them now and it shouldn't be too difficult to trace the ship, thanks to the speed of your discovery. I can't thank you enough, Mr. Boakes.'

'Please call me Percy. It sounds a whole lot better!'

After all, by now the two men were getting on famously. There were big smiles all round as the pair surveyed the garden and the chickens clucked happily nearby. It seemed a million miles from London's drug scene. Sensing his mood, Percy suggested Officer Brent sample a glass of his home brew before heading homeward. The pair disappeared into the old caravan, parked by the cottage gate. It was Percy's 'Man Cave' and it was where the concoctions were dreamed up. The combinations beggared belief - some were tastier than others, it had to be said. Suffice to say it was a way to use up surplus vegetables and fruit. That day, it is impossible to remember what mix was offered to the polite drug expert. He had rather more glasses of it than he should have done, and very soon it became apparent that he was not in a fit state to drive back to London, or indeed anywhere else. A phone call was made and two more officers were summoned down to the cottage on the corner, the one with the roses, the ferrets and every vegetable under the sun. One man to drive Brent's car back home and the other to have as a passenger a completely legless officer with his shiny, valuable load, a bunch of selected rhubarb, half a dozen free range eggs, and a bouquet of Pink Lady roses for Mrs Brent.

Percy's 'falling down water' had done it again.

19

Dave Fletcher

David was the less favourite child of two, born in the late twenties to Doris, a schoolmistress, and her brow-beaten husband, Arnold. David never questioned his mother and knew to always obey and respect her. His father had said as much, right at the beginning. Clearly, she ruled the roost. He was proud of his mother's achievements, since she was renowned locally in her teaching profession. What a wondrous thing was a female, especially a clever one, was his early conclusion. 'Just ask Mother' was the family's mantra. Sticking closely to a routine of schoolwork, homework and more work, David soon became the brightest in his class. He put that down to his mother's guidance. How grateful he was that gathering knowledge was a trait he'd inherited.

He didn't attempt, or perhaps wasn't motivated, to try anything even remotely athletic. Neither did he push himself in any field events the school curriculum offered. He didn't see the point of wasting any time that could be put to academic use. The brutality of rugby appalled him, and he thought cricket boring beyond compare. He was just not at ease on the sports field. Swimming involved far too much water, so that was out too. Though she'd have preferred him to multi task and spread his energy in at least a small selection of the sport on offer, Doris sorted everything out for him in a 'don't worry David, I'll attend to it' way. Husband

Arnold was never consulted so David continued to be an indoor prodigy. 'Your boy's a dreamer, a bit of a puzzle,' the teachers remarked when they called her in to discuss the absence of sporting prowess, or even an interest in it.

Puberty hit David unspectacularly. Doris did her best to explain the spots, greasy hair and lanky growth spurts, while *he* tried to ignore any strange urges. (He didn't mention those to his mother.) The years raced by and the brightest boy in class was replaced by The Boy with Little Ambition. Mother, by then despairing of his lack of drive, or lack of anything, was running out of answers.

David bumbled along, showing a distinct disinterest in every suggestion, firstly at his secondary school, but mostly at home whilst sitting around the table at mealtimes. On a whim he joined a walking group, exploring the countryside and villages near his Higham home. And it was while he was on one of the group's weekly strolls he spotted his inspiration. She was standing quietly by a fence. David was instantly smitten. Everything about the gorgeous creature appealed immediately. The conformation and colouring, her beautiful features, soulful eyes and especially the eyelashes. His future career was suddenly settled.

Doris felt a rare form of failure when teenage David left school earlier than she'd hoped. And of all things, to work as a cowman on a Cliffe dairy farm. Her son had stood up to Doris for the first time. It was a victory towards an independent future, and at last the lad had made a decision without interference.

'Come on, my darlin's!' David guided the herd into the milking parlour. His life was just as routine as before, but now *he* ruled. He had been allocated a small farm cottage; he did his own cooking, and twice a year he had a clear up. Nothing much altered from week to week. He relished working with the cows and felt contentment for the very first time. David had one speed. It wasn't rapid, but then he wasn't trying to prove anything. This was his niche, and he just loved the gentle nature of the cows. Their eyes seemed to look right into his soul. He went home each night a happy man.

Then those pesky urges started again – he'd met Connie. She was not in the first flush of youth but our David wasn't counting. He was thirty-five going on seventy, and Connie was pushing fifty-five. No-one said it, but everybody assumed he was looking for a mother figure.

The attraction was instant. 'Let them think what they like, I *know* this is love,' David mumbled, but he didn't really have much clue in the Romantic Attachments department, and he'd had zero experience to date.

'Don't worry dear,' Connie urged, her curly perm tightening around National Health glasses. 'We'll work it out.' She wore Crimplene and kitten heels, her teeth were false, and she wasn't about to lose him on her first foray into romance.

Connie and David were soon married and he changed his job, away from the doubters. Nothing dramatic, just five miles away to the Maclean's farm, in the next-but-two village of St. Mary Hoo. There he became more of a general farm worker and stockman too. It was a new start for them both and they shortened his name to Dave in celebration. The happy couple made their little cottage cosy and planted roses in the garden. He was blissfully happy. But it was only for a short while. Connie developed breast cancer before their first anniversary. Dave nursed her lovingly until she died before a decade of married life was up.

Mourning and moping through the years, looking as badly neglected as his cottage and garden, he continued to work loyally in the barns, at his one speed. He cared for 'his girls' and lavished on each new-born calf an endearing tenderness. He was also in charge of the fencing cart which, for reasons best known to Dave, had no sides and had sprung a sizeable hole in the bottom. The staples, nails, bits of barbed wire and spare parts had a bad habit of being jolted off here, there and practically everywhere. No amount of beseeching changed the frequency of punctures, and anyway, the poor chap could not cope with lectures. He turned a deaf ear to any suggestions, preferring to sulk until any threat went away. Dave was not for turning, nor compromise, though he did erect fine fences. When reprimanded, he'd tut-tut and say he was a silly old fool. We were inclined to agree.

Troubled by diabetes, and weary of the world, he was forced to retire at sixty, though he remained in his cottage. As with most other aspects of his life, signs of decay were seldom challenged. Dave was always greeted affectionately as he hobbled around the village, 'to get a little air.' He devoured library books in triplicate every week, though the pages needed ironing on their return. A trip to the library was the weekly highlight and he often took roses from his garden, or a small box of chocolates for the girls at the desk. Somewhere amongst the clutter of home was his set of encyclopaedias, legacy of Doris. His brain was still as sharp as any tack.

Dave's little blue Fiesta never ventured further than the next village of Hoo where he stocked up with basic provisions – to cremate in his oven. Cooking was not something he mastered, ever. His universe became smaller since he was lost for twelve hours on a trip to Wales to see his sister. After three circuits of the M25 he was put off motorways for ever and a day. The episode traumatised him and we all sympathised, though behind his back the district found it hysterical, as he became more melancholy. Any suggestions or cajoling to lighten up would receive the same response.

'I'm just a silly old fool, but thank you anyway,' he'd say, raising his cap apologetically. The good manners his mother taught never left him.

When he passed away, the entire village turned out to pay their respects, but that was only thirty of us. We soon learnt that Dave had amassed a few bob over the years, bless him. And out of the woodwork came his relatives who had been less interested in him beforehand.

Here on the farm, years later, we still discover random staples and nails on the tracks, and the occasional puncture reminds us of the cart with a hole and no sides, and the stubborn old fool who built a good, straight fence.

20

Arthur at No. 7

Random local characterisations leave the choices wide open. I'll plump this time for Arthur though goodness knows, almost anyone else would have been an easier option and perhaps more exciting.

Arthur was the village enigma. Not well known, but probably best known for doing nearly nothing at all. Nothing remarkable, even miraculous, and hardly ever anything normal. He was as boring as waiting for summer grass in a drought – though all of this is hearsay as I'd never met the guy, or spoken to him either. I'd merely spotted him now and again. Perhaps in the writing, I'll dredge up something, but right now, there's a dearth of information to go on, poor anonymous chap that he was. I just know he was dull, for everyone down in his row of houses said so.

Life in our hamlet could be explained thus: It's inhabited by impressive characters who have lived their lives surrounded by other similarly marvellous folk. I'm related to some and all of us are chums. Arthur lived in Number Seven, in a row of twelve terraced cottages, at the junction where the marvellous ones turn left and uphill, towards the church, where our houses form a sort of convivial commune. And yes, we do feel a little apart from the others.

Arthur was forty-five – yes, I know I'm using the past tense, but more about that later – so he was nearly middle aged. Until recently his mum and dad lived with him; or perhaps I mean Arthur lived with mum and dad. It makes little difference. They were also oddballs, which follows, I suppose. All I can tell you about his mum and dad is that every week they had twenty or more very large empty cardboard boxes piled up for the recycling lorry to collect. I deduced they spent some time each day unpacking. I am nothing if not quick to grasp things like that, but what intrigued me was that I could never work out what it was they unpacked, or what happened to it afterwards. Sometimes I glimpsed Arthur's parents bringing the empty cartons out to their gate, and yes, odd would be a suitable description. Their boy was never anywhere to be seen, year in, year out, and it was a surprise to me to be told some years ago that these two strange, elderly folk had a live-in son.

From the outside, Number Seven was a tip, a sad clutter of neglect and abandon. The overgrown garden encroached on a straggly hedge, which was in turn being strangled with some measure of success by wild blackberries. Neighbours either side cut right up to the boundary with their pristine borders, so the mess of Seven, The Street was even more marked, in a cheerless territorial way. From the jungle which was Arthur's environment, I assumed but perhaps unfairly, that the inside of Number Seven was just as chaotic. Probably even more so, if the contents of twenty boxes were scattered around the front room, waiting for distribution or heaven knows what subsequent fate. It certainly kept a few of us busy guessing.

Arthur neither sought nor apparently enjoyed any company. There were no visitors, nor random callers to the door. Even the postman was seen to hurry over his duties, anxious to be away from the cloying drabness. For whatever reason, the son and heir doubtless felt fulfilled enough waking, sleeping and eating in that house with his parents. He was single by choice. No fancy women, no blokes' magazines were delivered – for yes, we gossiped and the postman said as much - no signals either way. Arthur kept his sociability skills well under wraps. I can't say I'm warming to him yet, but I'll press on and maybe something will hit me – wham, bang, wallop. I do hope so, because there *were* easier options.

Mr Anonymous drove a beaten-up old car to his work at the nearby Army Barracks. His job was in the munitions store. He'd been there for about ten years and was reliable in an anorak type of way, so they later said. He was always punctual, and since the store wasn't peopled by many, he didn't have to make any social waves. He merely arrived, did whatever was needed in the store, kept his head down, ate his sandwiches, worked some more then went home to mum and dad. So, no big impression store-wise either, but he stayed and stayed and ten years were reached in a milestone which marked his unassuming qualities nicely.

Then his dad died. No-one in the terrace knew anything about that until the hearse arrived to take him away. Poor Arthur, what could they say? They tried, but it was too little, and certainly too late. They cared enough to look away. That left mum and Arthur to carry on with their listless, lonely life. It wasn't easy, it wasn't difficult, they just carried on and no-one noticed one way or another. Arthur came home and left again, and sometimes in the process nodded a good morning to Sue, at Number Five. But never much more than good morning. He reckoned, so she said, that was enough – any more and she was just being bloody nosy, or he too giving. Anyway, there wasn't the space to stop and chat, because the lorries thundered past en route to the local tip, all going faster than the limit allowed, spewing mud, dust or rainwater onto the feet of anyone walking on the road side of the hedges. And Arthur's hedge didn't leave much frontage, since it was mostly blackberry fronds snaking ever further towards the gutter.

All too soon, the hearse paid another visit. Mum, this time – leaving Arthur heir apparent, alone in the little house on the terrace. And I've been thinking, in a eureka moment - maybe

Arthur was a character because he *was* such a mystery. Would going solo be the makings of him?

What now for Arthur? Where did he shop? Did he even shop? No-one knew. There were nearly no signs of activity and just enough room for his old car amongst the boxes and junk which was their drive. It was difficult for Sue or anyone else, even if they'd wanted to after all the rebuffs, to form any impressions or to find out what made and motivated the man. All credit to them, they tried.

One Friday several years ago, Sue called out a morning greeting which was marginally longer than her normal one. 'Lovely day, Arthur. How are you? Off to work then?'

'None of your business. Leave me alone, OK.' Rude, even by his standards.

She did, until the Wednesday, and then, because Arthur hadn't been spotted since the previous Friday, she peeped through the kitchen window. Nothing doing – except six boxes, stacked high, unopened. She knocked on the front door. Again nothing. By lifting the flap and peering through the letter box, she had a good view of the stairs, straight to the top. Except that Arthur was on the bottom one. Very dead.

In no time at all, more local notoriety than most could wish for, certainly whilst alive and possibly dead also, descended on Number Seven. There were police, ambulance and bomb squad personnel – eight vehicles in all. This collective circus was busy all day, the neighbours entertained as never before, until they were evacuated. Arthur's house was full of shells and munitions. He did have one absorbing, spectacularly hazardous hobby, after all.

21

The House and Garden Machine

Extended Metaphor

Can machines have gender? Well, this one is definitely male, and I'll call him Cedric. It's not his real name, but I can't have him rusting up in embarrassment. For fifty years we've known this man machine, because we inherited him with the house. He came as part of the package, like a pet, the old owner thinks would be happier staying behind. And so it was that we had a Man Friday from day one; not bad for two green-as-grass twenty-somethings just back from honeymoon.

We grew into the relationship. A machine that can do most things is as rare a jewel as a jubilee clip. This one even tries to do the things it can't, but that isn't always wise and it's often messy. Cedric has more faith in his abilities than he should – his optimism knows no bounds and the 'bull in a china shop' cliché comes to mind as an apt description of his work in progress. Not every time, just often. Criticism is deflected via a pot-marked tin hat and then we feel bad – after all, he knew the house before we did.

Somewhere contradictory, deep in his cycle, there's a Delicate programme, and a gentler, feminine side comes to the fore. Territorial and protective, Cedric house-sits while we're on holiday. Leaks, fuses, dogs, cats, budgies and goldfish – it's immaterial to this jewel – he can cope. Burglar alarms are not a speciality (disconnection is) but then no machine is infallible. We return home to regimented spotless-ness, or a paint job, which is a pleasant surprise if you go along with his colour selection. On reflection, unpleasant would describe that incidence. Once inside the house our automaton spies sagging sash cords and the Jobs to Do List, previously ignored by the residents. Shelves feature and I'll mention plumb lines later. Toolbox at the ready, the gearbox needs triple warnings to slow down before the drill touches something it shouldn't. Short of electrocution, he is never fazed, and has never been known to utter the words 'I can't do that.' The 'can do' attitude has resulted in hospital attention often. Cheerful with it. Vertigo doesn't feature, and the top of any ladder is nearly up there with the sit-on mower in terms of popularity.

The bulk of Cedric's enthusiasm is reserved for hedges and edges, and for the device of his dreams – the mower. With this roaring, cranked-up hulk, vast swathes are devoured and speed is the essence, his essence. Naturally, spatial awareness has never been an issue. After all these years of edging and hedge cutting, his plumb-line is not what it once was (it never was amazing) and our hedges dip and sway while the lawns carry on getting smaller. But we forgive our robotic miracle - eight decades and just one replacement part – because he gives one hundred per cent, always.

This latter trait has been observed by the neighbours, who have poached his talents. Now we have to share our marvel and there are wavy lines next door too, while his slippers are under their spare bed when they zoom off to parts exotic, and their small canine is walked at sparrow's fart – that's dawn, apparently. He's a man of many aspects and now they have snapped up some of them.

In the vegetable garden the tools and-odds and ends kit makes an appearance. Something in his psyche tells him to put up flags and scarecrows to frighten birds. These can be seen from outer space – cats and dogs give them a wide berth also. Young children have been known to run. He builds Flintstone-like structures for beans and raspberries, elaborate rigging which collapses at the first fruiting. We reckon each bean costs fifty pence to produce, but tastes so good, the beaming machine continues to fire, digits dancing. We can't, just can't put a spanner in his exuberant apparatus. In times of drought his watering ways are legend and point of washout is reached weekly. This machine has its own timer (if only he knew.) Our multi-tasking miracle ticks over in its own space. Down is up, and right is left for our Cedric. Cogs greased, he's cranked up, firing on four.

Cedric's major parts are fired with creosote, and his carburettor efficiently maintained by Nescafe. Moving parts wallow in these substances with enthusiasm. Breaks are urgently sought, with an attentive audience a delightful option, for him. The creosote wafts its unique fragrance around for days, clinging to his clothes, our chairs and the washing, if we aren't one jump ahead of him. He loves to earn Brownie points by bringing it in if we don't notice the black clouds gathering.

As the years have ticked their way towards a long service medal, and the M.O.T.'s become more frequent, along with the fuel breaks, we notice the metal fatigue with sadness, because some machines – well, they're part of the broad picture.

Like Cedric.

For Cedric, please read Cyril.

'Honest to God'
Cyril Ingram

'It was time to bring Mary home from hospital in Swan Inlet. I was leading a spare horse for her. Old Trooper was quiet enough, so I helped her up and we strapped Julie in a saddle bag. They had to ford a river and both its banks and then ride another ten miles before we made it back to the settlement house.'

'But Julie had only just been born!'

'Yeah, she was only five days old. It was snowing hard too. Falkland women didn't have a choice in those days. Horses were the only transport. She was a tough old bird, my Mary, never complained, or anything. We brought all three girls home on horseback. That's why we came back to England – so the girls would have an easier life than she did. If I'd had sons we'd have stayed. Honest to God, I loved it there.' Misty eyed Cyril.

Every morning we'd have a story – sometimes Falkland Island, sometimes local. The pit was bottomless. There wasn't an inch of the Falklands we hadn't 'seen,' by horseback of course. His tales were always prefixed with Honest to God! Mostly the Falklands' stories featured the multi-tasking of Mary, who could butcher a sheep, shoot a cow, or milk it, make butter and keep the home fires burning with peat, until her man rode home from weeks away on another island errand. Meanwhile, our man (Cyril) also needed to multi-task, often miles from anywhere remotely near his family. He was regularly needed to guide the doctor all the way to a patient, giving him a spare horse, helping if needed with wounds and bandages, tourniquets, or something more serious. He was there while drunks and bodies were being pulled out of peat bogs or the snow-filled ditches, and while the cattle were swum over the inlet to another island until the spring grass returned. He'd break in a horse, work the bogs, despatch a sick animal, tend to hundreds of others, without a blink. 'No day was the same out there.' And we'd nod in agreement, having heard the variety so often before.

What Cyril made of the Falklands with the new-fangled roads, schools and hospital, after the 1982 war, remained to be seen. 'It's not the same, that's for sure. Ruined, I say,' said our man on the case.

He came with the house, did Cyril; our sort-of do anything, go anywhere man. Years and years of tales. Death and gore featured frequently, rather too frequently, actually. He was as familiar as his stories, having greeted us on day one. Always free with his advice... 'I see you're making bread, girl. Now Mary used to let hers go stale for a week, then the kids didn't eat so much of it.' There was a mutual respect; after all the years he spent part time on the farm or in the garden, and years of advice, wanted or not, he was practically one of the family.

When he wanted to share – recall - we knew we were in for the long haul. We'd escape if we could. He corrected every recollection with 'Tell a Lie,' ...Tell a lie this or that, and start all over again, until we were so confused, even our plate of porridge looked interesting. Honest to God.

(After returning to England from the Falkland Islands Cyril worked at the Grain Oil Refinery, but with his love of farm life so strong he sought part time work for the Macleans, first with Ian's Uncle, at St. Mary Hall and then Ian and me. He adored the farm and visited until his death, aged 92 in 2022. His ashes are scattered in the hay meadow.)

22

Little Man, Big Heart

Charlie Hazelden

Dear Charlie

Greetings to you, dear friend.

I know you'll need help with this letter but I really wanted to write it. I've been thinking of you, and sadly it's been a while now since we've been able to chat. And there are things I wanted to say.

This, for instance. Good things come in small packages, or something like that; I think that's how the saying goes. There was never much of you; a little chap for sure, except for your sizeable heart. And did you ever make enough of yourself or your immense and cheerful people skills? I never thought you did, to be truthful. I expect your well-meaning aunts and bossy mother were always telling you to do this or that, and teasing you when you got most tasks wrong. Your self-esteem wasn't overflowing, after all of that negative input, we could all see that. You were shy, rather than retiring, yet forever chirpy, so being in the background can't have got you down totally. With you, Charlie, it was a case of 'getting around to it' – this dream or that - but you never did follow them - or possibly you did, but in the wrong direction.

This scam or that, you were more on the ball with them. Scams and risks, you met them head on. I don't think anything worried you either, did it? Not ever, when really it should have, for some things have worry potential.

You, you little blighter, were forever skiving off school, and got more than a few clips around the ears for it. Perhaps that's why your ears stuck out a little? But in the process of never picking up your schoolbag you didn't pick up learning skills either, well not the ones you need a pen and paper for. How, but how did you manage to be so cunning and conniving without knowing how to read and write? I imagine the pen-pushers in all departments 'down the Social' trembled at the mention of your name. You didn't always get away with your scams, but don't let's go into that now.

Oh Charlie, how I miss you. How we all miss you. The cheeky grin, funny crooked teeth, nervous energy and cigarette about to be lit, or already burning; the teapot forever on the boil. Your teabag consumption could have built a small hay net. You'll smile at that bit – you loved all creatures, and saved anything sick or homeless, from a sparrow to a horse. Too many of them. They gobbled you into debt. That's how we became friends, wasn't it? Through our horses. When you were a little lad, you hung around the stables instead of going to school. You'd help them out and in return they taught you to ride. Now that **had** to be better than algebra and French.

They taught you well in those stables. You could break a horse with kindness not force, ride with gentleness not power, and tend the sick ones as cleverly and compassionately as many a vet. Somehow, I think you were more comfortable with animals, Charlie – they all loved you. And I bet you felt six feet tall on a horse.

When I think of you, it's almost always to do with horses; horses and kindness. My daughter, when little, thought you and Alec were the nicest neighbours anyone could have. You took her to the horse shows, while we at home knew she was safe and happy with you both and your handsome horse, Tom. And it is with you riding Tom, and me on my beloved Gigolo, that I recall the glorious daily gallops on the farm. We must have had the fittest horses around, for the 2,000 acres were often traversed in a slightly out of control half hour gallop. You taught me a lot about horses. That they can get hay fever from a field of oil seed rape, and how to treat mud fever caused by winter riding; how to pull a mane and plait it.

I felt comfortable with you. That was one of life's ironies wasn't it, Charlie? You had more girlfriends than a film hunk, but they were ever only friends, nothing more.

Amanda really got the bug for riding during that summer. Later, when she needed a 'scoop' for the Junior Reporter position on the local paper, you provided it – you, who were a never-ending source of adventure and mischief. It got her the job and a front page into the bargain. She'd had to tone it down though so it didn't get you into strife. Even lovable characters take risks, and there were a few of those on your patch.

You made the front page a decade later, Charlie and this time you'd got into so much strife, no amount of cunning could get you out of it. A risk too far, my friend. You paid the price that night, the ultimate price. The answer isn't always just around the corner, Charlie. I wish you'd known, you little blighter.

Yours ever fondly,

Kathy

23

Ross Farmhouse

(Joan's house for 35 years)

It is our house now, but for many years Joan Rogers lived here happily. She lived in one half of the 1930's semi-detached building, and her dear friend Kath Boakes, in the other. They were both widows of men who had worked for us. Percy Boakes was our shepherd for many years, and Ted Rogers was a general farm labourer for five. Their homes were in Ian's tenancy, and so that made them sub-tenants. In part of the complicated rules of the Church of England (our landlords) they were protected and able to stay put, even years after the deaths of their spouses. It seemed crazy to us, once we had decided we would like to live in the cottages after Ian retired, and once they were converted into one dwelling. And it was unlikely, obvious even, that the houses would ever be needed for farm workers. Machines had replaced that need long ago. We had to leave the ladies residing in Numbers 1 & 2, Ross Cottages and we had to be very patient.

Kath – everyone, including her bestie, Joan, always called her Mrs. Boakes, eventually became frail. As there was no heating in Ross Cottages, she needed wood chopped, coal delivered and constant visits and input from family who all lived miles away. Joan helped willingly as much as she could, but she was no spring chicken, and was cold and needy in her own half. Kath was subsequently moved into sheltered accommodation near her son, which left Joan without the companionship of her neighbour and friend. The hedges were high and overgrown, and the corner plot was bleak, with the glorious views all but obscured by a jungle of out-of-control trees. But Joan was not for moving. She had her little house, her cat and her special village friends. And yes, we still needed to be patient, but with a good deal of frustration thrown in.

When the cold and the isolation finally got the better of Joan, (her carpets were lifting when the west winds blew) and her health deteriorated, she relocated with reluctance to be close to her son. This finally allowed Ian and me to begin the lengthy process of purchasing two properties owned by the Church. It was anything but straightforward. 100 years of best-behaved Maclean tenancy possibly had something to do with the ecclesiastical souls agreeing to part with some bricks and mortar. From start to completion and eventually moving in, the time span was six years.

But what of Joan? Everybody loved her. She was part of the fabric of the village. She cuddled the babies born there, and watched, smiling as they went off to school. She was everyone's favourite babysitter in this village and the next.

From the first day we met Joan, it was so easy to get along with her. She was always upbeat, kind, helpful and comforting. And that meeting was a very long time ago, 48 years to be precise, but never once did she waver from being – well, upbeat, kind, helpful and comforting. In fact, it is the comforting aspect which always springs to mind when I think of Joan. I would pop around to her place, and there she would be, with a smile of welcome. We'd have a cosy chat by her fire, or perched in one of Percy's wooden chairs in the garden, looking over the little fence to where his two decrepit twelve-year-old sheep grazed amongst the jungle. We never heard her complain about anything, and it was as if she wanted for nothing. If only the world was full of Joans!

And then there was her interest in our extended family, remembering their birthdays, slipping a few pounds into their cards, when really, she shouldn't have. They loved her for that and we loved her for her continued interest in our little clan. Amanda and Spencer have wonderful memories of Joan and no doubt her patience was tried on numerous occasions when they were little terrors, convinced I expect, that they were helping. For three hours a week, she came to attempt to restore order to the chaos of a huge, busy household. She would work upstairs, while I beavered downstairs, and we would meet somewhere in the middle. Sometimes we would swap, for sanity's sake. By Friday lunchtime the house was ready for the weekend, and then disorder would start all over again. (I likened the Hall to Piccadilly Circus.)

Joan took the constant stream of our overseas visitors in her stride. She met all five of my siblings, their partners, and a never-ending trickle from Australia and South Africa. New Zealanders came often to the Hall, and in the midst of this cosmopolitan chaos, there was Joan, calm and collected. Her interest was genuine and she remembered their names. It was so touching. For years, her weekly Friday visits to restore order were welcome and appreciated, until we noticed she was puffing rather too much, admitting weariness, slowing down.

It was time to let her go – she was irreplaceable. And I didn't replace her, martyr me. When it came to moving into this house there was so much of her presence embedded in the property, and there is a continued feeling that she never really went too far away. Such a cosy feeling it is too. My morning view when having an early cup of tea in bed, would have been exactly the one she too enjoyed. Green fields and a stretch of Church Meadow all the way to the Hall.

In the garden here, the pink peony which grew alongside her path has been divided into six thriving plants. So healthy and huge that I am able to give friends pieces of it. But then I have all the special 'saved' plants from the gardens here - taken first to the Hall while we got organised - and then brought back to be planted in Ian's well-rotted FYM (I'll leave you to work out what that means.)

I can understand Joan's love for St. Mary's. It is a special place, and perched as she was, and we are now, on the corner, it seems a central pivotal point for all the action. Just like the view, which goes on and on, and down to the river. And I do know that the green fields were what she loved the most, where she walked when she was able to, with Kath Boakes and Percy's beloved collie dog, when they were both more mobile. That was what she always yearned for. Ten years on, in her sweet little house of relocation, she was still shedding a tear for those green fields.

We all mourned Joan's passing in 2020.

24

The Hat and a Rat

---◇◇◇---

Whichever one, be it a train, a bus, a plane; or whilst on a long journey, there's always an adjoining seat and it's a case of fingers crossed. Please God, let it be taken by someone interesting, someone who hasn't been eating garlic all week, and has had a wash in the last 24 hours. So it was for Margaret, returning from a journey to visit her sister and her soon-to-be-married niece. They'd continued to live in their birth country, South Africa, while Margaret had spread her teenage wings and migrated to England.

In Margaret's case, the empty seat was on a British Airways 747, economy class flight. She busied herself arranging her small amount of hand luggage; tissues, a book, sweets and a jersey for if it became chilly on the twelve-hour return flight to Heathrow. But what to do with the large and lovely hat she couldn't find room for in the overhead locker? It was a conundrum; the hat had cost a fortune, and the wedding she'd attended, at which the hat was a sensation, was such a happy time. Her wonderful South African relations had rallied around enthusiastically, ensuring that her two weeks with them were truly memorable. It had been exactly the bonded success she had dreamed it would be.

For the moment Margaret just laid the hat down next to her. The seat was empty and anyway, she was flummoxed and fragile as memories flooded back. She began to feel emotional, recollecting the warmth, the hugs and the belonging. A tear trickled down her cheek. She searched for her tissues in the stringed pocket of the seat in front of her, taking a few minutes to compose herself. She missed her husband so much. A solitary life had been so hard since his death eighteen months before. Stifling a sob and with all her concentration focused on controlling her sadness, Margaret suddenly felt the presence of a large body squashed against her right side. A man, she thought to be about forty years of age, was rummaging around and generally getting himself settled in the middle seat of her row of three. So much rummaging in fact, that she was pushed towards the window recess. She turned to investigate, and screeched indignantly. 'Excuse me! You are sitting on my hat. My beautiful, expensive, worn-only-once hat. Please get up!' And as if the poor, startled man hadn't heard, she repeated her order, louder this time. 'You're heavy! That's my hat. You're squashing it!' Nearby rows either side of the aisle, back and front too, were now very aware of the 'hat drama'.

The bulky forty-year-old in question stood up awkwardly. 'I'm sorry, I just didn't notice your hat. And actually, it was in my seat.' He retrieved a squashed version of something which was once rather more elegant and handed it to Margaret. She began to cry. The whole hat debacle was just the final straw. She'd been so torn about leaving Cape Town, and was feeling utterly homesick for her roots and her family. Being a widow and so far away from the comfort and closeness of siblings was never more painful.

The bulky man got out a surprisingly clean handkerchief and handed it to her. I'm so sorry.' He had an engaging smile, dark curly hair, and startlingly white teeth. There didn't seem much sense in continuing to rage. 'I'm Rob,' he told her, and smiled again as she calmed down. A stewardess eventually found a locker with enough space to hide the damaged accessory for the remainder of the flight. The pair began to converse, swapped smidgens of past history, discovering to their surprise, a shared love of Renaissance art and Classic FM, growing roses and bizarrely, chickens. Both were teachers, and both lived in Kent. Rob was unmarried, she learned.

Twelve hours is a very long time, and conversation continued throughout the night. Margaret found in a lull of their otherwise non-stop chat, that Rob's head drooped onto her shoulder. To her amazement, she didn't overly mind. It didn't feel strange. She knew she was being ridiculous and girly. One thing led to another, addresses and phone numbers were exchanged, and Rob was soon invited to her house to meet her two children, who were in their late teens. They were quite ambivalent about who their mother did or did not date. Rob wasted no time in courting his newly found rich widow and the wedding followed a whirlwind of introductions to neighbours, and passionate weekends away. Friends saw to her dog, cat and kids but they did question the speed of events. No-one formed an opinion either way, and anyway, they – or we, as I was a neighbour too – thought it wasn't our business. We merely wanted the best for Margaret.

It took about a year. The falling apart, and the fallout was so obvious. Rob, it appeared, had morphed into a prize rat whose actions and general behaviour towards his unhappy wife were truly terrible. She was stoic for too long, the children suffered and all in the garden was definitely not rosy. We felt for her and rued the haste of her uncharacteristically bad judgement. Like the elaborate hat, Margaret was reduced to a crumpled version of her former self. It was painful to witness the unravelling scenario.

Rob was eventually thrown out spectacularly and everybody involved or observing breathed a sigh of relief. Margaret stayed in the village until she retired from teaching, remaining steadfastly single and decidedly happier.

(Rob was not the name of the rummaging fellow passenger who caused hat havoc! Hopefully, he has remarried, to another widow from Outer Mongolia and remained there.)

25

Mr. Potter

Mr. Potter was an enigma. He arrived in the village in the dying dregs of '71, after a working life in the East End of London. He came with his shy wife and thirty budgerigars. We knew in time, that his name was Cyril, but none of us were brave enough to call him anything other than Mr. Potter, and his wife, Mrs. Potter. Actually, she also called her husband Mr. Potter in a quaint, respectful way. He kept his wife under wraps and she was seldom seen outdoors.

He'd amassed a sizeable pile of cash by setting up a barber's chair outside the Dagenham Ford Motor Factory in Essex. When the day shift ended, he had a queue of customers for these pavement cuts. He could complete one every three minutes. Needless to say, he was as bald as a coot himself and his manner was hardly bedside, though the queues continued enthusiastically through the years. So, there he was at sixty, with enough money to settle in the wilds of north Kent.

The house they'd chosen as their dream retirement pad was actually half a house. Not in the sense of it being a semi-detached, but because it had been badly damaged in a fire. The damaged half had been sliced off and boarded up, rather like a wedge of cake. This was the distorted view we had as we drove up the Hall Road, for Pond Cottage was directly ahead.

Mr. Potter immediately set about building a long row of cages for his budgies and also larger ones for his racing pigeons, which I forgot to mention previously. Then he dug a long curving pond for goldfish, filled it with little beauties and a water feature. His next job was to transform the neglected garden. And yes, he created a beautiful space – should anyone ever get to see it. He seemed busy enough to anyone driving past, not that there was much traffic, or passing villagers taking a stroll. He never seemed enthusiastic about engaging in conversation. Something alien to this village, I remember thinking and made it my business to get to know them both, or at least break the ice. It was hard work, but a mutual starting point were the birds and I went overboard admiring them. However, with two babies under three, the mutual admiration was spasmodic, I admit. Eventually though, Mrs. P and I were exchanging recipes and engaging in brief chats. It was Mrs. Potter who encouraged me to begin years of bread making.

Before long I was made aware that an entire room upstairs – and there were only two – had been taken over by Meccano. Theirs' must have been one of the most comprehensive collections of Meccano in the South East, and here it was in our street, up his stairs, surely unknown to the wider public, and deserving of much more attention. The man was a genius and had built incredible creations of, well, just about everything. They were running out of space and the spare room shelves were stacked high.

Alas, a few years passed in the manner of shy, retiring folk not really fitting in, and yet not making waves towards change. I took my mother across to Pond Cottage on one of her visits – to admire the goldfish, the garden, the budgies and gasp at the Meccano, and I swapped recipes with Mrs. P now and again. They were spotted on a Friday driving off to do a weekly shop in his 2.4 Jaguar. Sadly, there were very few waves from these Pond people.

By now, with Spencer's 7th birthday approaching, I persuaded him to give a Meccano display and a talk in our dining room at the Hall. On the party invites, I mentioned that parents were welcome to come a little early when collecting their children, in order that they might see the clever, painstaking work of years. On two trestle tables Mr. P had displayed motorised carts, circus clowns tumbling, trains chugging, a baby in a pram and so much else. Ninety parents had crammed into the room ten deep (I'd expected no more than a dozen) and the poor man was so nervous he could hardly speak. Mums and, it has to be said, mostly Dads were entranced. I could never understand why he hadn't displayed his genius with Meccano before, but perhaps he was just too shy.

Then I had the bright idea that he might teach Spencer the way to go with the craft. The first lesson went OK but in the midst of the second, our seven-year-old ran home to mum, announcing that he didn't want to go there anymore. There were tears. Mr. P was too intense and too strict, he said, and Mrs. P had insisted that he drink two glasses of fizzy lemon and eat a whole plate of biscuits, and what's more, Meccano wasn't his thing. Perhaps I should have asked him first.

Then Mr. P fell out spectacularly with the fairly new resident of the School House. The stronger personality won the day. It was practically pistols at dawn and tensions built up in an alarming fashion. The poor man obviously thought that the residents were taking sides and spent his remaining time (years of it) scurrying away, rather than to be seen or spoken to. The situation deteriorated quite seriously and in a damaging way. It was sad, and certainly unfortunate, and was the first time there had been anything but harmony in the street for a very long time. After that fracas, the poor couple descended into a solitary, secret life where no-one saw them, and if they went out in their car, it must have been under the cover of darkness.

Mrs. P became ill and died in '96 which shamefully means that their dream retirement in our quiet village had lasted for a mostly unhappy twenty-five years. Mr. Potter stayed in Pond Cottage for another year before moving in with his daughter. There was no farewell party.

The house was bought by the Clarkes in '98, extended beautifully; its name was changed to Pudding. All is pristine. There isn't a budgie in sight, but the goldfish pond remains.

26

Let Us Reflect

Those who live in the few houses in this select spot deserve considerable study. And possibly a whole book devoted entirely to their diverse and delightful characteristics. Perhaps the best answer would be to write at length about them in my next book, whenever that might be. It will give me the greatest pleasure, though I would need to be excessively polite. At least my dear departed Characters in this section cannot answer back.

Some, like Ian and I, have enjoyed the peace and quiet, the quaintness and the lack of bustle for more than fifty years, other couples and families have arrived over the decades, and as I mentioned before, few choose to leave. Visitors to the village remark on the views and the space we all enjoy. It is something we do not take for granted, given that new-builds are crammed together within shaking-hands distance of neighbours. And we have so much privacy as a village. We can water our gardens early on summer mornings in our nightwear, should we choose to. Dressing gowns have also been spotted – to little reaction. Bedding gets aired from top windows, and then, as I've mentioned previously, there is endless chat at each gate. Dog-walkers head off in twos and threes. Yes, we're a bonded lot!

Here, we have birdsong to wake us, owls hooting at bedtime, swallows nesting in our barns, and the everlasting routine of the farm, with colours changing as harvests happen. Although we have blissful freedom from traffic noise, there is rural activity to observe with giant tractors, and state of the art combine harvesters, trailers and drills. As if all of that isn't enough, the River Thames is merely walking distance away, blue – well, mostly it's blue – tidal, and an eternal talking point.

This then is the 'present resident' list of those enjoying life in The Street:

Charlie and Edie: Mark and Verity: Alan and Brenda: Darren and Julie: Andrew and Erna: Nick and Michelle, Olive: Charlotte and James: Amanda and Johnny, Amber and Erin: Sam and Hayley, Aurora, Arlo and Aubrey: Paul and Amanda: Lawrence: Philip and Alex: Pat and Kevin: Ian and I.

We are a delightfully eclectic mix in ages, shapes and sizes, aspirations and just about everything else. Enough, I suppose to potentially divide, but no, we are all united in the belief that this is a very special village and count our blessings to be here.

We gather whenever possible, at a party or a barbecue, walking our dogs, standing at our garden gates, gossiping or just 'being'. We are home.

Printed in Great Britain
by Amazon